# Theatre Connections

## a very personal story

Doreen Newlyn

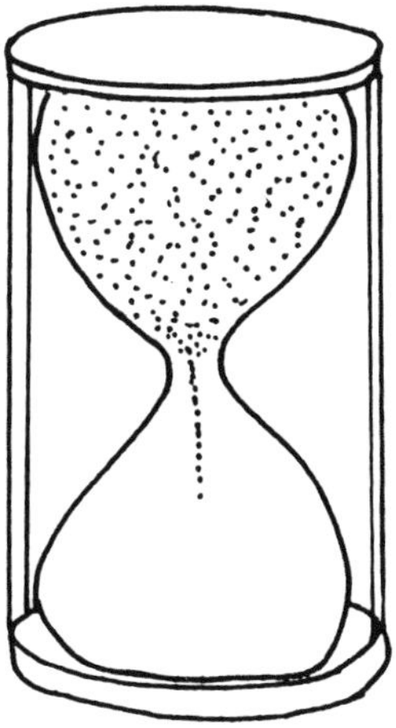

This book is dedicated to
the Campaigners for Leeds Playhouse

# Contents

'....the truth is that life is perpetually weaving fresh threads which link one individual and one event to another, and that these threads are crossed and recrossed, doubled and redoubled, to thicken the web, so that between any slightest point of our past and all the others a rich network of memories gives us an almost infinite variety of communicating paths to choose from'.

*Proust*: Remembrance of Things Past

# The Prologue

At either end of a span of more than fifty years stand two landmarks in my life: two points of time linked by 'threads crossed and recrossed' and by a 'rich network of memories'. The second landmark is in a playhouse in Leeds and the biggest part of my story is about the origins of that playhouse. The first landmark also is in a theatre where I first saw our century's noblest actor and where 'sitting at a play' I was, in Hamlet's words, 'struck so to the soul' that now it seems to me to have been unavoidable, the journey I took from there, zigzagging through many 'communicating paths' to the second landmark, the playhouse in Leeds.

It was December 1937, my fourteenth birthday. I had chosen for my treat to go to the Queen's Theatre in London to see John Gielgud in *Richard II.* It was a matinee; we were in the gallery and had queued in the morning, my mother and I, for the little wooden stools you used to hire for sixpence and which you substituted for your presence in the real queue while you went off to warm your feet and have a Welsh rarebit in Lyons Corner House. I had never been to the theatre. The cinema was my drama, the splendid cinema of Hollywood in the thirties, and my idols were the great tragic actors like Garbo and Bette Davies and Leslie Howard. For a railway clerk's family in an east-of-London suburb the West End theatre was 'too posh' and 'too expensive' for regular visits; and I hadn't heard of the Old Vic. So that day was a treat indeed. But my school had a lively drama tradition and a stage and a huge wardrobe of stage clothes from its productions of things like *Richard of Bordeaux* put on by the English teacher. And I had, by the age of fourteen, a very high opinion of myself as both producer and actress, in inter-house play competitions, classroom drama and even, once, in an outside festival. Theatre magic had already started work on me: I was already a keen amateur. Furthermore I had already done three or four Shakespeare plays, although I had never heard a live actor speak the words.

So it was a vulnerable but thoughtful girl that fell easy victim to the magic of great theatre that December afternoon; who was decisively enslaved by it; who came, in a numbed state, down the narrow stone gallery stairs at the Queen's Theatre into a London street that seemed suddenly completely unreal. I remember as if it were today feeling deeply cold, and being dazed by the shock of the streets and the traffic which were, sadly, *my* world: while the real world lay somewhere beyond the gallery stairs, not in time or place, but in a universe of deeper reality, a universe of marvellous sound where grief and pain were somehow beautiful and bearable; where tragic events somehow had a form that made them meaningful and endurable; where love and passion were at once familiar, recognisable but transformed into 'something rich and rare'. It was a world inhabited by the god-like creatures I had been watching and yet a world contained in the same space as that which contained the gallery, so that for a short while I too could inhabit it.

I know that everything that happened of importance in my life really started there. And what a 'there' it was; what a stroke of unimaginably good fortune for my first contact with theatre magic to have taken place where (a fact of no significance to me at the time) John Gielgud was launching a season of plays which was to be hailed by the critics as the most important that the English theatre had known for some years. What was of importance to me then was the immediacy of the tragedy and the passion; the sense of truth it gave me, in a way that the cinema had never done, so that I was part of it in a way I had never felt about a film; and then the music and the mastery of the voices, the gorgeous richness of the costumes, the swirling cloaks and glittering swords; all the rich paraphernalia of a traditional and lavish representation of mediaeval pageantry; all this as a vehicle for the glory of Shakespeare's language, the fullness of his dramatic universe, the intensity of his passions. I remember above all one moment, and I hear it and see it today as clearly as in 1937, the moment of parting between Richard and the Queen: two tall, tragic, lonely, beautiful figures, and two lines of the heart-breaking simplicity that only Shakespeare seems to give us at moments of agonising finality:

And must we be divided? Must we part?
Aye, hand from hand, my love, and heart from heart.

I was torn with grief which I thought would last for ever. In a way it has, for I still feel the desolation of it.

That was the first landmark in time. The second belongs to 1990 in a theatre in Leeds. A few weeks previously the West Yorkshire Playhouse had opened: a splendid new civic theatre, costing thirteen million pounds; a triumph for the City of Leeds that, with massive support from the Arts Council and from the West Yorkshire business community, had brought it into being. Most people who had shared in the celebratory opening knew that this theatre was the successor to, the replacement for, a smaller more modest theatre called Leeds Playhouse that had been in operation for twenty good years; some people knew that Leeds Playhouse had been built specifically as a forerunner to the West Yorkshire Playhouse, a first stage in a two-phase plan. But not many people knew of the long bizarre drama out of which had emerged that first, beacon-carrying theatre. There was no reason why they should know: what mattered was that the people of the region now had, at last, the result of a dream of twenty six years before, and that the magic of theatre was now accessible to them all.

We sat, my husband and I, at a little table on a raised area overlooking the foyer. Below us streamed in the audiences for the two shows for that night: all ages, many races, most social classes; no one we knew; just masses of people. It was noisy, festive, but not a special occasion; a normal one, a nightly one. There hummed a feeling of excitement and lively anticipation; there was music coming from the great public area; there were Tannoy calls, clattering cups, last minute queues at the box office; there were groups of friends meeting noisily; all the paraphernalia of a live theatre in a large community - production photos, packs of handouts for other productions and other theatres, a display in the art gallery, a group of children giving a folk dancing display just below us. And out of the crowd there emerged an old familiar face, that of an old friend from earlier days. 'Well, here it is', he said. 'At last. Is it how you first imagined it ?' And then he went on, 'Just think - if it hadn't been for you....' He was one of the few who did know that bizarre history and in some measure he was right.

But only partly so: this Playhouse would have been built anyway some day, some time. It was not the creation of a single vision or a single individual's effort. The making of it had little in common with the making of the Gaiety Theatre in Manchester, in the early years of the century: that was entirely attributable to the inspiration, wealth and generosity of one woman, Annie Horniman. But Leeds Playhouse belonged to its time, and it emerged from the conjunction of particular personalities with a particular point of time; because I was among the personalities and the times were as they were, it all happened as it did; and I realised that all the paths I had explored in my life, all the threads in my personal web, led to this moment in this theatre. The chances and choices of my life were as much a part of the story of Leeds Playhouse as were the state of the arts in regional cities in 1964, and as were the lives of the other people in the story.

For the story is not only an account of that unique, bizarre campaign: it is also about the coming together of a group of people who, one way or another, had all been bewitched; who shared a deep and unshakeable belief in the value of theatre; who saw that our neck of the woods was deprived and that something had to be done. We needed all the strength of our belief to survive the scepticism, the hostility, the cynicism and the meanness, and the sheer ridiculing lack of interest with which we were confronted. None of us was professional: we were all amateurs, lovers of the theatre. It is true that among us was a range of gifts of high quality, which were indispensable to our success. But for all of us it was a pure and passionate conviction that inspired each one of us separately: a concern for the cultural health of our society. And this quality of disinterested intensity created a personal bonding that held together a group of people as different as could be in their nature, backgrounds, conditions and talents: held us together virtually without breakage for six years. And from those six years emerged friendships of great depth and endurance. That is another theme in this story: how any intensely shared concern inter-weaves with personal relationships. You learn and come to care about people as you share your concern, and your dedication to the cause is reinforced by the knowledge and the affection that grows. It is a bit like theatre magic in a way: within a small and clearly defined arena the mighty issues are clearly perceived and intensely realised. Form and concentration: that is what the theatre gives; that is what makes a good campaign; and that of course is what makes profound friendships. Although we all worked for an objective that was not self-interested, we gained self-interestedly in the best possible way. So this story is also about the joys of working with other people for something you all care about deeply and are prepared to work for unstintingly.

One of the oddest things about the campaign was the unforeseen way, the unplanned way, in which it was born. Nothing could have been further from the intention of thirteen people who met one March evening in 1964 in my house than that of taking up the combined tasks of designing, financing, staffing and running a professional repertory theatre. Certainly nothing could have been less intended by me than the life that was to become mine for the next six years, and the changes that were to be caused in my professional life and in my own character. I can only tell accurately my own story and describe the paths by which I came to this task, but a glance at the thirteen gives as unlikely a picture as possible of the battling group we needed to become.

Four of the thirteen were third year university students, leaving the university within four or five months, and all of them have sadly faded out of sight and memory. They were members of the exceptionally talented Student Theatre Group of the university, which had a fine record of performance and indeed a very distinguished reputation, winning year after year the Sunday Times Award for student drama. Of the other nine, four were university teachers: Arnold Kettle, a distinguished scholar of English who went eventually to the Chair of English in the Open University (which, coincidentally, was conceived that very year, and which ran neck and neck with the Playhouse the race to opening night); Charles Barber, also a greatly respected lecturer in the School of English and a talented actor for the University Staff Dramatic Society; Bill Goldie, a dear and gentle medical academic and also an amateur actor; and Walter Newlyn, a development and monetary economist in the School of Economics and an amateur actor. There were three of the spouses: Barbara Barber, who was a full-time history teacher but also a fine director for the University Staff Dramatic Society; Mollie Goldie, another good actress for that society; and Doreen Newlyn, amateur actress, by profession a social worker and a drama lecturer but at this time currently emerging from an intensive period of being a full-time mother and engaged on an MA course in the Teaching of English as a Second Language. The other two were John Linstrum, a lecturer in Drama in a Teacher Training College and a talented ex-member of Theatre Group; and Ann Severs, who had also acted with Theatre Group and trained in acting at the Bradford Civic Theatre but currently, like me, a full-time wife-and-mum, married to the head of the BBC in the North. It was a fairly homogeneous group, linked by personal friendship and specifically by a passion for the theatre. All of us, in fact, spent a lot of our spare time acting, as amateurs, in various dramatic societies.

They came to be there on that evening long ago because they had been invited by me to consider the extraordinary fact about Leeds that, in contrast with all the other cities of comparable size in Britain, it did not support, as a public responsibility, a professional repertory theatre. It was all very tentative, exploratory, very relaxed. We discussed the quality of life in our city, within which in truth most of us enjoyed a privileged life inside the ivory tower of the university, with all its cultural and artistic amenities. We talked about the clear evidence in other cities of an unparalleled period of establishing, restoring or transforming theatres in those cities, many of which had never had a theatre of their own before. We contemplated the wealth of Leeds and the large sector of the society that we guessed must feel theatre to be as important as we did. We also contemplated the great divide in our city, the north Leeds / south Leeds divide: north Leeds housing the more well-to-do, the bourgeoisie, while south Leeds housed a predominantly working-class population, still in some of the meanest streets imaginable or in the great high-rise developments that were the misguided order of that day. None of us had any illusions about theatre being a majority leisure-time activity; we knew that the theatre audiences of Britain had become essentially middle-class and predominantly middle-aged. So we knew that in south Leeds there did not exist an already awakened enthusiasm; but we observed, had been ourselves beneficiaries of, the changes happening in so many of the other cities and smaller towns of the country. Everyone there that night was concerned primarily with south Leeds, and with seeing developments that might start to break down the divide in the city, as well as open up a pleasure vista that had been the prerogative of the more privileged. The dream was of a people's theatre, a community theatre, subsidised, accessible, popular and of the very highest quality: 'a great social force for good and evil.'[1]

Leeds, along with most of the bigger provincial cities, had a number of theatre buildings; or, more precisely, it *had* had. Many had gone in the course of development schemes, but there were still two. One was The Grand, a then rather faded and seedy example of the vast florid gaudy Victorian theatre, with orchestra pit and boxes and balconies and a large proscenium stage: an outsize version, seating about 1500 people, of the smaller and more intimate London theatres, like the Queen's, where I had first seen John Gielgud. This, run by a commercial management, staged the annual pantomimes which tended to run for four or five months and a series of visiting shows encompassing the whole range of type and quality of production. The ballet came, the opera very occasionally, musicals, straight plays in touring versions of London shows, sometimes post-London with perhaps down-graded casting in the star parts, and sometimes pre-London try-outs with the stars. Scattered through the season, blessedly, were occasional great productions, from the Old Vic or Stratford, or by a quality commercial company. It was a catholic programme, and although the really trivial plays drew poor audiences (not surprisingly), the high quality productions were usually packed; and the pantomime was a great theatrical event annually which did appeal to Leeds right across the social divides and did give popular contact with the magic of theatre. But straight drama, with its limited audience appeal, was not financially a good bet for management unless a famous name was in it, and so anything that was challenging, adventurous, controversial, tended to be a very rare experience in the Grand, in 1964: the year that the little group gathered to look at things.

The other extant theatre at that time was a really old fashioned affair, the City Varieties; the home mainly of Edwardian-style music hall and of a secondary pantomime at Christmas. It was a nice relic of an old-established popular entertainment and very well run by the Joseph brothers; a jolly, homely place, uncomfortable, rather primitive in its facilities compared with the

Grand which boasted, among other facilities, splendid star-dressing rooms much loved by many famous people.

The City Varieties was a relic of older times, with the variety acts, the stand-up comics, the brash vulgarity and the earthy smut. Popular and homely, it was perhaps an anachronism in a modern city, but it in fact continued a tradition as old as classical tragedy.

Most of the thirteen had been to the City Varieties: I with four small daughters to a pantomime once, and once for a lark to a very dirty show. It was nice, both times, being in a place of down-to-earth cosiness. In some ways it was more appealing than the pretensions to lost glory that I always felt pervaded the Grand.

But the places where we all saw serious drama were the places where all of us acted ourselves; the amateur theatre venues. If one wanted to find a well-spring for the West Yorkshire Playhouse there is no doubt whatsoever that one finds it in the old Mechanics Institute, in the Riley Smith Hall at the University, on college stages, rented halls and many a converted space such as the lawn of Temple Newsam House. The amateur theatre work in Leeds at this period was of the very highest quality. In the Mechanics Institute, renamed the Civic Theatre, there were companies like the Proscenium Players and the Arts Theatre which regularly through the year produced a repertory of plays of the greatest interest and of very good production quality. In the University both the Student Theatre Group and the Staff Dramatic Society were extraordinarily active. Although the University did not at that stage boast a Drama department, it so happened that a chance clustering of academics, who also acted, produced, translated and explored the drama of Europe, coincided with a few years of student talent of great quality. The old Riley Smith - a barn of an all-purpose hall - saw a constant flow of important, serious, adventurous productions from both students and staff, and often from them jointly. An early production of John Arden's *Sergeant Musgrave's Dance* was one of Theatre Group's greatest triumphs, with Ronald

Pickup (a student at the time) in the main role and the author, John Arden, in the audience - sweeping in, I recall, in a voluminous black cloak. One academic year contained a *King Lear* and *The Three Sisters* from the Staff Dramatic Society, with a Noel Coward one-acter thrown in for good measure to entertain a staff party. Some of us spanned two or three of the groups working in the city in the fifties: I for example acted in the Arts Theatre as well as in the Staff Dramatic Society.

Undoubtedly the amateur theatre in Leeds at this time was very flourishing and offered a wide range of plays. How much this abundance of drama was stimulated by the absence of a serious professional presence, and how much it actually succeeded in inhibiting recognition of the absence, is difficult to tell. Certainly for the purpose of serious theatre-going there seemed to be no dearth of opportunity; and certainly at a later stage in the campaign's confrontation with the civic authorities this was one of the arguments produced to confound us, 'What do you want with another theatre ? What's wrong with the Civic ?'

We considered in great detail at that first meeting what we wanted and why we wanted it, although at that stage, as I have said, none of us thought it would be we that had to create it. In our confidence and naiveté we imagined that a letter to the City Council from this newly-formed pressure group would result in an enlightened response to our approaches, and that perhaps within a couple of years Leeds, along with most other provincial cities, would be supporting with public subsidy a professional repertory theatre: appealing to all the population of the region, and as much a part of the civic scene as the museum and the library and the swimming baths; a home for a permanent resident company with a close relationship with the life of the city, and a programme containing the whole range of good drama; in a building that would also be a home for peripheral activities - music, discussions, films, community activities and children's theatre - a building that belonged to the people of Leeds, where they could feel at home, all the time; a place where an outlet would exist for the writing of local artists in the region that had nourished them and their artistic talent. Above all there would be the acceptance of the need for all this to be non-commercial, to be subsidised as art needs to be subsidised: so that experiments can be tried and failures assimilated; so that difficult minority pieces could find a home and a hearing; so that the success at the box office might not have to be the sole criterion for selection; and so that everyone could afford to go, because prices would be kept down.

In determining how to present and justify our proposals we discovered in ourselves a measure of diffidence about our status: it was to haunt us and daunt us for quite a long time. There was no difficulty for any of us in specifying the categorical benefits of theatre. We all enjoyed it and believed it to be important, a necessary part of a nation's culture, a force for good and evil, provocative, stimulating, as well as entertaining. We wanted it for ourselves - but much more for the community. This placed us in the posture of prescribing for that community; and who were we? A little self-appointed group of enthusiasts. How would we answer the question we would inevitably be asked: 'Why you?'? Had we the right to set about achieving an objective we had been mandated by no one to achieve? We were all privileged members of an educated elite with ideological and sociological motivation but no political status in relation to the community for which we were to prescribe.

However, the fear of appearing patronising, highbrow or elitist has surely to be overcome if the advantages and values of a privileged education are to be shared and to be of benefit to more than those who possess them: that is surely of the essence of democracy. One must not be afraid to speak out about cultural deprivation with the same certitude as about material deprivation. Most of us, as teachers, were used to guidance-giving in any case, so we found the will to overcome the fear, taking courage from our disinterestedness, our commitment to the ideals of a good society, and our absolute certainty about the importance of drama. We decided we would *not* be afraid to speak out; but we thought the 'speaking' would be the sum of our task and we retained for a long time a self-consciousness about our status that, for some of us, made it quite painful to endure the years of criticism, of abuse and of mockery, as the 'speaking' became public debate and the pressure group a full-scale campaign organisation.

When I recreate that time in my mind I see quite clearly how much our initiative was a response to the inspiration of our times. The year we began, 1964, was just one of the years in a whole decade that in many respects was a peak-time of hope and endeavour in our society. The decade is often referred to as 'the radical sixties'. There was overall a profound sense of thankfulness, a universal sigh of relief, that the world had drawn back, in 1962, from the very brink of a nuclear disaster in the Cuba crisis. The relief was not followed by complacency, but by what seemed to be a regeneration of a public will to influence events through protest movements. A greater awareness of the international scene seemed to come into being, perhaps stimulated by the growing impact on people everywhere of television. There was a mighty transformation at this time in the relationship between the developed nations and the countries that had for so long been their colonial possessions; the process of de-colonialisation brought to the ex-colonies the dignity of self-determination and to the ex-imperial nations a recognition of a new type of responsibility. The concept of international aid was born. The one-way importation of culture gave way to a reciprocal exchange, as old guilts in the west and old resentments in the new nations gave way to an appreciation of the benefits of cross-fertilisation. The disasters and the bloody violence that were to beset most of the ex-colonies were a little way ahead at the beginning of the sixties, and a mood of cautious hope for a new world order blessed those early years. They were years of idealism, but also of protest: the voice of the young was heard more clearly now than before. There was a widening of the social base of the student population, and a growth of its articulateness; and beyond that privileged sector was a whole generation that had a new set of expectations, enjoying a freedom from conventional and parental constraints that their parents had not known.

Flower power, the voice of the Beatles, the road to Kathmandu were all symptoms of a generation throwing off its subservience to the old; there was colour and noise and restlessness. They were the years of economic prosperity too, and there was a feeling of growth and progress in many spheres of social life. These too were the years when, following a Labour victory after thirteen years of Conservative government, Jennie Lee was Minister for the Arts and was introducing policies designed to open up access to the arts to the whole population. It was a decade of new universities - including the Open University - of new theatres, of local radio, of the Regional Arts Associations, of funding of the arts for ventures and buildings up and down the country. At last there was actually a positive step towards the creation of a National Theatre. In the regions there seemed to be an upsurge of creativity, particularly in writing, and very particularly in writing for the theatre; and in the regional theatres themselves - starting with the Belgrade at Coventry (the first theatre ever in the country to have been built entirely at the expense of a local authority) - there were exciting new attitudes and policies, with a new generation of directors fired with a concern for the regions: Colin George, Anthony Richardson, John Neville. Art and culture were definitely on the move in the sixties, and were both the product of and the inspiration for the radical years themselves. So we, at the first little meeting in Leeds, were a pretty representative sample of the idealistic enthusiasts of our time.

It is often a random spark that touches off a fire. The chance that caused me to touch off what became the Theatre Campaign was a burst of irritation on one particular day; and the cause was that, in order to enable four little girls, our daughters, to discover theatre magic, we were spending each Saturday driving them around the north to matinees in Sheffield, Manchester, York and

Nottingham; Leeds had failed us. Thus were the threads of our daughters' lives woven very early into the web.

I have strayed from the direct path between my two landmarks, and gone back along a different path to a mid-point. For the main thread in the story is itself woven into the complex fabric of the times, and the 'rich network of memories' does, as Proust says, give 'an almost infinite variety of communicating paths to choose from'.

So now I return to my starting point, to the moment in 1937 when I first looked into Shakespeare's universe of deeper reality opened up to me by the art of John Gielgud. And again, I am filled with wonder and gratitude for my luck.

# 1

# The first Act: A Travelling Theatre

I thought the luck had run out when the very year after that first meeting with great theatre my family movcd away from London, and thus, it seemed, away from access to this newly discovered world. Before that happened I saw from the gallery the rest of the productions that John Gielgud mounted in the Queen's Theatre. I did not know it at the time but that season in itself was a very important and unusual venture: it was a unique West End repertory season. In addition to *Richard II* the same company performed *The School for Scandal, The Merchant of Venice* and *The Three Sisters*; the season ran for nine months. The company established a quality and style of ensemble performance that had rarely been seen in the West End, or in London anywhere except for at the Old Vic, since the great days of the Vedrenne-Barker years at the Royal Court, from 1904 to 1907. In some of the first great provincial repertory theatres - Manchester, Birmingham, Liverpool and Glasgow - the concept of the permanent company had been combined with a policy of putting on high quality plays; and in the provincial repertory theatres that were established in a number of cities between the wars there was usually a basic core of actors playing weekly rep.

For a 'repertory company', which is what it was, to contain John Gielgud and Peggy Ashcroft, Michael Redgrave, Leon Quartermain, Alec Guinness, to name but a few, and to have such directors as Tyrone Guthrie and Michel St. Denis was very remarkable. It was a break with the old star system and was a company of stars. St.Denis himself said 'If good work was done it was because the conditions of work were so much better than in the average theatre'. Giles Brandreth, in his biography of Gielgud, goes on: 'And good work certainly was done....The plays were scheduled to run for eight to ten weeks preceded by up to nine weeks of rehearsals. Most of the actors had never known such a luxury, indeed regarded it as a self-indulgence, but all were convinced by the experience.'[1]

I had no idea on that fourteenth birthday that what I was seeing was to become a fabled passage of English theatrical history. What I knew was that something cataclysmic happened to me. It is hard to conjure up for those too young to have seen it for themselves the unique beauty of Gielgud's presence in the theatre: the Gielgud who was called the 'finest flower of the contemporary stage'.[2] Today his long unbroken record, down the years, of remarkable and varied performances which continue into his nineties and are still uniquely fascinating and moving, is perhaps most universally admired for the exquisite perfection with which he combined voice, movement, gesture and expression in the peak-time of his career. Michael Redgrave said of him: 'Ninety per cent of the beauty of his acting was the beauty of his voice. To this day I can see no way of improving on the dazzling virtuosity of phrasing and breathing'.[3] As I have listened to it over the years I have tried to analyse it: there was a singing, ringing tone, a clarity like the notes of a clarinet, with the vibrancy of a violin vibrato; there was a huge range of pitch and volume, and great flexibility in the handling of stress and pace which is entirely idiosyncratic; but there was also insight and perception which he brought to the handling of

Shakespeare's language in particular, a complete mastery of the verse which made the lines seem to come absolutely new and fresh at any time from the moment in the scene; and the effect of this in scenes of grief and tragedy was indescribably poignant. He had (still has) a fine-boned face of great sensitivity and deep, keen brilliant eyes; and there was a poetry in his movement that I have never seen in any other actor - lithe, nervous but economical, flowing, full of grace as well as of purpose. His gifts as an actor were surely without match in our time. It was not only new, young theatre devotees who were spellbound by Gielgud's magic and by the marvellous productions in that season at the Queen's Theatre in 1937/8.

The two Shakespeare plays were those that most affected me, for Shakespeare really is unmatched in the power to absorb you into a whole imaginative universe, within which he then subjects you to delights, shocks, griefs, perplexities, perceptions. Gielgud's Shylock, a 'shuffling, morose, malignant outsider'[4] introduced me to the strange excitement of the ambiguities in Shakespeare, which are only fully realised by the living actor on a stage. I had no idea how to handle the stress, tension and perplexity with which that Shylock filled me - so unlovable and ignoble but, in ways completely beyond an adolescent's comprehension, tragic, compelling my sympathy and my care. That perplexity, which grew into a life-long passion to search out Shakespeare's meanings, was the most important influence exerted on me by that production except for that of Peggy Ashcroft, whose beautiful incomparable voice became my model: the Quality of Mercy speech became my set piece at the family gatherings where my father sang old ballads and all the aunts played Schubert and Liszt.

*The School for Scandal* gave me little satisfaction, though I was dazzled by the style and polish and elegance of the production, and beguiled by yet another example of the range of Gielgud's acting; but it was emotion I sought, not wit, tenderness not heartlessness. *The Three Sisters*, by Chekhov, totally enthralled me although I was mystified by it: I had no idea how to think about the Chekhov world, how to comprehend the characters who were such strange mixtures of laughter and tears; all I knew, again, was that a whole universe of experience, of laughter and yearning and pain, existed on the stage and that the people in it - extraordinary people who laughed and cried and danced and nagged and longed for things - were as real as the people in my life and that they had something important to reveal. In few other playwrights is the text so unrevealing of the play's life, I think. I rushed to the library as soon as I could (indeed, I chose a volume of Chekhov's plays as the book-prize I won for that year's work at school) but found the play even more difficult to comprehend - quite apart from the difficulty of coping with the names and patronyms and pet names of everyone - in the absence of living actors to give flesh to them. And I ended up with the need just to accept and feel and remember it all without understanding.

The unique gift of the theatre is to effect receptivity on that level: to quicken subconscious perception, innate understanding; deepening sympathy and awakening awareness of issues and feelings that are not fully understood by the mind. Some years later I played one of the sisters in an amateur production of great insight and sensitivity, and I did enjoy the intellectual analysis and the detailed examination of the play's import; but I sensed all the time that I already knew about the heart of the play, that I was really coming back to something deeply familiar. How lucky I had been to meet Chekhov in that way, in a production of the very first order. Herbert Farjeon said of it: 'One is so overwhelmed by the poignant beauty of the production that anything written or spoken must fall short of what one feels. There is a tenderness in the acting so exquisite that it is like the passing of light'.[5] That was one of the occasions when the theatre achieves everything it exists for.

Another teenager, slightly older than I was, and considerably more gifted than I would ever be, sums up Gielgud's own power very simply. 'Gielgud...binds a spell', wrote Kenneth Tynan, who saw the production at the age of seventeen.[6] Certainly he did over me, during that unique season which is remembered by so many people in the same way as it is by me. And it was spellbound, by John Gielgud's personal magic and the marvellous productions in which he wrought it, that I came to the first real certainty in my life: that I wanted, above all else, to be connected with the theatre, in some way.

I believe that an appreciation of high standards was established in me when I was fourteen that remained for ever a criterion by which to assess the quality of drama in all the forms and various ways in which I have enjoyed it. And I have always believed profoundly that nothing but the excellent should be presented to young people, or to inexperienced audiences. Experienced and critical audiences can glean enjoyment even from mediocre performances, but not so the young or the inexperienced: to create an unexplained sense of disappointment is a terrible risk and may result in people not believing in the magic at all. One of the joys that came to me long after, in Leeds Playhouse, was the fact that the Theatre in Education company, set up at the outset as an integral part of the Playhouse work and one of the initial objectives of the campaign, was directed by a man who also believed this and who, along with his team and his successors, have put the belief steadily into practice to the benefit of thousands of Leeds and West Yorkshire school children.

But to return to 1938: in that year I had to leave London with my family and go to live in York. Desolate as I was at this enforced banishment - and such it was, for travel was expensive, and within a year the war came anyway and London was not a good place to go to if one could avoid it - it was in fact to present me with a unique experience of theatre of quite a different sort, operating in an utterly different context and in a way that I later, as a student of literature, came to learn mirrored a form as old as classical theatre: strolling players ... mummers ... commedia del arte ... the Good Companions ... all had their origin in the grass roots of popular entertainment; all shared the problems and challenges of presenting their performances with the minimum of infrastructure, in differing venues, to a variety of audiences and, as it were, on the wing. That is exactly the sort of theatre-making that I fell in with in war-time York.

Life in York seemed initially to be little touched by the war. There was food rationing, of course; there was the black-out, which was always a nuisance and a worry; there was Mr Churchill on the wireless, exhorting us to be ready to face the worst, and telling us bluntly of the disasters; and the ever increasing number of national anthems played before the nine o'clock news, as country after country in Europe fell to Hitler, and their free forces joined us here in Britain; there were false alarm air-raid warnings and the tiresome carrying of gas-masks, and fire watching at school (which grew very popular as it merged with that of the neighbouring boys' school's fire watching). Our small back garden, which had had flower beds around the lawn, became an Anderson air-raid shelter (an earthy hide-out with a corrugated iron facade and a turfed dome) and a large vegetable garden. The fields at the end of the garden were turned over to sugar beet; the dog had to be fed on horse-melt instead of horse-meat as the latter was used for people and we couldn't buy it for dogs. But we lived very well, for my father was a keen gardener and my mother was one who always managed to get something on the side - an extra sausage, an ounce or two extra over the ration at the butcher's, a pork pie under the counter from a friend. Our main contact with the actual war-events came in two ways: one was the busy traffic in the skies above us, for York was surrounded by RAF bomber bases,from which in later years they would drone out in their thousands to bomb Germany; and in the gossip about troop movements that my mother brought back from the WVS canteen on York station - where she shared duty with the mother of Judi Dench, and engaged in a rather unequal exchange of pride about the daughters' acting abilities. Judi was at that time a pupil in the neighbouring Quaker school, The Mount; a bit younger than me but apparently already known to be gifted. I never met Judi then - I think - but a quarter of a century later I exploited rather ruthlessly the tenuous link in order to wheedle a favour from her.

Mother usually brought stories of a rather boring domestic sort - rows with fellow-workers, matters of status and hurt pride; but in June 1940 she started to come back with tales of trains packed with tired, grey soldiers, and we knew before Mr Churchill told us that France had fallen. It was some time before we heard the full story from him of the little boats that had in their hundreds braved the German Luftwaffe to cross the Channel to rescue those men, of the British Expeditionary Force, in an operation of such courage and daring and skill that it will live always in the memories of those of us who were alive then; and for which I personally will always be grateful as the man I was, a lot later, to love and marry was one of those - one of the last- who left on a little boat.

So the war was always there, although York itself was a haven of peacefulness compared with the London I had been so sad to leave and which, soon after the passing through York of those grey soldiers, became the target of intensive and sustained bombing. We in the sixth form at school went about our business of working for Higher School Certificate, and I for Oxford Entrance as well. Although by now drama was my passion, my parents were too poor and cautious to encourage me to go on the stage; so I was resigned to trying for Oxford as a second best - hoping secretly that from there, if I got in, I might find one of the ways via which many of our actors had entered the profession. Those were the days before mandatory grants for Drama School - or indeed for university itself, for which one needed one of the limited number of State or local authority scholarships.

It was at this stage of life that I became therefore as full-time a part-time actress as was consistent with the duties of life. There was all the school drama, in which I was soon playing all the leads: Mrs Malaprop, Hamlet, Macbeth - a single-sex girls' school gives a girl more chances in Shakespeare than the real theatre does! There was also a Virgin Mary in York Minster with the bonus of a commendatory word from the great Archbishop Temple himself; there was a concert party, playing in old people's homes, with the bonus of supportive reference to public spiritedness in testimonials to universities; and there was an Extra-Mural drama group of which I was the only young member, in which I consequently played all the young leads in entries for drama festivals, notching up quite a number of awards and secretly gaining some hopeful expectations. Life was full. And in addition there was theatre to watch: York Repertory Theatre, a good, old fashioned weekly rep.(the oldest in the country as I later discovered) kept alive through the war; and although the plays were varied in quality, and the productions the same, nevertheless they kept the magic doors open into the world of theatre.

There were at this time two other exiles from the South, living for the duration of the war in York, who were also great theatre-lovers and gifted and experienced spare-time actors. One was an architect whose practice had shut down for the duration and who was just too old for war-service: Geoffrey Ridley, who took on temporarily, while the permanent incumbent was serving in the forces, the post of secretary to the Yorkshire Rural Community Council; and Jane Lawrence, who was a professional actress. They had been jointly involved in a number of Shakespeare productions in a tiny theatre which Geoffrey and his first wife had created in a mediaeval barn in the grounds of their house in Sussex.

In normal times the YRCC ran and encouraged drama activities in villages all over rural Yorkshire, but by the time Geoffrey came they had suspended this side of their work, partly for the need to cut down on fuel consumption for all but essential purposes, and partly because of the currently prevailing pressure in all spheres of activity to cut out everything that was not directly geared to the war-effort. But on 19 January 1940 was set up in Britain the Council for the Encouragement of Music and the Arts - CEMA - a milestone in British artistic history. It was the first Government initiative ever of its kind, and it was the progenitor of the Arts Council. Its purpose was to encourage the arts throughout the country in the knowledge that art is never so much needed as in times of trouble and anxiety. One of the first members of the governing board of the Council was Maynard Keynes - a great economist and one of the most cultivated and civilised minds of our times, who knew that the life of work and endeavour and sacrifice needed to be supported by the life of the mind and the spirit and the imagination. Where theatre was concerned CEMA's purpose was to 'endow theatreless areas with dramatic diversion'.[7]

Geoffrey Ridley perceived the need for diversion that existed in the many villages for whom the black-out and transport cuts brought a growing isolation and dreariness - villages where dwelt the essential work-force that produced food, and which were increasingly the centres of new concentrations of population: air-bases, anti-aircraft emplacements, training camps. In co-operation with the North East CEMA representative, John Groves - a small dynamic Scot with a populist attitude to drama, Geoffrey and Jane set out to found a Travelling Theatre - unpaid, part-time, subsidised initially by the YRCC - that would travel the villages bringing plays 'to boost morale and to show by example rather than exhortation what could be done in war-time'.[8] Of course the motivation was not exclusively altruistic: it was, for Jane and Geoffrey, as much that of having a whole lot of fun themselves doing the very thing that had formed so large a part of their lives pre-war. But then, what better to fuel a creative activity than self-fulfilment?

Although Jane and Geoffrey wanted to go straight into the best and start with a Shakespeare, with scenery and costumes, John, although sympathetic, was less confident and ambitious. They agreed finally that the start would be modest, both in respect of the scenic demands requiring transport, and of the demands upon the receptiveness of the audiences; and they chose a play by A.A. Milne, *Sarah Simple,* a trivial comedy with only six characters, a light-hearted piece that John thought more appropriate for dark war days. It required no scenery or costumes, and was not likely, as he put it '...to scare the villagers in the way the mere word "Shakespeare" was bound to do'. No transport would be needed for the furniture and props as the sofa and chairs and bits and pieces that were used could be borrowed from the villages.

There were two teenage parts in this play, a boy and a girl; and it was for one of these that I was recruited. I well remember the recruitment occasion, although I had no idea at the time that that was what it was. It so happened that it was at the time when I was playing Macbeth (his very self) in a house play competition at school, and a professional was to come and do our make-up giving us instruction in make-up technique at the same time. This man was John Groves. I remember awaiting my transformation under his hands into the gloomy Scottish hero, little guessing how he would subsequently describe the occasion: '...and then along came this little girl who murmured that she was Macbeth - I couldn't even hear what she said at first'. John was, unknown to me, scouting for the Travelling Theatre, and he must have found my Macbeth revealed the potential for playing an adolescent ingenue in a drawing room comedy, for soon afterwards I received, to my complete astonishment, a phone call to ask if I would take on a part in this enterprise, about which I now heard for the first time. Of course I accepted and then it was that I first met Geoffrey Ridley and Jane Lawrence.

Geoffrey's experience in amateur theatre had been acquired in a privileged context. In the great house of a tiny village near his family's home a well-to-do family had, in the early years of the century, mounted annually a production of one of the Greek tragedies translated by Gilbert Murray, who was a friend of the family. They involved friends, their large staff of servants and the village people in the productions and the performances took place for a few days in the summer, in an open-sided barn, or on the terrace of the house. Audiences consisted of the local gentry and intelligentsia, as well as the friends of the cast and the local people; it became a local tradition, a tiny, elite-led community theatre. Geoffrey, a local architect, became one of its leading actors. When he married the daughter of the house and moved into a neighbouring manor house in the same tiny village, he and his wife, both of whom wanted to produce Shakespeare, converted a mediaeval barn on their own estate into another Barn Theatre and established their own tradition of an annual three weeks summer Shakespeare season. Furthermore, Geoffrey's wife, who had a keen interest in local history, wrote a number of plays herself on local themes and these were also produced, though for shorter runs, in this tiny theatre, for local audiences.

It was, and still is, an enchanting place; it has all the original timber vaulted roof-beams, and a great open hearth on one side of the auditorium; it has a tiny gallery which presumably was once a storage loft; and Geoffrey built at one end a low stage, at the back of which is a great double door letting into a backstage area which is now converted into living space. There is room to seat about two hundred people on rows of folding timber seats. All the scenery, costumes, furniture and properties were made by Geoffrey and the groups of friends who constituted the casts. Geoffrey was an imaginative and ingenious designer and craftsman, as well as an accomplished actor; but he also invited friends who were in the professional theatre to take part, and it was in this way that Jane, in the early stages of a stage career, came upon the scene. She lived in the area, and had been working both in London, and in a small theatre in Tunbridge Wells with Christopher Fry.

All this drama in this tiny village in a remote corner of Sussex provided an exceptional amenity for the local people, for, in a village, involvement tends to be of a whole community; and in this village there were *two* Barn Theatres, for the Shakespeare and the Greek plays were at one time both still being produced. One wonders what Lady Bracknell would have said! It must have offered a cultural experience which would otherwise have been entirely inaccessible, both geographically and socially, to the lowly country people of pre-war rural England, while at the same time it provided idyllic conditions for the privileged groups that were creating it. Geoffrey and his wife gained additional notoriety for their somewhat anomalous left-wing sympathies -

doing plays and being left-wing was a fine combination of oddities in these gifted gentry.

The tradition of drama continues to this day in the village: Geoffrey's grandson, with his partner and two children, happily vacate the Barn, which is now their home, for a period in the summer, while the local amateur players, bearing the name of the great house where the Greek tragedy was performed in the old days, put on a Shakespeare.

When I met Geoffrey and Jane all that was over: the war had come, and he was no longer living with his wife in the house with the theatre. But twenty years of experience of small-scale, non-professional theatre activity in a small rural community had implanted in him an absolute confidence in the viability of taking good drama to village communities in Yorkshire; not only did he have expertise in staging with simplicity, but he had a deep confidence in the power of good drama to engage the most unsophisticated of audiences. He may have belonged to a privileged elite, but he understood village life and rural people, and had been much involved in rural affairs before he left Sussex, as a County councillor, as a magistrate, in the Council for the Preservation of Rural England. But above all he had a warm and compassionate nature, with a generosity that delighted in the prospect of making delight for others out of the past-time that he enjoyed so much himself.

Together Jane and Geoffrey made an inspiring team: perfectionists both, they expected - indeed demanded - of others the same dedicated commitment which they brought to anything they undertook. They never hesitated to be frank about the suitability or otherwise of would-be players of parts when auditioning, and this provoked the odd crisis of offendedness in smug and vain amateurs who were not up to their standard. There was no place for compromises or for the mediocre in their productions. Their combination of talents gave me unprecedented insights into and understanding of how good theatre is created. In addition to their own acting skills, they had a range of abilities - carpentry, costume making, set designing -

*The Barn Theatre*

*The stage*

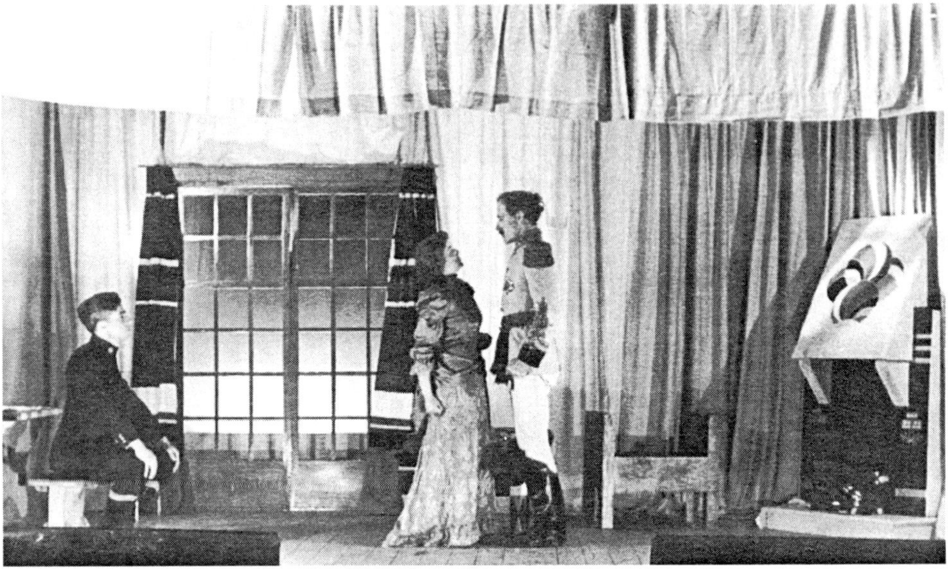

*Shaw's 'Arms and the Man'*

*Hall at the end of Farndale*

*Twelfth Night. Sir Toby (stage right) is played by Geoffrey*

rehearsal phase; and it was then that I discovered that, for the really committed amateur, rehearsing is much more delightful than performing. There was a mixture of ruthless criticism and lunatic hilarity that I found terribly exciting, while it could be also quite humiliating.

The first performance was given on 23 November 1940 in the tiny village school in the remotest village at the very end of Farndale. As it happened, for this engagement the troupe set off in three separate convoys: it was a Saturday, and it had been decided that a matinee show was to be given for the village children as well as the evening show. There was to be a song act by Pamela and John, followed by a performance of Mozart's *Bastien and Bastienne*, that had been prepared by the also-re-established Music Organiser of the YRCC: a three-part feast of music and fun and drama for a tiny cut-off community, in a dale famous, now as then, for the oceans of tiny wild daffodils that engulf it each spring. The first convoy arrived early morning to get things ready, including locating and shifting all the furniture and props needed for *Sarah Simple*. The music people, and we two teenagers, came mid-afternoon; such a cold grey gloomy day and no daffodils in November! I was numb with the cold of nerves, too. Jane was to follow separately and alone - by ill luck her work (with the Archdeacon of York, no less) included a Saturday morning shift. We of the second convoy arrived in the middle of a rather frenetically dramatised version of 'There's a hole in my bucket', performed by Pamela and John with the children participating in high glee. The Mozart went on next, very prettily and to much acclaim; and it was only as it was coming to an end, and tasks for which normally Jane was responsible had to be completed in preparation for *Sarah Simple,* that an anxiety began to take hold of the company: Jane had not arrived; our first engagement, and disaster had struck.

To play for time, another - also acclaimed - performance was given of 'There's a hole in my bucket...' and how, then, I admired the nonchalance and panache with which an old trouper like John Groves could gag and improvise to prolong the act and delay the ending! And it worked; for as we were thinking that it might have to go on for ever, Jane arrived; she was just not *too* late for us to be able to open on time. She was hustled in to her place on the sofa in a clinch with Geoffrey and the play started, for the first time.

The mishaps that had delayed Jane were of the sort to be expected by a troupe negotiating the remoter roads of Yorkshire in war-time, when the predictable hazards of remote country routes were increased by absence of sign-posts, all of which were removed in war time in case of invasion. The way up Farndale had (still has) one critical fork - at which she made the wrong choice. She happened also to be driving a borrowed car which she was unable to manoeuvre into reversing, although even if the technical mystery had been soluble she would still have been committed to a very long drive to the end of the wrong track, as there was - just as today - no place to do it until the end. So along she drove to the very end of one side of Farndale, where she found herself in 'the most isolated anti-aircraft battery in Yorkshire', where she was 'greeted with rapture' by a small community that 'hadn't seen a girl for weeks'. The problem of reversing the car was solved by the grateful airmen, but only after a little delay caused by what Jane calls discreetly 'a sentimental interlude'. I am sure that with the good trouper's horror of ringing up late she did what she could to balance compassion with urgency, but the trump card of car manoeuvring was not in her hands. But she did arrive in time; our first performance opened on time if with more stress than planned; and we were never late in starting throughout the whole life of the Travelling Theatre - one of our proudest boasts. That first performance was wonderful: we did it well; the audience loved it; the magic worked; the idea was proved to be a sound one; it was viable; strolling players still had a place in English theatre life.

I think it was after that performance - but I cannot be sure, for the play had a long run and in fifty years since then it has got confused in my mind - that we stayed, as on several other occasions, for the night in the village, arrangements having been made to distribute us among the villagers, as it was too far to get back so late at night. Jane and I were billeted in a cottage with dear people who cosseted us and fed us nobly, but forgot to inform us that in the country lavatories are somewhere at the end of the garden. Our hosts pointed out the bathroom, went to bed and left us to do the same. Jane went in first, and returned horror-struck - a bath, running water, but no loo! What to do? Well, there was only one thing, so we did it, together, side-by-side. A useful lesson learned - take stock of the stage before you tread it. Geoffrey the while was being royally entertained by the local great lady in the manor house: Lady Margery Beckett, mother-in-law of Sir Anthony Eden. We were to meet up with her again on many occasions, as her domain included many of the villages where we performed.

The organisation of the run was meticulous: Geoffrey had undertaken the preliminary reconnaissance and arrangements in the villages; transport was minimal - normally just two cars; the advance guard during the day, comprising the YRCC and the CEMA personnel, whose whole days were available; then the people in other employment - Jane, freed from the Archdeacon's commands, and we two school attenders at the end of the school day. How marvellous it used to be, being met outside by a beautiful actress in an old though classy car, and taken off to some far corner of Yorkshire instead of going back to high tea and homework and Mr Churchill. My family never owned a car, and they were rare on the roads anyway during the war, so that in itself was a thrill. We actually saw little of the Yorkshire countryside at the beginning of the first run, for the journey was mostly in the dark and we could hardly tell if we were on moors or in a village, as the blackout covered all. But arriving at the villages, to the bustle and the tensions of the last stages of setting up, we were given all manner of stage management tasks - we all were for we had no production team - and then getting into clothes and make-up. The make-up! That uniquely evocative smell of Leichner sticks, and the glistening translucent removing cream, and the queer little rabbit foot for removing surplus powder (scrounged by my indulgent mother from her pal the butcher) with which I really felt professionally equipped ... then the kindness and gratitude of the villagers afterwards ... and the good country fare we were often regaled with ... it was a dream world ... a magic world.

*Sarah Simple* was performed in villages from Farndale to Bardsey, in the dark and fearful winter of 1940/41, when the blitz raged in London and Britain stood embattled and alone in the face of the greatest peril she had ever known. People were only too glad to have some escapist diversion to take their minds from the shortages, the fears and the deprivations that affected everyone. The play was always a success. The halls ranged from tiny ones in village schools to great barn-like hangars on Air Force stations, to which we occasionally extended the tour. The stages ranged from the neatly conventional ones to the wobbly plank one which gave way as we took our final bow, neatly dropping one of us into the space below, from which a bow was taken with just the head, the only part visible. There was also the one that had a wickedly low tie-beam on which we all recurrently crashed our heads. Our set was different every time, gathered as it was by the advance guard from around the village. We never knew before we arrived how low would be the sofa, how big the distances between articles of furniture, how obstructive the occasional table; another lesson - or perhaps the same as the last one - take stock of the stage before you tread it. It became second nature, the quick appraisal before the curtain went up, the on-the-spot amendment to a movement or a timing.

Sterner lessons were learnt too. There came a time when George Lee, who played the man-servant, could no longer spare the time from Rural Industries. At short notice no replacement was available, so for the subsequent performances I was directed to double the part with my own part. That is when I first began to revel in comic character parts: we converted the aged man-servant to a gawky Cockney female; with little difficulty I resuscitated the language of my birth and found with mixed delight and consternation that a splendid Cockney lay very close at hand. The company was pleased with it. But on the first occasion that I played the part in a performance I took liberties with it, and put in some bits that I found so funny myself that I started to laugh. It was the silly line 'Was you referring to the night hair, sir, or the 'air on the 'ead?' that did it. I might have been able to suppress the initial giggle but Pamela, who shared the scene with me and Geoffrey, also found it funny and also started to laugh. As is the way with nervous laughter it generates more; we became helpless; the scene was wrecked; the audience loved it; John, Jane and Geoffrey did not. I shall never forget the icy silence in which Pamela and I returned, in disgrace, in John Groves' car; it was worse for Pamela for she was a professional; but I felt in the depths of shame. It never happened again to me. It was a lesson painfully taught by the silent censure of comrades: the lesson that theatre illusion must be sustained, and that laughing at your own performance destroys it, no matter how tolerant and beguiled an audience is.

Another lesson is the one that would have been of most use, I think, if I had gone on the stage: bearing the disappointment at a chance lost. One day John phoned me up to say that Jane had gone down with mumps or measles or something. Could I learn her part in the next six days, within which time we had our next performance? He would convert my two parts to a twin brother and an aged Scottish male servant, playing both parts himself, and hoping that the discrepancy in twinhood ages would pass unnoticed. I was thrilled: forgiven for the awful act of laughing; trusted with a large part - of, I may say, a comely stately older lady; and believed to be capable of miracles - to learn a large part in a few days. Oxford Entrance and Higher Certificate went for six, and on the evening before the performance, when we had our one rehearsal, I got through pretty well. But, alas - or perhaps I should nobly say 'luckily' - on the day of the performance I was picked up as usual by Jane; she had recovered. I had to remind myself that rehearsing is more fun than performing ... though I should have liked to put my week's concentrated effort to the test.

As the run of *Sarah Simple* came to an end the next production was ready. Geoffrey had been determined to do a Shakespeare, and already *Twelfth Night* had been in rehearsal for some time. I was not in it, which was desolating for, of course, I longed to take part in a more challenging play and especially in a Shakespeare. But it was perhaps a good thing that there were others cast in the play, for the pressures of Oxford Entrance and Higher School Certificate were growing, the school was rather anxious, and my till-now-tolerant parents more so. I am sure I would have heeded neither if I had been given the chance.

The production was staged with much greater elaboration; it had a large cast, of course, so a lot of costumes; it was a triumph of achievement in the context of the shortages and difficulties of the time. For at last Geoffrey had brought off his original intent, of having a complete set, and moreover a complete structure to contain it so that the play could be performed no matter what the conditions in any hall where it was to be given.

> He designed and made a skeleton box set adaptable in size to any stage by means of seven upright posts of 4 x 4 timber with 4 x 3 tie-beams which could be bolted together to the required size. There were double sets of wires strained all round and across the traverse beams on which were hung the sets of curtains, one blue, one cream, and one green.....For lighting we built a portable switchboard (with six circuits and three dimmers) which could be plugged in anywhere so that it was independent of any existing stage lighting. We made three biscuit-tin floods, four standing battens and three floor battens, and we also had one borrowed spot.....There were only three pieces of furniture necessary - a long seat, a chair and a throne. The seat and the throne Geoffrey brought up from The Barn, where he had made them for *Othello* in the late 1920's, and the chair he made in the same style in our long-suffering living room. All the props were made from bits and pieces - nothing in the house was safe.
>
> To transport all this we had to make a small trailer: a box-like affair of about 2 feet 6 inches x 4 feet 6 inches x 1 foot deep. In and on this were packed all the curtains, props, furniture and

timbers, plus the switchboard and lights, with a tarpaulin sheet lashed over all. To keep the breakables safe, everything was very tightly packed. Loading was an art, down to the correct positioning of every matchbox, and after each show the loading took place in the blackout, usually with the Air Raid Wardens swearing at us to switch off our torches.[9]

Thus did the YRCC Travelling Theatre finally come into its own, and join fully the gallant ranks of travelling fit-up troupes that had performed down the ages all over Europe; and with *Twelfth Night.* I think our Shakespeare would have liked it, and the combination of high seriousness and laughter, and good companionship and adaptability to circumstances that made the whole enterprise work. It had a run of ten performances, between 23 April (Shakespeare's birthday, by a happy chance) and 31 May 1941; a remarkable small paragraph in the history of English theatre. It was played, as *Sarah Simple* had been, all over North Yorkshire. But the difficulties of keeping the company together grew all the time. During five weeks there were eight changes of cast, caused by the call-up. There was some clever doubling involving some re-writing (Sir Toby with Orsino, for example) but even so nine players were needed, and that, in those uncertain times, was too many. But it remained throughout the run a splendid production, beautifully acted to a very high standard, with lovely music, played, as it happens, by the principal oboist of the London Symphony Orchestra, who happened to be stationed at York and married to the actress who was playing Olivia. The scale and intimacy of the production and the smallness of most of the venues enabled audiences to be engaged very easily in the action; the problems of comprehending Shakespeare's unfamiliar language seem to me always to diminish in direct proportion to the size of the theatre; and this play in particular has so much that makes an immediate and direct appeal to the most unsophisticated audiences. The Yorkshire Post reported that 'crowded village halls for productions of *Twelfth Night* are proving that there is a strong demand for worth-while drama in the rural areas'.[10] Overcoming the awe felt for Shakespeare was a problem. Jane tells how the children were:

> herded into the front rows and obviously under severe instructions to behave properly. They were suitably subdued during the first scene, but Sir Toby's boisterous entry in Scene 2 would raise surprised titters, hurriedly "shushed" by anxious adults; but by the time Sir Andrew was skipping higher and higher laughter became uninhibited as it dawned on young and old that it was meant to be funny. At the end of the show they would cluster happily round us with "Eh, we never knew Shakespeare was laike that".[11]

The timeless magic of the great magician was at work, in its proper place, a theatre; and many children may have had their first glimpse into that same universe of deeper reality that had been opened to me by John Gielgud: for them in a school hall in a village in North Yorkshire, but in a space magically transformed into a theatre by a troupe of strolling players that had a lot in common with those who may first have kindled the fire in Shakespeare's heart.

More sophisticated audiences were equally satisfied. At a performance in St. John's College in York it was said of it that

> it was a production of considerable interest, both from the point of view of its attractive setting and original approach...a simple curtain set...curtains decorated with heraldic designs...varied lighting....In all it was proof that simplicity handled with imagination achieve the best results.
>
> The production showed a departure from tradition and though the comedy was stressed there was a good sense of poetry. The riotous drinking scene, with the players silhouetted against a brightly-lit rose-coloured curtain, was one of the outstanding scenes of the evening and was excellently played.
>
> Sir Toby was played not as a fat and red-nosed tippler but as a gentleman of wit, roguery and charm....Feste with wit and polish.[12]

It was a great achievement, to be so good in quality in the light of the problems of those changes of cast and all the other difficulties or war-time. There were, of course, crises and disasters, the worst being undoubtedly that of the occasion when the trailer broke loose from the tow-bar; it happened on a downward hill after a steep climb onto the Wolds. Geoffrey found that what he took to be another vehicle was drawing alongside, and rapidly overtaking him. He was mildly surprised, for in the war there were very few cars on the road at all. However, he gave a friendly wave as it passed him - and then realised to his horror, that it was, in fact, the trailer. Aghast, he watched it careering down the hill, gathering speed as it went, to turn turtle at the bottom. The rest of the story is one of desperate measures taken against time: of superhuman efforts at unpacking, righting the trailer, repacking, limping along, with the trailer tied to the car and the contents mostly loaded into the car, to a garage to get a repair to the tow-bar; and finally of the miracle of a curtain-up on time. The even greater miracle was that nothing (apart from the tow-bar) was damaged - a tribute to the skill of the packer.

*Twelfth Night* came to an end in May 1941; it was miraculously revived for three performances the following year, with many cast changes, but clearly a play with a smaller cast was desirable for another concentrated run. For a few months there was a lull in the theatre's activity, and in the meantime the villages were entertained by a mobile cinema which Jane and Geoffrey took round. I myself set about doing the necessary work to catch up on preparation for the Higher Certificate and Oxford Entrance, and by the time the year ended I knew that the following year, October 1942, I would be going up to Oxford to read English. I thought my work for the Travelling Theatre had ended, with only *Sarah Simple* achieved; and I half wished that I could stay in York.

And then - there was a production of Shaw's *Arms and the Man*, in the spring of 1942. Apart from being a delectable play with very popular appeal, it has a small cast which made it a viable proposition for us as the difficulties of keeping a group together grew. This time I was in it: as Raina - the first major part in a full-length production in which I felt completely at home; and played in splendid costumes made by Jane (by hand, for she had no machine) out of fabric remnants and swatches of furnishing fabrics gleaned and begged from kindly shops, for clothing and materials were by now rationed. There was a three-scene set, designed and built by Geoffrey of course - in his living room. Geoffrey was the second most resourceful man I have ever known. (The first, also an architect, was to play a key part in another theatre project a quarter of a century later). An ingenious, endlessly inventive man, he seemed as happy doing the basic carpentry necessary for each performance as designing and making sets, playing the main parts, liaising with the village gentry or packing the trailer. He seemed to find everything a lark; no matter what the set-backs and problems he had encountered during the day, he was always full of high spirits when the rest of the company arrived for a performance, and always childishly excited about the show. " Hey diddly dee, an actor's life for me " he used to sing gleefully over and over again. He was doing a full-time responsible job as Secretary to the Yorkshire Rural Community Council, but it was in the theatre that he was most happy.

*Arms and the Man* was an inspired choice: it has a first-rate, well-structured plot, a small cast of engaging characters of considerable variety; the comedy is romantic, satirical, farcical and witty; it is benignly, amiably ironic, and above all it is one of the most intelligent and perceptive critiques of war and heroism in our language. Shaw's language is as much a delight to speak as it is to listen to: economical, purposeful, graceful, as well as witty and original. There could hardly have been a more appealing play for those audiences at that particular time, in drab, dreary anxious days of war, when laughing at it all was a relief. No better account of its impact, or of the whole inspired enterprise that was the travelling theatre, could be given than that which appeared in the Yorkshire Post. Here it is, in full.

Over the sweet-grassed shoulder of a hill, villagers in their war-time best make their way in ones and twos to the hall. Next to a first-aid point sign-board, at the bottom of an orchard thick with white-washed fruit trees, a small poster flutters on a bill board:

Yorkshire Rural Community Council Travelling Theatre presents
Arms and the Man by George Bernard Shaw

The village folk are excited by this unusual event. A real live company in a theatre play.

"Eh", says Sarah, "Ah've seen t'pantomine, but Ah cannot mind Ah've ivver seen a play. It'll be an experience like".

Others are more sophisticated. But they, like the children who have occasionally been "to t'talkies", have an air of eagerness. They file into the doorway of the village hall with a certain amount of good humoured crowding, settle themselves on the round-seated chairs with a great preliminary rustling, flouncing and arranging of handbags and coats. "Footlights", the more knowledgeable nudged their neighbours.

Doubtfully, as one who scans a new Government form, they peer at the one-sheet programme with the queer names - Raina Petkoff, Louka, Captain Bluntschli, Major Sergius Saranoff - "one of those Rooshian plays", decides Mrs Bardsey.

Promptly at half-past seven - the advertised time - the curtains swish apart. This does not occasion the stunned surprise among the audience that it would to those familiar with the Grand Tradition of amateur drama in England.

The scene is in Raina's bedroom. The tiny stage is cunningly flood-lit. A drapery of stone-coloured curtains delimits the set; the right entrance is a trellissed door-frame. The furniture is sparse, simple, effective: a dressing table, a chair, candles, a swinging kaleidoscopically-glassed lamp, a crucifix.

Before these wonders can be taken in, Raina Petkoff enters, a Botticelli angel oddly rigged out in the kind of night-dress-like garment worn by figures in Victorian paintings...the play begins.

Not a sound from the packed hall as Shaw's story of the soldier who took a realistic view of heroics and war unfolds. Intent, agog, the village audience reacts to sound and spectacle; most eagerly intent of all is the first row of stalls - boys and girls presumably allocated to these seats in order to provide a clear view of the stage for the rest of the audience, herring-packed on the level floor. When the curtains swing together at the end of the first act there is a drumfire of applause.

Backstage, the closing of the curtains is the signal for demonic activity by the cast. The YRCC players are their own scene shifters electricians, stage managers, carpenters, scene painters. "There will be an interval between the acts" announces the programme. There is....

"Part of the fun", says the producer, Miss J Lawrence laconically. "We make all our own props, paint them, design the folding furniture, devise the drapes and what little scenery we use".

Miss Lawrence is the only professional actress in the company. The leading lady, Miss D Harrington, is still at school. Major Sergius Saranoff is the Secretary of the Yorkshire Rural Community Council. Other members of the cast come from the Services and from Civil Defence Units.

"This is jam to some of the stages we have played on", says Miss Suzanne Rae, workmanlike in slacks and overall. "In some villages we have played in the schoolroom, on a stage just big enough to fit the bed across the angle of the walls".

Relief from the strain of the war, Home Guard, and Civil Defence uniforms are sprinkled in "stalls" and "pit".

In one way and another all present between the ages of 10 and 70 are taking some part in the war effort. This one rare, deeply appreciated visit indeed provides a break in the everlasting tension of life in Britain today.[13]

We could have gone on playing *Arms and the Man* for a long time to more audiences, for it never failed to delight. But it all had to end, the whole wonderful enterprise. We were all on the move: men and women alike were subject to the constraints and demands of a war-time life, and I was going up to Oxford. Furthermore, petrol was beginning to get impossible to obtain. So at the end of April the last performances were given - of a revived *Twelfth Night* on 22 April, and of *Arms and the Man* on 25 April. Appeals for more shows continued but by now the times were too difficult to make a new start possible for Jane and Geoffrey, with a new set of people. What an achievement it had been, that inspiration and its realisation, and what a miracle, its achievement in the face of the continuing shortage of people to take part! Jane (who is still teaching and producing although she is half-way through her eighties) wonders:

> ...how we managed to do it all. Costumes, rehearsing, even casting were as nothing compared with the logistics of travel and set-up. We reckoned that it took two people six hours to erect the timbers, strain the wires, hang the curtains, run the cables and set the lights. Generally Geoffrey and I would set off soon after 9am. The drama organiser would bring the rest of the cast in the office car after they had finished their daytime jobs. On a long journey this was often a close-run thing, but ... we never rang up late. Conditions varied in every place. Sometimes we would find the hall open and ready and on other occasions we would have to waste time tracking down the caretaker for the key. Some stages were dreadful, others so pristine and perfect that I had to divert the watchful caretaker's attention while Geoffrey was putting screws in the plaster.
>
> Not many people are left nowadays who can appreciate the difficulties we had to overcome. Blackout, for instance. Every hall we played in had to be inspected to make sure that no window let through so much as a chink of light ... scarcities of little things like reels of cotton or nails: Geoffrey used to stop at every ironmonger's shop he came to in remote villages and even forges, in search of nails. Little inconveniences like air raids. We returned from one long journey into York's Baedeker raid [14] and next morning I rushed round to a bombed area to see whether we still had a Raina. We had - just. There was a crater at the bottom of the garden.[15]

What a time we had! Hey diddly dee, an actor's life for me - and especially that of a strolling player: coming, setting up, playing, and going on to the next stop; with good companions, with whom you shared conviction that theatre is important, that drama works - binds its spell, stimulates, entertains, enlightens - wherever the performance, if it is good, meets an audience, and that with a simple portable set and something good to act a group of players can create the magic as well in a church hall in a war-time Yorkshire village as in a traditional theatre building inaccessible to all but the privileged minority.

The privileged gentry who in the early years of this century brought Gilbert Murray's translations of Greek tragedy to their tiny village community, would possibly greet with astonishment an acknowledgement of their place in the history of a playhouse in the industrial north. But from their inspiration came that for the lovely little Barn Theatre which Geoffrey Ridley created, and where he developed a style and scale of production that served as a model of what could be done in the Yorkshire villages. And I was then, by great good fortune, early awakened to the power and the delight of drama in unsophisticated communities, which led me in my turn along the paths to *our* theatre. The threads which link me to the Playhouse in Leeds also link me to the YRCC Travelling Theatre, and to a tiny mediaeval barn in West Sussex.

There was a particularly happy coincidence in the fact that it was in York that this travelling theatre was created: for York was one of the centres where the great mystery cycles of the fourteenth and fifteenth centuries had flourished - indeed was the home of the *only* complete extant cycle, consisting of forty-two plays, each one of which was a self-contained episode in the story of the Bible, from the Creation to the Day of Judgement. The YRCC Travelling Theatre had some things in common with the companies which performed these plays: different companies for each play and organised by the Merchant Guilds to produce the whole cycle at the Feast of Corpus Christi. Those companies were the craftsmen of the guilds and so, like us, were part-time, rehearsing and performing in their spare time; they had mobile stages, but on wheels and horse-drawn, as their circuit was smaller than ours - the streets of the city, where there were a number of 'stations'; and their stages, which were called pageants, were very elaborately designed and constructed, with all manner of staging devices; but they, like the YRCC Travelling Theatre took their plays (in their case a sequence forming a complete whole when viewed by the standing crowds who gathered at the stations) to the audiences.

That is how drama in England began. Although the inspiration was a religious one, and derived from the churches' early efforts to convey the scriptural messages to congregations that were mainly illiterate, the form developed when it left the church setting and took to the streets; the long process began of secularisation, no doubt stimulated by contact with older forms of travelling entertainment. The first audiences must have been completely bewitched, and looked forward eagerly each year to the Festival; and then perhaps they began to join in, to modify, to participate - we don't know. Certainly they must, as the years passed, have got to know the parts and the regular actors very well so in this respect our audiences were perhaps rather less experienced than theirs, for ours - farm labourers, village policemen, war-time school children - had never seen any play, let alone Shaw or Shakespeare (to say nothing of A A Milne). It must have been a really dramatic experience, the descent upon the village of this colourful band.

The YRCC Travelling Theatre had few parallels in its own time, although today the concept of 'taking drama to the community' is very well established and is practised by a number of very high quality professional companies. But pre-war it was very unusual. I had, in fact, seen a performance in 1937 at my London school by the only such company: the Pilgrim Players, formed and directed by E Martin Browne ( a fine professional actor, and incidentally the founder of the British Drama League) whose objective was to take a repertoire of religious and predominantly verse plays to schools and churches. I had seen James Bridie's *Tobias and the Angel;* and during the fearful summer of 1940 they took this production, and T S Eliot's *Murder in the Cathedral* to the people living in the dangerous and threatened southern counties of England, with the brave ideal of helping to keep up morale as they suffered continuous bombing and the threat of invasion. Our work was much less heroically set, but it did attempt to lighten the darkness that could engulf remote places in those unpleasant times, with all the anxieties that lowered spirits and enervated people. As a result, people may well have been introduced to the theatre who would otherwise never have made an effort to try it.

Certainly for me the involvement in that brave and happy venture, with the comradeship and the hard work, depending so much on ensemble spirit and on adaptability and improvisation, generated a wider and deeper interest in drama and its roots in society than working in a conventional dramatic society would have done. When, soon after my last appearance with the Travelling Theatre, I went up to Oxford to read English, I found an immediate rapport with early drama and in particular with the mystery plays. The thread in my life that is connected to the mystery plays is woven into all my story, and there is a point in the web where threads cross. Jude Kelly, the first Director of the West Yorkshire Playhouse where the dream of 1964 was finally realised, was once the Director of the York Festival which contained the York mystery plays. The whole Cycle had been revived in 1951 for the first time since the sixteenth century, and it became a triennial event. Jude was the Director in 1988.

But the web is even thicker: as a post-graduate student I lived in York again for a year after Oxford, in 1944; and I spent regularly an evening a week in the city doing voluntary work with young people; I had a drama group; and I conceived the scheme, unrealistic but nevertheless supported by the Youth Organiser, of mounting a version of the Mystery Cycle and performing it as it had been originally, on pageants - with individual youth groups throughout the city undertaking each one play, thus replicating a production as it would last have been seen in 1572. The York Cycle was at that time 'almost unknown except to a comparatively small number of students of Middle English, many of whom showed themselves strangely unresponsive to any kind of merit in the plays...'[16] The proposal went, I think, as far as the Education Committee and, not surprisingly, no further. It was still war-time and it was a crazy dream and who was I? An amateur, a twenty-year old student heading for a life in social work - not even in the theatre - with no professional status or experience. But I can't help wondering: did the idea linger in one or two of the memories of the Education Committee; were they less unreceptive than they might have been when, in 1951, the proposal was made to mount the Cycle in full but to do it on a larger and more prestigious scale, - with Martin Browne of the Pilgrim Players as Director - to do it for the Festival of Britain festivities and thereafter as a three-yearly event; was I just minimally connected with the enterprise on which, by then an established event, Jude Kelly worked in 1988? It may be idle fancy, but perhaps 1990 was not the first year in which Jude the professional played a part in this amateur's dream.

Twenty years were to pass between that grandiose conception and the even more daunting one of a full professional resident theatre in the great city of Leeds. But they had a lot in common. The great difference was that the 1964 dream was not mine alone but shared, at first by only that handful of friends, but as the campaign grew, as we turned *faut de mieux* from a tiny vociferous pressure group into reluctant entrepreneurs, we had to gain strength from the only proper source: 'the people'. It was the concern and interest and dynamic of a sizeable section of the Leeds population that brought the thing into being. The way that came about, at the same time as the process of negotiating and consulting, designing and planning and fund-raising, is one of the most interesting features of the Leeds Theatre Campaign. The mobilising of public support, the stimulation of interest and conviction out of nothing, the brain-washing, the inspiring, the bullying into action, into generosity: all those *were* the campaign. How often I wished during those years, when my life was completely taken over by this enterprise, that the bright idea of 1964 had gone the same way as that of 1944, - that I could step back from a very daunting commitment and be just a theatre-goer and an amateur actress again and with luck find that mysteriously, and without involving me, the objective had been realised!

Indeed, for me personally the years between 1944 and 1964, the years of the two dreams, were filled with theatre delights on both sides of the curtain. I see now how they led, as had the work with the YRCC Travelling Theatre, steadily towards the Playhouse in Leeds. In search of the threads in the web, I explore some of those years in my own life. I know there are many others whose lives also have threads that cross and recross in this same web, but mine are the only ones that I can follow. The thread of the mystery plays runs unbroken through all the years. I did finally realise, in a totally unpredictable and unlikely place, the desire to produce them; the influence of that drama of 600 years ago established in me a firm conviction that theatre should be for everyone, not a privileged minority; the Travelling Theatre had given me my first chance to see in practice how it worked at grass roots; and the theatre that finally embodied the dream of 1964 is, for me, the trustee of that right, as much as it is the upholder of the tradition of great classical drama.

# 2

# Between The Acts: Some Amateur Scenes

> A severe cold usually prevents me from attending amateur performances. I do not wish them ill: it is just that I am tired of hearing that amateurs are more sincere than professionals because they do it for love. It seems to me unjust that the man who foregoes regular employment and devotes his life to the fluctuant rewards of stage pretence should be held less sincere than the man for whom acting is simply a more exhibitionist alternative to bridge. [1]

Kenneth Tynan's view has long been shared by the majority of theatre-goers, and not only in respect of the amateur's hypocrisy or his indulgence in exhibitionism: his standards are assumed to be inadequate, his technical skill deficient and his artistic accomplishment minimal. 'Amateur dramatics' are all very well in a Jane Austen novel, or for school children, students and Women's Institutes. For the average Englishman the word 'amateur' does not mean 'lover', but something more like 'dabbler'. It connotes second-rateness, ineptness. 'Amateur theatre is often stigmatised; people think of village halls and expect the scenery to fall down, people to forget lines and trip over things'.[2] This is an observation by David Wildman, an amateur director and designer for the Ilkley Players, a company formed in 1929 which owns its own Playhouse and gives eight shows a year of twelve performances of each one: an established feature of Ilkley artistic life. The real truth, as Wildman knows, is that 'there is a vast amount of talent in the amateur theatre and standards are very high. Just as high as professionals'. Indeed, to be just to Tynan, he too was obliged to make reservations: after one very fine Student Drama festival he conceded 'if this is amateurism, then we can do without professionals'. Which of course is exactly what Leeds did insofar as serious drama was concerned for a large part of the time before Leeds Playhouse. But, because of the deep-rooted prejudice, the amateur theatre rarely serves more than a very small minority and is not an adequate alternative in a large community, no matter how good it is.

It is true that some part of an amateur's motivation is exhibitionism and vanity: a delight in showing his skills, and in exercising the power over people to make them laugh, cry , think or be afraid. Many a timid, reserved, self-conscious person finds in acting the opportunity to free himself for a short while from his inhibitions by engaging in relationships, and situations, and dialogue not of his making and therefore not vulnerable to mockery or criticism of himself *ad personam:* he can feel powerful and effective and profound - all the things he would like to be in real life. And for this therapeutic experience he needs an audience.

But there is another reason for the presence of an audience, even for the amateurs who are primarily interested in exploring drama: only in the presence of an audience is the act of play-making complete. To some extent this is true of all performing arts: the performance of a string trio or a pas-de-deux is, like that of a play, the culmination of a long creative process, the climax of sustained practice; and the tension created by offering it to an audience concentrates all the artist's endeavours into a supreme effort to achieve its final perfect form. However, a play has a far more fluid relationship with an audience than the other performing arts, for it uses more methods of communication than any other and, above all, it uses language, the medium common to us all. It engages an audience at the level of ordinary life. When a character in a play addresses another, he knows the words that are written in the script and the response that is written in the script; he and his director and fellow actors have come to their conclusion about the meanings to be found in the words. But in an actual performance there may be as many different responses to the words as there are members of the audience; and the audience response will impact on the actors, subtly influencing and perhaps modifying their own perception of the words and meanings; the actor who truly enjoys the act of performance will feel the compulsion to respond to a newly created situation in all the ways that are part of his medium - gesture, expression, stress, emphasis, timing, but always within the constraints imposed by the overall artistic interpretation of the entire cast and director. All the performers are doing this at the same time. All are conducting a three-way communication, though one of the three is the rest of the cast, the other the number in the audience. This is the great fascination of acting to an audience, for an amateur as it must be for a professional. It is frightening and very taxing, and one can never know in advance how successfully this complex operation will be conducted; it is an extraordinary multiple act of mutual communication. 'The play' is not the same play night after night. And it is certain that without an audience no actor, whether amateur or professional, ever feels his character has come to fruition.

So the amateur needs an audience as much as the professional. Unlike the professional, however, he does not depend upon praise and approval for his livelihood, so may seem to like the praise and approval for vanity's sake. The amateur 'does it for love' as Tynan says; he prefers it to bridge. It is just unfortunate for his image that he needs an audience to respond even if not to praise and approve. In some ways, however, the most enjoyable part of amateur acting is in the rehearsing and - oh yes - all the fun: of relationships, of dressing up, of testing yourself, of trying things out, of discovering the meanings of words, of entering the magic world of make-believe. And it must not be forgotten that amateur drama does in fact give a great deal of entertainment to audiences who may have no other access to drama.

This is how it had been for me until, in 1964, I gave up perforce being an amateur actress in order to help create a stage for the professionals. I had spent more than twenty years acting and directing in a great range of amateur companies, from the partly professional one of the Yorkshire Rural Community Council Travelling Theatre, to a multi-racial group in Uganda in which work of remarkable quality was produced by men and women who had not only never acted before, but who had in their society no indigenous tradition of drama.

The earliest and most committed of the campaigners had similar backgrounds. First among them was Alec Baron who came into the campaign on the second wave: bringing with him a life-time of experience as a director of high quality in the Leeds amateur world, and knowledge of and passion for cinema too, which had started when he was fifteen and had founded the first Film Society in Leeds; bringing furthermore a standard of criticism and judgement equal to none, and an intense interest in experimental theatre. It was said of him that whatever good thing happened in the theatre, wherever it was, he could more often than not say 'I was there'. Thus did he call his autobiography, an absorbing documentary of sustained commitment to theatre. His actual productions with the famed Proscenium Players in Leeds were of the highest quality, and the range of his play selections was wide and adventurous.

Another early campaign figure of great renown in city drama was Charles Gardiner, who trained as a teacher and took additional qualifications in drama, which was his real passion. After the war he became a headteacher and presided over an extraordinary Secondary Modern school in West Leeds: a school, serving a predominantly working class population and a generally under-privileged housing area, which established a national as well as a regional reputation for its work in the performing arts - dance, music, and above all, drama. He staged annually in the summer term a great Shakespeare production, which would involve practically the whole school, staff and students, for a good part of the term. All the technical work was designed and executed by the school - costume materials dyed, lighting equipment constructed; and performances of astonishing competence were created by youngsters from homes where little was read - performances which contained insight and depth beyond normal expectation for their age, the result of group exploration of the plays in an atmosphere of passion and commitment, and genuine encouragement. Charles was himself a talented actor and worked with the Leeds Arts Theatre for many years. He, like Alec, joined the campaign within the first three months, and stayed to the end and beyond.

Many other amateurs who joined the growing theatre campaign will appear in later pages of this story. It was in truth the case that amateur work in Leeds, fostered by the absence of a professional presence, flourished with remarkable, sustained artistic achievement and, let it be said, with stalwart support from the City Council. The old Mechanics Institute (where Dickens, giving one of his famous readings, once walked onto a platform to a reception in which '...the whole audience rose, and the applause became almost deafening ...')[3] had been converted into a Civic Theatre for the use of any society wanting to stage a production. It was subsidised by the Council and run by a Civic Arts Guild, a voluntary co-ordinating committee, to which individual societies belonged and on which the Council was represented. And I shared with many of my fellow amateurs a snobbish feeling that the work of some of these groups, together with the University and College groups, had an integrity, a high seriousness, and a much greater commitment to good drama than anything that went on in the Grand, or in the Theatre Royal in its last days in the fifties when it was hosting Harry Hanson's Court Players - one of the last survivors of the commercial touring repertory company which played twice-nightly weekly shows on a circuit of venues: '... dreaded as the last funk-hole for any actor...' as John Osborne describes it. [4]

But amateur theatre was a minority activity and it tended to be a bourgeois one. It made little impact on the great numbers of people in the city who were potential audiences but who were neither friends of the actors, students of drama, parents of the children, nor interested in the work of various, otherwise unperformed, writers. So the amateur work, in the Civic Theatre, in the schools, in the University and the colleges, made no substantial contribution to the cultural life of the city as a whole. However it was prestigious enough to be used by the City Council as an argument against the demands for the new theatre; although paradoxically we, the campaigners who were amateurs, were consistently referred to slightingly as 'just' amateurs who, by definition, could know nothing about professional theatre, nor appreciate that its value to a community would be greater than our own.

Although this did present us with the very first line of opposition to overcome, it never really shook our inner confidence. It is true that our status, or lack of it, disadvantaged us and we had a great deal to learn about the professional theatre world and its workings; but our inner confidence was based on a profound shared belief that drama was an art that was of prime importance to all the people; and several of us had come to that belief by way of amateur work.

My own work as an amateur was done in a variety of groups, and a history of it gives a not incomprehensive account of the range of this form of theatre where, in Leeds, the origins of the Playhouse are to be found. And so, leaving for a while the main thread of this story, I now pick up the network of threads that connects me with the Leeds Theatre Campaign.

It was to a privileged closed community that I went on from the Travelling Theatre, for in 1942 I went up to Oxford. It was the precise moment, I suppose, when I made my final vow to stop longing to go on the stage, to plan to make a different career and to settle for a life in which my work in drama would remain amateur. It was not the glamorous Oxford of Brideshead, nor the comfortable (albeit perilous!) one of Morse. For it was war-time. We in the women's colleges suffered from inadequate heating and from boring minimal food; we lacked the social stimulus of a large male undergraduate presence; our academic working time was limited by an obligation to do eight hours a week war work; and our general comfort was eroded by such minor irritations as bath rationing, butter rationing, coal rationing, and the blackout. The men's colleges were variously populated by pre-service young men, by those unfit for service or exempt from it; the pre-service men were up only for a year before going off to the war. We women were urged to stay and complete, but were given only two years unless we were going on to be teachers.

I was completely blank about what I was going to do. I suspect that contrary to my vows, I still secretly hoped for a 'break' that might lead to the stage. So I was pressurised through the Shortened Honours Course, of six terms plus a six-week extra stint in Oxford during the only long vacation. It was quite tough going, and had the curious result of sending us forth with Honours Degrees in English Literature having studied no English Literature later than Milton. And of course it was a deeply troubling time too: for those years were the most urgent and the most vital in the conduct of the war, and the pursuit of learning in the ancient city of dreaming spires seemed agonisingly irrelevant. But I suspect that for me that serious, intensive, rather sombre time was more suitable than the Oxford of May Balls and punting romances and extravagant parties would have been. I was enough out of my social element, in the Oxford of those days, among the gifted daughters of the upper and upper-middle classes. We had not benefited from the Education Act of 1944, and there were no automatic grants for those who could gain a place. Only if one managed to get one of the limited number of local or state scholarships was a daughter of a poor man able to enter this world; and the local scholarships, one of which I got, were very meagre, as I discovered. We were in a minority, we of the poorer classes. But war is a great equalizer, and that one at least tossed us all into the same boat insofar as, for example, dress was concerned. None of us had anything to wear, for rationing at that stage was draconian. So all of us, whether from Roedean or a state secondary school, looked pretty rag-tag; except that the absolute formality of academic dress was maintained. I think one of my most bizarre memories of being a war-time undergraduate was of the days in 1944 when I took my Final examinations - or, as it is termed in Oxford, 'sat Schools'. It was glorious June weather and we, rigged in black stockings, white blouse and black skirt, black tie, cap and gown, sat in the examination hall, writing papers on Chaucer and old Anglo-Saxon poets, while the war-planes flew non-stop overhead to the beaches of Normandy. It was a stressful guilt-burdened time.

Perhaps the disadvantage I most lamented on my own behalf about being up at Oxford in war-time was the suspension, for the duration, of OUDS - the Oxford University Dramatic Society 'whose productions since their inauguration in the 1880's had launched a number of stars'[5] and for which, I knew, Gielgud himself had in 1932 directed a production of *Romeo and Juliet.* I cannot think why it was suspended, for the immediate reaction was for alternative groups to fill the vacuum - the Experimental Theatre Company (ETC) and the Friends of OUDS. So there was still opportunity for doing drama in the small amount of time left in those very over-filled years; and I in fact became heavily involved very soon. Within two weeks I joined forces, by way of what I can only describe as a dating service within the ETC, with one Anthony Besch, who was later to become a very distinguished international opera director. For the purpose of showing our form to the established people working in the Company, we were invited to offer either a solo or a two-hander piece in a competition judged by Lord Berners and Neville Coghill. I was certainly in luck, in the arbitrary pairing that was brought about for freshers who preferred the two-hander option but had no already-established contact with the other half of a pair. Anthony arrived one day in my college with very decisive ideas as to what we should do and how we should do it, and he was clearly by then already a most accomplished and experienced director. We put on a scene from *The Way of the World*; and I found myself being directed with precision, with style, with fanatic attention to detail, even for this scene that was to last some twenty minutes. We won the competition, and received the grand sum of ten shillings prize money - the equivalent of fifty pence - as well as the honour and the reputation. We divided the ten shillings and I went on to work for Anthony in a production he did of *The Beggars' Opera*, as stage manager and assistant director. This in effect started him on his opera / music career; and to me too it was important. It gave me a first experience in directing, for two of the leading characters sang divinely but were not very experienced actors and were put under my tuition.

As ever, the production time brought all the fun and the hecticness, as well as the intense relationships, that are part of the fascination of this 'alternative to bridge'. One occasion I remember with special delight: a day in London for which none of us had obtained the necessary passes. (Oxford was a tightly disciplined place in those days - passes for a day away from the city were de rigueur.) The object was to choose the costumes from Nathan's the theatrical costumiers: they still had the costumes from the 1920 Nigel Playfair production of the Beggar's Opera at the Lyric, Hammersmith, and these were, in fact, the ones we hired; they were used again by Anthony in another production he did in Oxford after the war, in 1948.

This was the first time I had ever entered the gorgeous domains of a costumiers, and seen the acres of rich velvets and brocades, the rows and rows of shoes of every period and style, the baskets of 'extras' - cod-pieces, hats, belts; the cupboards filled with weaponry; and everwhere the strange, elusive, powerful smell of 'the stage'. I felt I was penetrating the base foundations of theatre life and never since have I failed to feel a shiver of fear and excitement at the moment when the hampers arrive for whatever play I am acting in: fear, because this is the moment when the secret activity of preparing the play is coming to an end and it has to go public; excitement, because it is now to become real theatre. The smell of costumes from a theatrical costumier is unmistakable and incomparable. That day I smelt it for the first time: no more were costumes things that appeared from the school needlework room, or from the miraculous hand of Jane, run up out of black-out material or bedspreads; this was the authentic smell of theatre of all time.

We had a lovely day, the being illicit making it the more so, and I ate hors d'oeuvres for the first time. How the memory fastens upon the trivial: a strange taste; the strangeness of a new smell; like the hawthorn and the madeleine for Proust. Odd to think of the mighty issues and dreadful horrors that were engaging the world at that precise time when all that meant most to me seemed distilled into a new smell in the basement of a theatrical costumier.

So my first year in sombre, war-time Oxford had its share of theatre magic. The second-cum-final year claimed time back for work. And I did no more drama, but concentrated on getting a degree. Many of the men who had been up for that first year went off now, to serve in the forces, and some of them to return after the war to complete their degrees. It is irritating to know that I preceded by only a year or so the great galaxy of theatre devotees who poured into Oxford after the war, and poured out of it as the new generation of directors who were to bring such profound changes to British theatre: first among whom was Peter Brooke. I had come and gone by the time the war ended and Oxford began to live a full life again; and I think that the really most important thing I brought away with me - apart from some life-long relationships, a degree, and the experience of working with a very talented young theatre fanatic - was a passion for mediaeval literature and a sense of identification with the spirit of the middle ages. It was at this stage immediately after Oxford, while I was doing a post-graduate course in Leeds, training to be a social worker and living again for a time in York, that that vision of the Mystery Cycle production came to me. But that could not be realised; and so I settled myself to the prospect of an immediate future without drama, while I completed my year's post-graduate training.

Stage drama, at any rate, was in abeyance for me; not so the great drama of the war, which reached its final phase as 1944 drew on. The bitter struggles that followed the invasion of June 1944 went on, and hope and despair alternated as the fortunes of the West waxed and waned. It is difficult - and mercifully so - for later generations to imagine what life felt like for civilians in those strange and terrible days. The ultimate fear, of the war being lost to Hitler lay deep inside, but unreal like a sleeping mythical monster, unheeded except in fleeting moments of horror, or in nightmares; and covered up by layer upon layer of different consciousness: the boredom of the diet - nutritious because designed by the Government, but dull, stodgy, basic, giving rise to wild longings for a banana, a lemon, a real egg,; the struggle with clothes, on a clothing ration that posed such choices as that between a pair of wearable shoes and a skirt to replace one adapted from a school tunic three years before. That inspired miracles of ingenuity: I still have, kept for old times' sake in a patchwork bed-cover, a piece of the parachute silk I was given once and with which I made - yes - a pair of French knickers. Such were the times that one never asked where the parachute had come from.

There was the ever-present irritation and danger of the blackout. And above all, even for the lucky families such as mine that had no close loved one in the forces, was the presence of death: death in the little buzz of an approaching plane, even in our privileged part of the land, which had seen only two massive air raids; death in the south from the new monstrosities being launched from across the channel - the buzz-bomb and the rocket, awful sudden forms of death-giving more widespread than from the bombs of the beginning of the war; and all the deaths of the battles - just numbers until the sleeping monster stirred: numbers that went with the reports and the battle maps and the arrows on the maps that went one way and then another. And death made by *my* hands, in the smooth thin shape of propeller blades to be covered with gauze and soldered down the edge (a hand tearing job) and then to become part of a death-carrying bomber plane. For six weeks I worked in the aircraft factory that had been set up in Terry's chocolate factory. It was with the friends that I made on the shop floor there, tough, kindly comrades, that I celebrated getting a degree; and few friends could have more generously rejoiced than those women who had left school at fourteen, and had certainly never heard of York's Mystery plays. I think they would have enjoyed them, actually; they would have liked the directness, the lack of classiness and pretentiousness, the straight, homely humour, and the deeply affecting conviction that contribute to the abiding power of those old plays. But they were certainly not theatre-goers to York Rep; the middle-class, snobby atmosphere would have made them ill-at-ease, though goodness knows the stuff of the plays that constituted the regular fare in repertory theatres of the time was not very demanding. Theatre at that time, particularly in the provinces, was generally a cosy, bourgeois affair, and my mates on the shop floor would have felt out of their element, as did I, with the respectably clad ladies, with the tea-trays passed over the knees in the interval, with the little trio playing away in the orchestra pit, and with the family feeling of an audience that each week returned to their accustomed seats, coughed discreetly, and applauded circumspectly.

The war in Europe had ended, a great election land-slide victory for the Labour Party had taken place, the atom bomb had been dropped on Hiroshima and the war in the east had also ended (and the founder members of Leeds Theatre Campaign had all been demobbed), by the time I went on to my first job and a new phase as an amateur actress.

Where two of three are gathered together there will be formed an amateur dramatic society: so urgent seems the need to act, and to make theatre. In the enormous factory in Manchester where I started my professional life as a personnel officer there was a flourishing and respected society, which did work of good quality dramatically, but of no less than stunning quality technically: this factory was Metropolitan Vickers, a vast empire of 22,000 employees on one site, and having perhaps the highest concentration of skilled electrical engineering experts in the land. It had also, during the war, developed the gas-turbine engine. In the little theatre which was part of the social building in the factory, the lighting, the sets and the technical effects were always of the highest professional quality, and never since have I belonged to a society that had such a large and expert stage crew. Writing for the theatre was, at that time, producing little of note and the society produced the work of stalwarts like Shaw and Priestly and Rattigan; and once, daringly, a piece by a now-little-remembered dramatist called Charles Morgan. It also did Gilbert and Sullivan, and the revues and satirical sketches that in an in-group in a closed world are always successful with the willing but captive audience who enjoy the carefully engineered jests at the expense of targets in the hierarchy. The serious work, though, was really seriously undertaken. The members of the society were drawn almost exclusively form the graduate elite of the research and management sectors: there were *no* members from the shop floor and there was no parallel society among the 'workers'. Metrovicks mirrored the class-structured society of pre-war Britain accurately. Most of the members of the dramatic society were University graduates, and many had taken part in student drama and came to their participation with the high seriousness that is to be found in good student theatre work. Rehearsals were very long; all one's spare time was given up to it - and there was little enough spare, in the long working day (7.30 am to 5.00 pm) in a five-and-a -half day week, with week-end duties thrown in occasionally.

The amateur theatre world has a rhythm of its own. Productions tend to have long rehearsal periods, and the amateur lives with a commitment that initially makes modest demands and leaves a lot of time for the cultivation of the relationship bonds that flourish with such intensity in the theatre: a commitment that slowly takes over his life completely, until in the week of the performances themselves nothing really of any importance happens except in the evening when the play goes on. The affairs of the factory seemed, to me, very insignificant in that week; shop-floor problems could come and go but in that last week they could not expect to get solved. Perhaps gas-turbine engines might have gone into production a little earlier if Metrovicks had not, for so long, had such a vigorous and absorbing dramatic society; and who knows how *that* might have affected the course of history? Certain it is that one of the most carefully and sensitively directed productions I was concerned with in many years of amateur work was that of the brilliant young engineer in charge of the development of a vital part of the jet engine: a production of Charles Morgan's rather pretentious, but thoughtful and high-minded play, *The Flashing Stream* - little performed and now virtually forgotten. It appealed to the society because it took place on a research station, set on an island in mid-ocean; most of the parts were played by men whose own records of scientific research achievement were of a very high order, and there was a quality of inner truth and integrity about the production and the characterisations that gave it an intense dramatic power; it was an unusual example of the value of identification by actors with the inner world of the play they are acting in - in this case a process that needed little effort on their parts.

Acting for the Metrovicks society was not only something I took for granted, from the first moment that I knew about the society soon after I joined - as the most junior member of staff - the very distinguished Women's Personnel Department of that great empire; it was an activity I would have been swept into anyway even without a passion for acting, for 'the staff' contained very few women. It was an almost exclusively male-dominated world; and I was additionally rare in that I also had a lot of acting experience. Within this quite self-contained world of tough basic industry, which had a large female work-force, I led a completely double life: factory society was a divided society consisting of the two major sectors, 'works' and 'staff' with a carefully sustained hierarchical structure within both. There were different eating areas for works, foremen, staff, superintendents, directors; there were different hours for staff and works; works personnel clocked on while most staff personnel did not; there were different methods of payment, and different frequencies according to whether you were weekly-paid in cash, weekly-paid by cheque or monthly paid. Except for Christmas parties, which were departmental, social activities were separate. This microcosm of class-ridden British society affronted and dismayed me, and I found my position as a member of the 'staff' class a hard one to occupy. I found superficial solutions to this personal dilemma in personal relationships, and in working as hard as I could to achieve welfare improvements. But it was a double life that I led. The women fettlers in the brass foundry, the tough Irish immigrant women in the iron foundry core shop, the all-powerful foremen with whom I battled and flirted and haggled, knew little of the secret life that their young, fervent social worker led, although the networks of individuals, within which we were all intertwined, overlapped.

Life in the factory was a drama in itself; and for me especially it had a highly dramatic 'set'. I was responsible for all the women in all the foundries, and the hyper-tension that took over the vast, cavernous, murky iron-casting shop when a really enormous casting was to be made moved me profoundly. For a critical short period a huge cauldron of molten metal swung across the upper space of the shop, watched intently by groups of tiny dark figures beneath, to the huge core that had been prepared; and then the flaming liquid was poured into the core. There were all sorts of hazards, many of a technical, metallurgical nature that I never understood; I simply sensed a tension that was spread throughout the whole shop, where superintendents, foremen, and foundrymen shared the crisis moments, and which seemed to me to resemble some of the most dramatic scenes in Milton's *Paradise Lost*. My best friend, the brass foundry foreman, a great bear of a man who treated me with fatherly kindness, and grudging tolerance when I did battle with him, always used to let me know when a big casting was to be made, and he always went with me to give guidance through the perils of the shop floor: perils which were not only 'health and safety' ones, but also of a more personal nature. There were very few women in the iron foundry, and a young one from 'the Welfare' was a target for a great deal of minor harassment. Not that I minded; but my friend the foreman had old-fashioned gentlemanly ideas and insisted on acting as chaperone on such occasions, when there was a lot of standing around being done.

My job had its own drama too. Battles to achieve things, from decent loos to human respect for the women foundry workers, seemed to follow much the same pattern as the productions I was currently in in the theatre: I would be operating a carefully worked-out strategy, a plot in several acts, with as far as I was concerned, a pre-determined dénouement. It was a job to ensure that the climax weeks of each did not coincide. This was a world into which, male-dominated as it was, women had been grudgingly accepted for the duration of the war, but where they were always second class citizens in spite of the tough male work they did. The conditions in which they worked, and the problems that derived from the low esteem in which they were held by the majority of the old male work force, gave rise to many of those battles. But I am sure that the tensions, the passions, the intensity of my commitment to drama fed and fired my commitment to the job. And equally that the passions engendered by the work helped to enhance my acting ability; and I found in the job a delight in battling that was to be very useful later on, in the Theatre Campaign.

It does seem strange to me now that I should have found no way to synthesise these two commitments: started a drama group that straddled the divides; seen the potential for dramatic material in the tensions of life within the factory; written a play about women in a male industrial world, or Irish immigrant girls adjusting to English factory life or the absurdities of the class structure as evidence by Metrovicks. But that did not happen to me; and the lessons I had learnt about the universality of drama with the Travelling Theatre seem not to have struck me as relevant. Perhaps the explanation lies not only in my own inadequacy and inexperience, but in the nature of the times and the rigours of life in them.

The years following the war were very stark and impoverished in many material ways, although there was a great spirit of excitement and confidence about the new Welfare State society being created by the Labour government that had swept to power in 1945. But there was little relaxation of war-time shortages and constraints: food rationing and clothes rationing continued and bread rationing came in; only the blackout went - but then that was a transformation so marvellous that if made up for a great deal. I did not belong to an 'affluent society': I was extremely ill-paid. My salary as an Oxford graduate with post-graduate qualifications was £5 a week - equal to two and a half times the rent of my bedsitter - and somehow I never managed to resolve the problem of how to cope with a calendar-month salary-payment of twelve instalments, while paying rent on the basis of a four-week month. This resulted in some terrible months when *two* payments for the bed-sit had to be found out of one month's salary. The hours I worked were long and with little money to spare, I rarely explored the professional theatre on offer in Manchester, and so missed out completely on the work that Joan Littlewood was starting in the Library Theatre - and certainly would have lacked the courage shown by just one member of the Metrovicks Dramatic society, who gave up being a research engineer to go and work on lights for her. Indeed, I had little idea of what she was doing or the beacon she was to be to the post-war theatre. I was blinkered, I think, by the agreeable and accessible satisfaction of my work on the amateur stage.

The 'Works Dramatic Society' is in a rather special category in the amateur world. It has the great advantage of a closely knit community, of easy communication, possibly of management-provided facilities, of a network of relationships which can make much easier the business of talent-spotting and recruitment. It also has a guaranteed audience, and easy outlets for ticket sales. But more common and very numerous are the dramatic societies that exist *per se* in centres large and small; attached sometimes to churches or clubs or organisations such as Townswomen's Guilds or Women's Institutes; but most commonly self-standing within a town or a suburb or a village; usually drawing on the immediate community for both acting members and audiences, and often being important centres of social life in their community. The size, competence and standards vary considerably, from the small groups like the first one I had belonged to in York, which was based on an Extra-Mural class and put on a one-act play two or three times a year for a drama festival; to the Little Theatres, few in number but prestigious, owning their own buildings, putting on several productions a year which run for a week or so each, often engaging a professional director for some or all of the productions. This group has a distinguished history, and includes such names as the Maddermarket in Norwich, Bradford Civic, the Questors in Ealing, London, and that to which I referred at the beginning of this chapter, the Ilkley Players.

Amateur theatre in England has a long history. Charles Dickens, for example, formed a group that performed all over the country - having the specific objective of raising money for charitable purposes - for friends, or causes; he himself directed and acted, and as often as not had written the plays himself. '... the idea of a play stirs my blood like a trumpet' he said.[6] His company took with it a theatre made by the designer of the Crystal Palace, Joseph Paxton, on account of whose ingenious construction design it could be unpacked within a matter of hours: a feature it shared with the YRCC Travelling Theatre. (and, as it happens, though with a different objective, Leeds Playhouse). Dickens' amateurs, after a debut in Devonshire House in the presence of Queen Victoria and Prince Albert, travelled to Bristol, Birmingham, Manchester, Sheffield and many other places - though sadly not to Leeds. Indeed, 'it has been suggested that the travels ... marked the first occasion when actors toured the country with a complete play'.[7] They met immensely enthusiastic receptions, and must have taken dramatic entertainment to places that had no other resources. And it is still the case that amateur theatre brings entertainment to many sectors of the community that otherwise have no access to it. Life can, too, be greatly enriched for those who participate. Involvement in a local dramatic society is, and always will be, a thoroughly absorbing hobby, for people with a wide range of talents that need not be acting ones: putting on a play involves a huge range of crafts - woodwork, needlework, electrical skills, painting, making artefacts - there is little limit to the ability of an amateur production to find a job for anyone who wants to get involved. From 1919 to 1990 the British Drama League acted as a source of encouragement and advice to the amateur movement all over the country, with a library of plays to lend, a network of regional organisations to guide and stimulate activity, and a year-long programme of festivals and competitions. Sadly, it died in 1990. But amateur drama goes on.

A good example of the Little Theatre, one of two that existed in Manchester, was the Altrincham Garrick, to which I belonged and with which I acted frequently, alternating productions with those for the Metrovicks society. It was a wealthy society, and possessed a beautifully equipped theatre with a conventional end-stage auditorium, and truly splendid audience amenities and backstage facilities. It was run by a committee of local people, who engaged a paid professional director for the six or seven productions they put on every year. The membership was socially homogeneous - middle-class, middle-brow and predominantly, though not exclusively, middle-aged. It was not really my sort of social group: radical political views, a limited wardrobe and an even more limited budget mixed uneasily with the affluence of the comfortable businessmen and their conventional wives; my little bed-sit was no place for post-rehearsal drinks and dalliance with fellow members who had grand houses, proper flats, cars and good wine glasses. But I intended to act wherever I could; and I was a good and useful (and young) actress, so they were glad of me in the theatre. I was greedy for parts - any parts in any plays wanting varied technical acting experience even though in plays of inferior quality. I learnt a lot, not only about acting but a sector of society that would otherwise have been quite unfamiliar to me. I played every sort of part they offered me, from Mary Magdalen to a middle-aged comedy wife-and-mum (the children in this case being played by actors older than myself). I learnt in that part a great deal about make-up and style and voice-range. Little dynamic Kit McCullough - the name comes back across the years - the paid director, was a compendium of professional jargon and practice and attitude, and those too I learnt. I must have been insufferable: so many amateurs are - borrowing and using with studied nonchalance the thought-to-be professional terminology, and affecting histrionic attitudes that are, I later found, quite unknown to the real professional.

Altrincham Garrick was at that time a typical example of the amateur theatre that engaged its members in serious, meticulous, hard technical work, but largely on material of little value or depth. The satisfaction for its members was a craft satisfaction - and none the worse for that; the satisfaction for audiences was in the undemanding nature of the entertainment. Discussions in rehearsals were about how best 'to put it across' rather than about the meaning and significance of the words and the action. Discussion after the performance was non-existent. But the theatre was highly valued in the limited sector of Altrincham society which it served, and the audiences were always large and appreciative, if uncritical. It was a regular, conventional audience and for that reason, as well as by its very nature, the Garrick produced no plays that disturbed or exercised the mind: only comfortable, conventional, predictable plays for comfortable, conventional people. And many a comfortable predictable marriage comes about between the acts of amateur productions in groups like this. Friendships as well, for acting is a marvellous hobby to share with other people: pursued in atmospheres of high emotion and tension, it demands exclusive commitment, which forces people to push aside the nagging trivia of monotonous everyday life; it offers a magic entry into places and rooms and clothes and situations that are remote from the everyday round. Then there is the 'bonding' - the close linking together of the one with the group: you share the slow build-up to the terrors and tensions of 'the show'; you share the stage-fright, the horror at disasters, the agony of the hitches on stage, the misery of a dull reception; and you all get very fond of each other or you hate each other - one way and another the feelings are strong.

Then you share - for one or two hours - the 'flatness' after the last performance, before you all break up and part, and you feel as if a family you belong to is being torn apart. And you go away feeling that there really is 'nothing left remarkable beneath the visiting moon'. There may be a couple of lines perhaps in the local press to dwell over and remind you; perhaps a press photo that recreates for a moment the best moments. But life lacks lustre when it is all over, unless it has become enhanced by the relationships formed during the work. It is for this that many societies do, really, exist; as a hobby to share, through which to make friends, and on which to spend the time. And, as it happens, doing plays, unlike playing bridge, can serve another purpose - the entertaining of other people.

For better or worse, and unknown to each other until twenty years on, this absorbing, engaging world of amateur theatre is what was engrossing most of the small group of people who eventually came together in Leeds to campaign for a professional theatre, all of us convinced that no matter how beguiling and delightful we as amateurs found the amateur theatre, it was not in that form that our community, our City of Leeds, would benefit most from drama. By the sixties I had moved a long way from the sort of work I remember in Altrincham; and others in the group had for much longer than I been creating work of greater importance and value. I had left Manchester, worked for a year as a social worker in Leeds, acting the while in the city societies that performed in the Civic Theatre, before joining the staff of the University when I immediately became involved in drama with the University Staff Dramatic Society. Although being an acting member of that society afforded most of the same delights as any other society I had joined, the work that was undertaken was predominantly of great artistic merit and high quality, and the frequent productions were, in fact, for the actors, a sequence of quasi-academic explorations of the great dramatic literature of the world.

In a way, the Staff Dramatic Society of the University had things in common with a works society: it was an in-group of a larger, closed professional community; contact and communication was easy; rehearsal arrangements could be made without difficulty, in lunch hours for example - a benefit of campus life. But more important was the unanimity in respect of the aims of the society; it was taken for granted that only plays of real literary and dramatic merit should be produced; there was no case for putting on plays of light entertainment value only - except perhaps for light-hearted occasions. In 1949 there happened to come together in Leeds a glittering group of academics who were distinguished in their scholarly fields and at the same time eager to bring into the full life of production the drama that they were teaching, editing, researching and translating.

The central figure was the great Wilson Knight, one of the greatest names in the field of Shakespearean scholarship, a noted writer on the theatre and on drama, and an experienced actor and director. Arnold Kettle, who was so key a figure later in the Theatre Campaign, was in the School of English, and was a subtle and skilled actor; so was Kenneth Muir, another important Shakespearean scholar and editor, gifted with fine stage voice and presence. There was a remarkable triumvirate in the three main language schools of Spanish, Italian and French: brilliant young men who translated, edited, produced, and acted in the great old and new plays in the languages they taught - John Boorman, Frederick May and Richard Coe. All took part in production after production that were of considerable competence theatrically and that far exceeded in significant content the work of most professional theatres in the regions. I remember a *King Lear* in which Wilson Knight as Lear engaged in protracted textual and interpretative discussion throughout with Kenneth Muir, who played Gloucester and who was in the very act of editing it for the Arden series. The rehearsals were like long seminars. I remember a *Love's Labour's Lost* in which every pun and every piece of word-play, every double-entendre, was exhaustively examined. I remember a production of Granville Barker's *The Secret Life* - rarely performed - which, deeply and carefully explored, thoughtfully directed and immaculately dressed, played nightly its four hours to a near-empty hall, a condition that hardly at all diminished the pleasure that the cast had derived from the production. I remember Strindberg, Ibsen, Pirandello, Chekhov, Lorca, Claudel, Gogol, Arden - all in our repertoire, as well as the old classics, and as well as Noel Coward and Labiche and N F Simpson whom we performed at staff parties, and for which we were highly regarded by even the least literary of the dons.

Working in this way, with this quality of drama, was quite a different experience from that with the Metrovicks society or the Altrincham Garrick. Contact in the theatre, during the creative process, with the greatest dramatic writing, in the company of specialists and scholars, emphasised for me that a deeper satisfaction is to be attained in searching out the inner content of plays than in achieving the most polished performance. The fun was in the latter still but the real purpose and the real joy was in the search; and the revelation of the heart of the play, when the miracle happened and both understanding and a good production resulted, was uniquely the gift of the theatre.

We too, in that rarefied atmosphere, had our inter-act dalliance: another product of this rich and fruitful time for me was getting married to Walter, who was also a member of the society - a very accomplished one who, among a succession of diverse parts, had played in *King Lear* a Cornwall so terrifying in the blinding scene that there was a high count of faintings in the

*Shaw's 'Arms and the Man' (Metrovicks)*

*'They Came to Leeds' by Alec Baron and Luis Seipe (Proscenium Players)*

*'The Dybbuk' by G. Anski (Proscenium Players)*

*'The Brontës' by Alfred Sangster (Leeds Arts Theatre)*

***'Pantagleize'* by Gheldérode** , *translated by George Hauger (Proscenium Players)*

*Wilson Knight's King Lear (University of Leeds Staff Dramatic Society)*

audience. Simultaneously with getting married, however, I also changed my job - to teaching drama, instead of teaching social work. And that was how I came, at last, back to mediaeval drama and had the first real opportunity to try out my ideas about the Mystery Plays. It was in the rather sedate context of a Women's Day Training College in Manchester that an anarchic and riotous production of a single play from one Cycle took place, in the round, with a lot of loud and messy business that entranced the previously rather hidebound elderly senior English lecturer, while shocking the prim and critical Principal into whose lap landed a large half-eaten apple. Most important of all it captured the affection of the students, and led to some very rewarding work with them. I feel it may also have been the cause of a strange event in a lesson taken by one of the students on teaching practice. She, filled with enthusiasm for participatory drama, engaged in a dramatisation of *The Pied Piper of Hamelin.* It was so successful that her entire class followed the Piper out of the classroom, out of the school and away out of sight, while she watched helplessly. I cannot remember if she got her Diploma, but I think she deserved to.

Over the next few years my own, married life was based on Leeds, but interspersed with longish spells of living in Africa, where Walter's work in the economics of developing countries took us. We both continued to act with the Staff Dramatic Society during our home spells, turn and turn about as necessitated by baby-sitting. The Staff society continued to flourish and to do regular major productions, with a great deal of inter-production workshop activity. This is not the place to recount the development of Drama Departments in the universities of Britain; and in fact the recognition of the subject came later in Leeds than in Bristol and Manchester, for example. But, in the devious ways in which things are brought about in universities, there had come into being a small Studio Theatre; it was the brain child and inspiration of Frederick May, one of that group of academics who were at the heart of the staff society and also of the student theatre group. Resisted bitterly by a strong force in university politics that had no time at all for all that acting nonsense, it came to be a centre of excellence from which came forth a steady stream of talent and expertise. Leeds' first Fellow in Drama was Martin Banham, who became, from the moment he was appointed to the post, an integral and indispensable member of the Theatre Campaign and made an important contribution to the actual planning of the theatre building; he subsequently became the first Professor of Drama in the University.

So drama in the academic sector in Leeds slowly grew to be recognised as a serious and important subject, while it was still far from being so regarded by the City authorities. The story of Leeds Playhouse owes some of its inspiration to this fruitful period in the university drama, which coincided with the period of maximum decay in the city's professional theatre provision for the half million people living outside the ivory tower of the university. But movements grow slowly and imperceptibly out of their origins: we in the university - largely separate from the also flourishing amateur world at the Civic Theatre - simply observed with irritation that we rarely went to the professional theatre in our own city. We accepted this, together with other defects that seemed to us to be a price to pay for living in Leeds, a rather run-down city with unequally developed cultural amenities, that happened to have a marvellous university - a really perfect ivory tower.

Then in July 1956 I, for whom for some reason the task of starting a theatre campaign was lying in wait, was suddenly transported from the ivory tower to a very far away world, and to a quite new experience of the workings of theatre magic. With one little girl, and with another child on the way, Walter and I flew off to Uganda. We had already spent a year in 1953 away from Leeds, in Nigeria, where the indigenous drama, with its deeply rooted place in society, had fascinated us. Now, with expectation of similar discoveries and delights, as well as the excitement and challenge for Walter of his job as Economic Adviser to the Government of Uganda, we embarked on a longer adventure: three years that, as it happened, were as full of theatre involvement as all the years before had been, although of a completely different kind from that we had expected.

# 3

# The Second Act: On The Road In Uganda

British Colonial Uganda in 1956 was a curiously anachronistic territory. Although within six years, along with most of the African colonies, it was to become independent, there seemed few signs of urgency. No political leader had arisen to mobilise pressure on the colonial power to speed up the independence process - no figure parallel to Kenyatta in Kenya, Nkruma in Ghana or Nyerere in Tanzania. There had been no bloody uprising like that of the Mau Mau in Kenya. Even rival political parties, such as we had observed two years before in Nigeria, growing vocal and aggressive, were not in evidence. An urgent political will seemed to be lacking, or dormant; and the same seemed true of a cultural assertion of national identity. The reasons for this are hard to fathom, and this is no place to hazard explanations of a phenomenon so complex. Only two factors seemed unquestionably contributory: one, which in any case was common to most colonial territories, was that the 'nation' was an artificial creation by boundary-makers in the nineteenth century. Although there were ethnic links between some of the kingdoms that made up Uganda, there were very distinct cultural differences, and to some extent hostility and rivalry among the kingdoms tended to evoke more concern than the common resistance to colonial domination. There was also a considerable amount of suspicion of the sizeable Indian community, in whose hands was held a large proportion of the commercial and industrial enterprises. The inter-tribal hostility was to contribute very considerably to the tragedy that overtook Uganda some years after independence; but that too is a sad story common to most of the ex-colonial territories.

The other factor was a benign one. Of all the British colonial territories, this was that most approximating to a land of milk and honey (a description that is singularly apt for the possession once suggested by Winston Churchill as a possible Jewish homeland). It was a region blessed with fertile soil, a kindly climate, and sufficient land for the subsistence farming population. It had a sound economy, based on coffee, cotton and sugar as export crops, a textile industry and copper mining. There were no white settlers; the sugar estates were exclusively in the hands of the Asian community; but there were a number of rich, land-owning African families. The African peasant farmers grew much of the cotton and coffee, and the produce of subsistence farming was sufficiently abundant to result in a moderately good standard of living. Droughts and famine were very rare in Uganda: only in one part of the north were there areas that were to any extent arid, and these were sparsely populated by tribes of migrant herdsmen who were the least advanced of the Uganda people. But overall, Uganda was a country where people were not battling against hostile nature. The mighty Nile rose at the country's heart, in Lake Victoria, and ran through the country's length, yielding the huge bonus of electricity from the harnessing of the great Falls at Jinja. Uganda seemed, as they say, to have everything going for it, with the natural resources and potential for a gentle progress into a successful life as an independent nation. For many, even the staple food 'grew on trees', literally: it was the banana, or *matoke* as it was called in the state of green under-ripeness in which it was used by the people - steamed in packages of its own leaves, and succulently delicious. The staple of most people of the world grows at ground level - potatoes, yams, cassava, rice, wheat - but the banana grows on a lovely tree with leaves that act as shade from the sun, as umbrellas, or as steamers for matoke and wrapping for anything that needs to be wrapped. It grows in graceful, curving bunches that curl upwards to the sky and look like accepting hands or courteous gestures; it is gathered by people in a dignified upright position not a back-breaking bend; and as it is perennial, it comes year after year without too much effort in cultivation.

For a good proportion of Ugandans life was modestly agreeable, and perhaps the incentives to political or cultural assertion were inadequate; it may be that there was lacking the stress and tensions and discontent out of which political activism - and great drama - are bred.

A year in Nigeria had been, for us, a marvellous introduction to an ancient and highly developed drama that existed at the grass roots of an African society. Even in the tiny village where we worked and lived, where I was - even in 1954 - the first white woman the one hundred villagers had ever seen, the complex drama, based on one of the great religious festivals, was played annually with expert acting skill handed from generation to generation and in costumes, also hereditary, of ingenious workmanship and exotic richness quite out of proportion to the poverty of the village. Drama in ritual form grew among the people, based on religion, and was as familiar to the poorest as was the voice of the talking drum and dances and stories. All the forms had flourished for generations of Yoruba people. Wole Soyinka, who was many years later to win the Nobel prize for Literature, and the many other Nigerian writers of high quality are the products of a culture rooted in the common people. Many of them, Soyinka included, write in English as well as in their own languages, and we in the west, who invested a mite in the education system of Nigeria, are blessed with a rich yield in the access we have been given to this cultural richness through the writers who span the cultures by using our language.

When we went to Uganda Walter and I set out immediately to learn about Ugandan culture. We learnt that there was music and dance and story - telling, and a body of oral literature. But in this oddly decorous society we learnt of nothing that brought the other arts together in drama form. Predictably, at University level the students were familiar with western drama and acted in it in the great hall of Makerere University College. There, too, various productions were mounted by local amateur societies: none were African; some were Indian; most were European. In the clubs that were the centres of white society in the various administrative centres throughout the country, there were dramatic societies whose raison d'être was providing entertainment for the expatriate population. A National Theatre was in the process of being built by the Government (and Walter was its first Treasurer, representing the Ministry of Finance); even before the building was completed a Director was appointed - a European, with a conventional British Drama League background and no previous knowledge of Uganda or Uganda culture. A competitive festival along BDL lines was held annually, always judged by a visiting expert from Britain. The secondary schools did their Shakespeare plays and other western classics. But there was no tradition of drama at the grass roots, in the villages. It was very difficult for us, so early in our life there, to understand, and the comparison with the vigorous drama tradition in Nigeria was most marked.

Many years later, at a conference in Kampala[1], it was suggested that the Christian missionaries in the early days of colonial power had suppressed a popular drama along with other 'native' practices; and it seems not unlikely that there had existed a form of drama based, as in Nigeria, on pagan beliefs, customs and practices, and that this had fallen victim to missionary zeal and racial arrogance. Whatever the explanation, at the time when we were in Uganda there was no indigenous drama tradition. Many western-educated Ugandans teaching in the schools, as well as many expatriate teachers, were in the early stages of stimulating an interest in drama that was, it seemed, no longer in the nature of the people. So it seemed.....

This was a great disappointment to me, on my own account. At this stage of my life I was predominantly a wife, a mum and a mum-to-be. I expected that bit by bit I would get worked into Uganda life in my own right somehow - teaching a bit of English here, doing a bit of Extra-mural teaching there. I had certainly hoped that there would be interesting indigenous drama to see and learn about, perhaps even to become involved in. Above all I had looked forward to discovering in what form the old magic operated there.

An additional problem was that as Walter was to be a quasi-colonial servant for three years, we had to live in the seat of colonial government, in Entebbe. On first seeing it, and in many ways for all the time, we felt that Entebbe was an idyll for a family with young children. It was an imported paradise, created by the first colonial rulers along a stretch of white sand beside Lake Victoria; it was actually on the equator, but 3000 feet up and so with a lovely temperate climate, lots of rain to keep it all green, ravishing sunsets across the lake, great swathes of inviolate grass, specially cherished as it was mostly golf course; there were lovely swimming pools, great shady trees and bougainvillaea, and roses, violets, lilies along with exotic tropical flowers and shrubs; there were troops of servants and a round of social life that could have come straight out of *Tales from the Raj*. We had stepped not only into a different continent but a different century. And the oddest thing of all was that initially we met no Africans, apart from the large armies of servants. Senior Government at this stage (six years only before independence) was almost exclusively white. There were two 'token' ministers who were Ugandan; but apart from them and their families no Africans lived in the same residential area as ours. The Ugandans who were in the Government service were in lower ranked jobs. They lived in a different part of the town, and were not invited to the round of cocktail parties into which we found ourselves thrown. We did not know quite how to get to know the people of Uganda, and this we wanted far more than to spend our lives with these, in many ways alien, fellow-countrymen of our own.

My first friend was, as it happened, a woman of mixed race, Olive Kagwa. We met at the doctor's clinic, both awaiting an inoculation for our children, who were of the same ages. She was the wife of one of the very few senior African professionals, a Cambridge educated lawyer. We chatted at the clinic, realised a rapport had come about, and I said, 'Shall I see you at the swimming pool?' Then came the shock: neither she nor her husband were allowed in the swimming pool, which was a part of the club facilities. It was for whites only. It suddenly became horribly clear that our life for three years was destined to be lived in another ivory tower - one that perpetuated an archaic power structure - with the sort of people with whom we had little in common.

As a token gesture, useless but necessary to us, we resigned from the swimming pool, never joined the club, and began to work out a strategy for making friendships with African people through our contacts and friends in the University College of Makerere, which was, however, situated in the commercial capital of Uganda, Kampala, twenty miles away. Another source of contacts was the great family network of my friend, whose husband in fact belonged to one of the ruling families of Buganda, the part of Uganda in which both the capitals and a lot of the wealth of the country lay; he had friends and relatives in all sorts of places. Gradually I became involved in various groups, met some interesting people, particularly among the cultivated higher-educated women of Uganda (including one who had become a film star), and eventually found myself doing some extra-mural work: a set of classes on English Literature in a small town on the border with Kenya. It was a momentous occasion, for it was then that were sown the seeds of another travelling theatre, the second in my life.

It was the oration speech of Mark Anthony in *Julius Caesar* that did it. To give body to my lecture on the play I asked the large class to bring it to life by 'being' the crowd. While I orated, in the circle formed by the students, and conducted and directed at the same time, a most vocal, inflammable and aggressive crowd came alive around me. It was amazing. The scene was as alive and dangerous as if it were, in real fact, happening for the first time, there and then. How can this happen, I asked myself, when they don't make drama, never see it, and seem by nature to be very reserved and private people? I thought what a shame it was that some random factor had apparently inhibited the growth of a form existing at grass roots in so many civilisations: a form which clearly these people had as much capacity to enjoy as people everywhere else - indeed, which they seemed to have an innate ability to practise. Most of the people I was lecturing to - junior clerks, shop-keepers, technicians - had never seen a play, for outside the European clubs in the towns (clubs from which they were debarred) and the senior schools, no plays were performed up-country. And yet, once a drama had started to take place, they were swept into it.

Slowly in my mind the idea took shape. Memories of the YRCC Travelling Theatre, and my love for the mystery plays, helped it along. What fun it would be to bring plays to audiences like this - and perhaps in doing so help to plant and cultivate seeds that had somehow blown over Uganda! As I saw it in those terms I saw the parallel with mediaeval Europe, and the growth of drama in our own culture: the mingling of two traditions, both handed down the centuries by conquest and scholarship - the popular drama of the people and the classical tradition from ancient Greece, via the scholars and churchmen. And there I was back again at the beginning with the mystery plays: evolving from the church's early efforts to dramatise the holy stories; taken over by the Guilds and produced by ordinary men and women, who themselves inherited another tradition, equally ancient, equally shared with the rest of Europe - the anarchic popular comic tradition carried along by travelling troupes, jugglers and tumblers and entertainers of every sort, through the great mediaeval fairs, in the inns and market places, surviving all attempt to expel or prohibit; and keeping alive in the common people a delight in the magic of theatre in some form.

The diffidence with which I initially rethought the idea, and the fears of being an agent of yet another item of colonial superimposition, diminished as I saw that this could be just one of those routes of continuity that are necessary to the fertilising of one culture by another. The University, the schools and the National Theatre were all operating at the level of the classical, scholarly tradition. As the reality of independence came about, the small educated élite would grow in number and would diffuse the influences upon them of their education in world wide culture: a nation's culture should be open to and partly formed of influences from other cultures. But its strength and integrity comes from a popular root; and at that time there seemed in Uganda to be no drama growing from the native soil. It seemed not impossible that a way to stimulate, even revive, the growth of a popular tradition might be to bring entertainment, albeit foreign, of a type and performed in a style, that would make an immediate appeal; and to *take it to* the people, instead of causing them to seek it out and get to it.

This was the theoretical base for the concept that quickly developed in my mind. But the actual dynamic was quite selfish: it was a sudden vision of the fun, the sheer, glorious fun, of starting a drama group, with a membership to include Africans and Asians, in - of all places - Entebbe, where no activity was racially shared; where even the Government hostel banned one young African civil servant from visiting white colleagues who lived there... I saw that in this way we could break through the idiot barriers that existed, in the place where we were to spend three more years of our life, between us and the people we really wanted to make friends with, while at the same time enjoying sharing the intense and enriching world of drama. And then, of course, there was the gratifying delight of realising that the *most* suitable drama to work on (apart from improvised pieces) would be mediaeval drama. Here I was, back at last with the mystery plays, and the chance to try them out with audiences much closer in many ways to the original ones than I would ever be likely to find again. The concept was almost at once complete in many details: the sort of acting space we should use; the style of production; the sort of place we should try to act in; the scale of the productions, and the rejection in them of all sophisticated paraphernalia.

All this posited a quite new status for me in the world of amateur drama. I had not before actually created a group, let alone a travelling group, with all the organisational problems that involved. We knew, still, very few people in Entebbe, except for Walter's colleagues, their wives, and the Kagwas. This situation was to be, in a way, reproduced six years later, in Leeds; and the same rules operated both times. The smallest handful of people who share a conviction or an objective can achieve their end if they maintain their personal bonding and their conviction. Each one of even the smallest group has links with another group through perhaps only one individual; even by casual connecting the ripples spread out. If the group sets about systematically to multiply itself the rate of growth of involvement is quite astonishing. This is a truism of campaigning of any sort. In Leeds it was to be a much grander exercise in scale and organisation than the one we now set into operation in Entebbe, but the process was the same - enlarge through contact and persuasion.

Quite quickly in Entebbe, as we talked and followed up connections and startled people with our excitement, a group of whites gathered who shared both our delight in drama and our shame about race attitudes; and almost as quickly the first contacts were made with potential African members. There was a junior officer, for example, in Walter's office - a Makerere graduate - who responded with immediate delight; some of the younger whites who joined had African colleagues whom they approached; Olive Kagwa's sister-in-law came in, and as she worked in the Department of Rural Development she knew of several young men and women who became interested. The lower ranks of the government departments in Entebbe were filled with the new men and women of Uganda, graduates of Makerere, who within a few years would be top administrators of their country. I think we had the best of them: men and women who, amazingly, were not too cynical or disillusioned about whites; who brought their high intelligence as well as dedication and warm friendship to the group. Few Africans who joined us had acting experience, but most joined because they were profoundly attracted to the concept, on their own account, and because they confirmed, on the basis of their own experience, that drama indeed did not exist in the villages where they had grown up. For all of us, black and white, there was the quite explicit welcome for the opportunity to share a leisure activity, to make friendships and to do something valuable while having fun.

There were several problems to solve, but choosing a play was not one of them. On the principle that it is easiest to attract people to a specific project than to an indecisive one, I had already decided what we would start with: the Second Shepherds' Play, from the Wakefield cycle - the best of all plays in the extant cycles. Since the time of which I am writing, the mystery plays have been widely revived and have taken their rightful place on the popular English dramatic scene. But at that time they had been but rarely seen - indeed, until the 1951 revival in York, hardly at all. In his foreword to his 1957 edition of the plays, J S Purvis writes about the 'grave misgivings' with which that first production was given; but he goes on:

> 'The first performance showed how unnecessary those misgivings had been. The performance was hailed by the critics as a quite startling revelation of the power and beauty of the mediaeval plays....It was not only the critics who were impressed; the effect on the great audiences made up of all sorts of people was truly remarkable in its depth of impact....The actual performance was, indeed, a real revelation, of something fresh, direct, and powerful and of a greatness hitherto unrecognised....There was a noble simplicity and a direct and powerful handling which belong only to great art ... above all, a sincerity, a natural aptness of expression....' [2]

York had discovered its own at last.

The plays are now well known through performances all over the country, from the National Theatre to the streets of Wakefield or the Cathedral in Birmingham or the precincts of Coventry Cathedral. There are four major cycles: only the York cycle is complete; but each of the others, the Coventry, the Chester and the

Wakefield, contain some masterly work; and in this last there is the small masterpiece which most scholars believe to come from the single hand of a real artist, rather than from a joint effort by the men of the Guilds. It is a comedy that is partly farce, partly satire, based on a study in depth, as it were, of the three shepherds of Bethlehem. It introduces two other characters who are arguably the first real comic pair to be created in English drama - a wily sheep stealer, Mak, and his wife, Gill. The play divides into two sections, the one an ingenious and hilarious story of treachery and retribution, with five characters naturalistically drawn, of their time in social reference, but of all time in character type. I was certain that with changes in the social reference the characters would be totally at home in Uganda, recognisable and entertaining to the peasant farmers who would predominantly form the audiences. The second half of the play is quite simply the arrival of the shepherds at the manger in Bethlehem, a scene of great tenderness and humour and simplicity. This too would be familiar to most people in Uganda, where the mission churches had run primary schools and clinics since the early days of colonial rule. The two sections, each a masterpiece, are linked by the enduring characters of the shepherds, and divided by a scene of homely slapstick comedy in which Mak is, for his sins, tossed mercilessly in a blanket by the three who have foiled his thieving plans.

This was presented as a fait accompli as the first production-to-be. We planned that eventually, quite soon, we should organise ourselves and establish less draconian methods of play-selection but to start, to get off the ground, was the main objective at the moment, and generously and uncritically everyone came in on that basis. But there were other problems to be resolved and it was during this process that the foundations of the group's identity and character were laid, and that were born deep and abiding friendships that were the strength of the group as well as its joy.

The first problem was exhaustively discussed at the very first group meeting: the problem of language. Although the language of government, education and commerce was English, and although English was widely understood at all levels throughout the country, it seemed to us all that its use as a medium for entertainment at village level was incompatible with the 'grass roots' concept, and that it would be presenting drama as essentially a foreign import. However, there was in fact no viable alternative. In the first place our African members belonged to a number of different language groups, from different parts of the country and different tribes; the common language for them was English. In the second place most of the whites were in the same position, having only one of the Ugandan languages, if that: many were in the same position as myself with a halting knowledge of greetings in Luganda, the language of the part of the country where we were all living, and a functional ability to speak Kitchen Swahili - a debased version of another authentic East African language. Thirdly it was generally agreed that in the first production the principal acting parts should be played by those with experience - and this was exclusively the whites, who, as I have said, were not necessarily apt enough in the local language to act in it. (I had, incidentally, planned the production to enable the inexperienced, black and white, actors to gain their first experience, in performance, in a special way that I hoped would be of multiple value to the whole production).

English it had to be; we looked to a longer future when we might move into the vernaculars. In terms purely of communication I had no real anxieties. Drama operates on so many levels, of which language is only one, and I had little doubt that one way or another we could make our play work. Of course, it had to be modern English not the Middle English in which it was written, so the translation was a technical job that I had to get out of the way quickly, and I did.

The second problem (task, rather than problem, actually) was to plan an itinerary of possible performance places, make the necessary approaches and make the appropriate arrangements, and get our performances agreed to and known about by the local communities. This is where the advantage of being in a capital of colonial government emerged. Among our white members were one or two senior and experienced ex-District Officers, and one or two other officers with power, if not of life and death, of administrative influence in the country. Between them they got out a list of small towns and villages where they knew of a space, where they had a good relationship, where they knew of a lively headmaster and so on. For our first tour we wanted a representative sample of communities, so we included two schools at different levels, bush clearings in villages, market clearings in smaller towns and, for good measure, we decided to try ourselves out on the University. The contacts and planning of the first tour were soon in hand.

Thirdly was the problem of staging. All had to be done on a shoe-string - a 'whip round' in fact. Moreover, we had to plan transport to our performances on the basis of a fleet of private cars, one of which - ours - by great good luck was a huge thing: a standard Vanguard station wagon built like a tank for journeys over the roughest of murram roads and as large as a small bus, for we had a growing family that travelled around Uganda with us when we went 'on safari'. So whatever 'stage' we were to use had to be in sections of a size that would fit onto or inside the Vanguard. Furthermore it needed to be easily and quickly erectable: our time constraints for performances were quite tight. All our weekday performances had to fit into the three hours between offices closing at 4pm, and sunset at 7pm: there are no long twilights on the equator. We intended to act in the round anyway, so needed very little in the way of settings. We designed a very simple rostrum, in three sections, with a self-standing frame to stand behind it and hold an all-purpose curtain, which could serve to hold alternating curtains for backgrounds and as a place for properties, costume changing and so on, That was all. It was made by Walter and a handful of helpers in the garage of our bungalow. And this was one of the first indications to the decorous world of Entebbe that something odd was going on: the Economic Adviser to the Government was to be seen doing rough manual work in company with a jolly group of black men. Our traditionalist servants were shocked but our children were entranced; and the sections of the rostrum did off-duty service as small tables for small people to paint on.

Oh, what a gallant time it was: the house buzzing with activity and excitement and tension; rehearsals going on in places throughout Entebbe; costumes being designed and made out of local textiles by a group of the women; the music - two drums and a recorder - being rehearsed in another house; the news of agreement to have us, sometimes eager, not infrequently perplexed if not downright suspicious; above all, the play growing into its strange new identity - a six hundred year old English play transported to Africa beside the equator! Quite soon the numbers of Africans in the group had grown considerably and the production was such that there was no limit except transport to the numbers we could involve, for I had early on decided to incorporate a 'trained audience'. They were to be a mob of rather unruly spectators who formed a part of the arrival of the whole company through the real audience, marking the beginning of the play by rollicking about, chatting with the audience and with the actors and - this was the secret objective - easing an unaccustomed audience into enjoyment by telling them, in the appropriate vernacular, what was happening, what they were going to see, who we were; then they were to scatter themselves throughout the audience for the same purpose, to keep up a constant line of communication - answering questions, translating and giving authority, as it were, to uninhibited responses from audiences who were more accustomed to seeing the whites in dignified situations of authority than larking about in funny clothes in bush clearings after office hours.

A latent talent for acting in both the men and women in the company was soon revealed to an astonishing degree. There was a spontaneity, a freshness, an integrity in the African style that was to give to all our performances an attack and an impact that could not have been achieved by the play alone, or by an orthodox mode of production. Of course, all of us were fired, not only with idealism and conviction that what we were doing was worth while, but with sheer glorious delight in the fun of it all, and in the old magic of make-believe.

Every amateur knows the panic that takes over, together with a sense of disbelief that it can ever happen, as the opening night approaches. 'Never again - I can't endure it' are familiar words, I think, to us all. And we were not just facing a first performance, but, as it happens, a load of scepticism and criticism from several directions, and, oddly, not least from the University where our early attempts to get co-operation and advice had been met with dismissiveness. There was also the very real suspicion of colleagues and mighty ones in the colonial administration in Entebbe, with one unexpected exception: one outrageous piece of protocol-breaking on my part - refusal of a summons to dine with the Governor on an occasion when I had a rehearsal - was treated with tolerance and an interest that might not have been aroused except by an act so unprecedented; and I was very touched when, on leaving Uganda and the service two years later, the Governor's warm letter of appreciation to Walter made special reference to the work we had done with the travelling theatre. Some priority-weighing had gone on, clearly; economic advisers were not to be judged by their economics alone.

We had by now a brave assertive name: the Uganda Pilgrim Players. We took it, of course, from that company formed in England in the thirties by Martin Browne, the Pilgrim Players; and in answer to our letter asking his permission to use the name we received a most supportive and encouraging letter, which was especially significant in view of the fact that it had been he who produced the York cycle in 1951. It just seemed a nice coincidence, for me one of the threads that interweave in the web.

The name made us feel established, real, gave us a status; and this helped to assure us that the whole enterprise really was there, would actually start to operate, in the very near future. The usual pangs of stage-fright were bad enough; but in addition none of us knew what to expect from audiences. We were all harrowed by panic, doubt, self-questioning, and we all kept it from each other until later. It was a happy arrangement that our first performance was actually one of the school ones and that the school, a primary one, had as its headmaster the husband of my friend the film star, both of whom were already good friends of ours, and who had in some measure prepared the ground with staff and pupils. We need not have worried, and in the event it was quite clear that such preparation was not needed; but our confidence in a friendly welcome helped us as we set off in convoy from Entebbe, for the first time. Amongst us was a rather naughty and over-vocal actor, a young goat borrowed for each performance from the veterinary department. There were no sheep in Uganda; we wanted no truck with a stuffed one; so a goat it had to be. Our property mistress had the unenviable task of collecting this member of the cast on every occasion, and acting as its chauffeuse, chaperonne and prompt throughout.

The opening lines of the play are 'Brrrhh, how cold it is...' It was a very hot day, high on a hill overlooking Lake Victoria. How readily audiences will suspend their disbelief! I shall never forget it - the marvel, the miracle, of that first triumph by an old English play over incongruity, anachronism, unfamiliarity. For it *was* a triumph; it *did* work. The audience of youngsters and their staff quickly abandoned themselves to their delight in the plot, their recognition of the character-types and a tale that did not, for them, pose a credibility problem. The mirror was held up to a nature that they recognised and they revelled in looking at the reflection. It was *we* who were swept off our feet - literally -when the excitement reached such a peak at the end of the first act, in which the scheming Mak is tossed in a blanket, that what seemed the entire audience converged on the scene to help in the tossing. A riot seemed about to take place, and that first performance was a tough initiation for our troupe, the plants in the audience. They alone were in a position to control things, and the way they rose to the unexpected situation was a great achievement. Between them they managed to restore calm, rescue the actors, change the back curtain to that for the second act, get through to the audience that the play was not yet over, and prepare a seemly atmosphere for the second half. And then the old magic of the play got to work once again. The homely tenderness of the scene in Bethlehem is a masterly piece of writing, and it was not the last occasion that it touched and enchanted audiences - although the first occasion was the one that meant the most to us. I think we felt a bit like the first farmers

*Setting up the stage*

*Notice of a village performance*

*First performance*

*The Shepherds (Olive in the tall hat)*

*Tossing Mak*

who had ploughed the first arable plot and sown the first seeds of grain.

*The Shepherds Play,* as we called it, did its modest tour as planned and there is little doubt that it brought enjoyment to a great variety of audiences. Many of those audiences had little or no English, comprising as they did local peasants, shop-keepers, farmers. There was one little village where the chief sat in state under an awning, and exchanged gifts of chickens with us. There were always women with babies on their backs. There were the officious, managing types, lowly clerks perhaps, who kept up a fine dignity until the tossing scene, when they restrained themselves from participating but fell into helpless laughter - and no laughter is more grand than African laughter, deep, gusty stuff that has no rules. The implanted audience *did* bridge the gap until the play took over; and then it was wonderful to see it over-riding the barriers of language, race and time. The farce, the slapstick and the good plot could hardly fail to work no matter how unfamiliar the language; and Mak always got well-tossed, poor fellow. (He was played by the headmaster of the European primary school - one venue where the play was *not* performed!) But the value of the production, and the work we went on to do, was more substantial than one afternoon's entertainment, valuable though that may have been: it was that it presented unsophisticated audiences, predominantly for the first time, with theatrical illusion, with the total dramatic experience - telling a story, simulating real people in conflict situations, exciting, perplexing and entertaining people all at the same time. I like to think that we opened the door into the magic world of theatre for some Ugandans as it had been opened for me when I was fourteen and when John Gielgud filled my heart with the wonder of it.

The Uganda Pilgrim Players became and remained for two or three years a popular enterprise with the audiences as much as with the participants. Two more major tours were mounted, both on a larger scale and covering a much wider geographical area than the first by the use of weekends, which enabled the company to travel further and stay overnight. One venue was the small town where the idea had been born - and I, alas, was unable to go with the company myself that time because I had two little sick children to care about; but I was glad that the place of the oracle was honoured. One of the two productions was of a French mediaeval comedy, *The Farce of Monsieur Pierre Pathelin* translated as *Peter Prattling's Payment,* which had a predominantly black cast, a mixed marriage, and was played in a mixture of languages, English, Luganda and Swahili: all the unusual features - the mixed marriage being one of them at that stage in Uganda in the less sophisticated sectors of the population - were accepted without difficulty by audiences; and the use of a mixture of languages achieved the rapport that the trained 'troupe' had been so useful in establishing in the *Shepherds' Play*; we still played in the round and used our device of close involvement with the audience - prompter, property mistress and characters were in the audience when they were not on the acting area. The last play, performed after we had left Uganda, was *Macbeth*, with an almost exclusively African cast.

In addition to the performances, we ran workshops for our company; we staged a workshop performance of Yeats' *The Kings Threshold*, and of Obé's *Noah*, and we had classes in voice and movement. We also entered a production for the Drama Festival in Kampala, stepping into quite a different style of work not natural to our real purpose, but we were motivated by a wish to present ourselves and our growing expertise to the conventional theatre-goers in the country. Furthermore, it gave experience to the company in more complex types of stagecraft and scene building. It was an act form Betti's *Queen and the Rebels* and gave the opportunity to the actors to play parts of considerable power. Walter produced that work, while I at the same time was producing *Peter Prattling*: we were actually running true repertoire! Our company had become a very popular activity with the younger people in Entebbe. There was a remarkable amount of talent, and the varied experience gave them confidence and courage and kept the enthusiasm alive. In the absence of a professional training ground, an amateur movement was providing some opportunity in which expertise and craftsmanship could develop. It is just possible too that, simultaneously, in out-of-the-way places in the country a feeling for drama was being stimulated, perhaps stirring old memories of a long-forgotten tradition. But whether the seed was newly-sown, or whether it became cross-fertilised with dormant seed, we all hoped that it might result in a flourishing growth. For me there was a singular satisfaction in the fittingness of having started with a piece that figured in the early stage of English drama.

The Uganda Pilgrim Players transformed our life in Uganda. We got to know and understand people we would never have met in any other way - whites as well as blacks; and we found that not all our prejudices against the colonial servants were justified: many of the younger Europeans were as thankful as we were for the chance to break an old mould and engage whole-heartedly in an activity that had a purposeful objective and that at the same time opened the way for us all to rich and meaningful relationships between the races. It is perhaps difficult for readers of today to imagine the tenacity with which most colonial administrators held to their sense of superiority to the people under their rule.

Walter and I left Uganda, as we had known we would, at the end of the three-year secondment. We returned to Leeds with three children more than we had left with three years before: our second daughter was born soon after we arrived in Uganda and our twin daughters, conceived simultaneously with the conception of the Uganda Pilgrim Players, had been born conveniently between *The Shepherd's Play* and *Peter Prattling's Payment*. They spent their first year in a frenetic household, but in the status of honoured creatures, for twins in Uganda are reverenced and have all sorts of privileges, above all that of being doted on by all. Even the Uganda Pilgrim Players felt that the twins belonged in a very special way to the company. The two older daughters had the fun and the buzz and excitement of a house that always seemed to be rehearsing, designing, hammering, or just filled with people talking and planning; and little as they were they came along to performances and were spoiled and doted on in their turn. When we left I felt I was leaving not only dear friends but a commitment and a task that had justified all the years of 'messing around' in plays. The amateur and moralist in me had found each other and synthesised. It was a hard thing to leave. And in the context of the great changes that were to come in the following years in the African territories under British colonial rule, I wondered how much the work would endure.

The stories of all the members of the company took different courses, and in fact the Uganda Pilgrim Players did not endure more than a year after we left. All the members were on the move: the whites beginning to look to their lives after colonialism, the blacks moving up to busy posts of final authority, and in many cases moving away from Entebbe. It had actually been something of a miracle that the group had been given the time it did to stay together. But within a year it quietly folded up its last costumes and became a memory: but one that, as I was to discover a few years later, remained alive and did bear fruit. That path will be traced later in my story. Many paths crossed at that time, many threads in my life-web were interwoven in the Uganda venture: my own deep, long love for mediaeval drama; memories of the travelling theatre in Yorkshire and the inspiration it had been to me; a belief in the special bonding power of doing plays; a desire to spread the magic of theatre so that everyone could discover it. All these were of seminal importance to me and connected with the moment in the West Yorkshire Playhouse, when the sound of an audience gathering in a northern city was the same as that of a crowd gathering in an African bush clearing. Finally, the whole operation in Uganda was a confirmation to me that anything, everything is possible if you believe in it enough and if you put your heart's core into achieving it. Surmounting the obstacles in Entebbe and climbing that small hill were good exercise for the mountain climb that was to come.

# 4

# The Third Act: Action Opens - In Leeds

During the rich and fruitful years that we spent in Uganda there had been taking place a major revolution in English theatre. A number of influences came to bear upon the professional theatre scene, and they seemed so to coincide that it is difficult to tell which influenced which. The crystallising of an attitude to the arts, which had been born during the war and had created the Council for the Encouragement of Music and the Arts, CEMA, and the concept of public responsibility for encouraging and supporting the arts, had led to the setting up of the Arts Council in 1946; and legislation empowering the local authorities to spend a certain amount from the rates on promoting 'entertainment' shortly followed.[1] The whole concept of public patronage was so unfamiliar in Britain, as distinct from most continental countries, that change was slow: but it came. Gradually local authorities began to allocate, in varying degrees of generosity, some of the rates to their local arts. Alongside this infrastructional development came the beginning of a great surge of new writing for the theatre. The single most influential work was *Look Back in Anger* - John Osborne's decisive blow against the dramatic stagnation that had for many decades dulled writing in the English theatre. A new play 'in which you can hear the authentic new tone of the Nineteen Fifties, desperate, savage, resentful, and at times, very funny' as T C Worsley wrote in the *New Statesman*; '...intense, angry, feverish, undisciplined. It is even crazy. But it is young, young, young', was the view of John Barber in the *Daily Express*. The production by the English Stage Company at the Royal Court, on 5 May 1956, was significant as the first outstanding success for this newly formed company, under George Devine, whose declared aims were of 'being primarily a writers' theatre, where new dramatists and new drama could obtain a hearing.'.

Other initiatives were being taken: a few years earlier, in 1951, the Festival of Britain committee had financed a play competition, which John Whiting won with *Saints Day*. In 1956 the *Observer* financed a play competition and several new writers emerged from that - Ann Jellico, N F Simpson, for instance. In Stratford East, Joan Littlewood's Theatre Workshop had found a permanent home, and was producing Brendan Behan, Shelagh Delaney and Wolf Mankovitz. In Scarborough Stephen Joseph's Theatre in the Round gave a first showing to David Campton, James Saunders and an unknown young writer called Ronald Alan, who later became somewhat better known as Alan Aykbourne. A year or so later the Arts Council was trying to 'encourage the repertory movement up and down the country by offering, in addition to the individual grants already being made, a special grant to mark the fiftieth anniversary of the opening of the Gaiety Theatre, Manchester by Miss Horniman; the grants were made available to any rep producing a new play'.[2] Thus it was that the first important work to result from a specific Arts Council subsidy for performance was produced not in London but in a regional, subsidised theatre: in Coventry.

Coventry was the first local authority to take a direct part in providing subsidised theatre for its people. The Belgrade Theatre in Coventry opened in 1958 (by coincidence the year that had been so important to us in Uganda). The Theatre became a beacon to the theatre world in the regions and it did more than establish a good ensemble company with a coherent and enterprising play policy, which included a high proportion of new plays: it established from the outset a programme for children and set out from the beginning to take seriously the value for children of drama, both as entertainment and within education. Its Young Stagers Club, by 1961, had some 3000 members; it gave talks for young people in the schools and in the theatre, and ran courses for Youth Leaders. It took productions under the title 'Theatre as Entertainment' out into the schools, and so in effect established for the first time a direct link between a working theatre and the schools within the community; and its children's theatre, Unicorn Theatre, ran Saturday morning programmes of mime and plays. The Belgrade, furthermore, designed and set a pattern for the financing policy of subsidised regional theatre, with a Trust on which ten of the fourteen Governors were local councillors. The artistic director had full artistic control, but the Trust retained financial control; and the local authority by 1962/63 was contributing 1/3 of a penny rate - equivalent to £6,750 a year - towards the theatre's total expenditure of £111,627; the theatre recovered eighty per cent of its running costs in box-office revenue, and the Arts Council grant of £15,000 covered the deficit.[3] The theatre was purpose-built, the architect being the City Architect: it was not an exciting or adventurous design, but the whole concept and ideology was of a real community theatre. It was the first theatre ever to be built in Britain entirely at public expense, and to operate on the basis of substantial subsidy from central and local governments.

It was here that the first of Arnold Wesker's trilogy of plays, *Chicken Soup with Barley, Roots* and *I'm Talking about Jerusalem*, was the first produced. He had been 'discovered' by the Royal Court but, in order to activate the Arts Council's scheme of grant-giving to provincial theatres that produced new plays, the Royal Court passed him on to the Belgrade; and it could hardly have been a better place for this fine play about the working class - another land-mark in post-war writing, and a work that fitted well into the radical attitudes and the adventurous play policy of the first subsidised theatre in the country.

Within a very few years of 1958, may of the theatres in the provinces were taking on a new look, as well as the new name of 'regional'. Building and re-building was going on at an extraordinary rate - Nottingham, Leicester, Bolton, Stoke-on-Trent, Watford, Crewe - all, with local and Arts Council support, were, in the early sixties, establishing theatre as an integral feature of the life of the communities; Theatre in Education companies were set up alongside the acting companies; in Nottingham, when the new Playhouse was opened in 1963, John Neville worked a true repertoire system - a daring alternative to the three-or-four-weekly run (and an expensive one). Many of the new theatres operated activities and amenities that were additional to the plays - discussions, workshops, talks. And plays for children were being taken seriously: no longer was the provincial child offered a yearly pantomime alone; the programmes of many of these regional theatres, with their increasing subsidies, contained specially written children's plays, many of them of very high quality, which were an integral part of the year's work in the theatre. In some cases there was a resident writer; and it was the work of one of these, Allen Cullen of Sheffield, that first made me perceive the gap in Leeds' cultural life.

Some two years after we got home to Leeds, when our daughters were of ages ranging from three and a half to seven, we joined another family with three children in the same age range who lived in Sheffield, at a matinee at the old Sheffield Playhouse - a modest theatre housed in a converted Temperance Hall but directed by Colin George, one of the best of the new generation of theatre directors - and, incidentally, one of the best friends of Leeds Theatre Campaign. The play was called, I think, *The Play of the Winds*; it was the first I ever saw that attempted to deal with issues of high seriousness but in a vernacular comprehensible to young children. It was a deeply moral play, but full of magic and excitement, a lovely production visually, with music and dance and some splendid theatrical effects. Our seven small people were entranced, and the meaning and values of the play were talked about very eagerly by our four on the journey back to Leeds.

That journey, in those days, took longer than it does now on the M1: through Barnsley and Wakefield we would drive, their markets busy and their streets crowded on a Saturday afternoon, and the journey slow - a journey that was to become very familiar to us in the years that followed, in which, Saturday after Saturday, we trekked down to matinees in Sheffield Playhouse, with a carload of children. But Sheffield did not always have something on that the children could enjoy, so, as the years went by and their interest grew, we discovered other theatres that we could get to. It was not only for children's plays, but for adult plays that, with some preparation by us in the knowledge that only some of the play would be comprehensible, gave the children a constant experience and enjoyment of theatre magic. Our circuit was expanded - to Nottingham, Manchester, York, and Harrogate. But Sheffield remained our favourite: the nice old building (to be replaced by the *Crucible* in due course) always seemed to be friendly, welcoming, homely. I think the front-of-house staff had a special recipe for making children feel respected and comfortable. The theatre operated a young people's club, the Pegasus Club, and saw its work as 'establishing a strong, vigorous and exciting theatre, giving the best to an audience which Pegasus will have helped to create, and which will demand nothing less than the best.[4]

Both Walter and I had returned to our leisure-time activity with the Staff Dramatic Society, and I in particular found acting the great parts I had in some splendid plays - Ibsen, Gogol, Arden works amongst them - was an enriching way to offset the stress and wear and tear of caring for four little children. But it now became very important to both of us that we should enable the children themselves to enjoy theatre-going. Although theatre magic makes quite formidable material attractive to quite young children, as we had already found, we needed to search around for the most suitable productions. One of the reasons why enjoyment seemed to be readily attained by them was, we felt, that they had started so early. The two older ones saw as their first full play *The Shepherd's Play* in Uganda, and the younger ones also, by curious coincidence, saw as their first another of the Mystery plays. During the 1960 production of the York Cycle, one or two of the individual plays were performed on pageants and were taken around the city to fixed points to play to audiences gathered there. It was what I had dreamed of doing back in 1944. We took the children over to York and we joined a crowd gathered around the *Abraham and Isaac* play, in the space outside the Minster, on a chilly spring day. The crowd gave way for the children to get to the front, and our four little girls stood in a row, in a street in York, to watch a play that children had watched there six hundred years before: a play that was part of a body of work that had been central to my own search after theatre magic. The younger children were then only two; of course they could not comprehend in any depth the content of the play. But it lasted barely twenty minutes, and for that time the magic of strong and fearful actions, taking place between people who spoke in language strangely more powerful than the language of everyday life, seemed to enthral them.

Along with that next special occasion in Sheffield Playhouse, which then led us on to the circuit of playgoing treats, the very early contact with theatre made it early on a part of their lives. Playmaking at home became the most successful shared activity (and we adults enjoyed that too, of course). Then they got a puppet theatre, in which they experimented and in which productions by us became the established way of celebrating birthdays. We acquired a big 'company' of puppet actors, and quite a big repertoire of plays. But the live theatre was the best, and by the time each daughter arrived at the age of six we felt able to take the plunge and show them Shakespeare; each sixth birthday traditionally was celebrated with a theatre trip. The twins were particularly blessed in that their sixth birthday coincided with Shakespeare's four hundredth and we all went down to Stratford, a festive and celebratory Stratford, and saw a splendid Henry IV.

By then we had covered many miles of pilgrimage to theatres all over the north of England. I cannot remember precisely on which of the journeys home I said 'Why do we have to go so far for this?' No doubt it was one of the more harrowing ones when pitched battle raged in the back seats and all tempers were pretty frayed. Having said the words they echoed in my mind. Why indeed? Here was Leeds, at the centre of one of the biggest conurbation's in the country, lacking an amenity that existed in all other centres of comparable size and many much smaller ones as well. It suddenly seemed, also, so unfair that the children of parents with cars, with opportunity, and with faith in the theatre, should have a privilege that was unknown to hundreds of thousands of children in the region. And the same applied to the adults; only the privileged and those who had an interest already could readily become theatre-goers.

That moment of perception was not unlike the moment in Uganda; the words of an instant reaction echoed, became specific and ended up as a thought: 'Why not DO something about it?' It was not a timely thought for me personally: when the last batch of children had started full-time school I had started the process of getting back to full-time work; I was in the middle of an MA course to enable me to become a teacher of English as a Foreign Language. But untimely thoughts have a way of creating an unintended momentum and a few weeks later, after a few casual chats with people, we had that first gathering in our house. That was on March 12th 1964.

I have already told how everyone agreed that it was a doleful situation; but perhaps, we thought, it was just chance that the idea of subsidising theatre had not arisen; although Leeds City Council was not a leader in the field of the arts it had excellent policies in other leisure amenities, such as the provision of open spaces and parks; and, although it had allowed the Yorkshire

Symphony Orchestra to fail for want of funding, it nevertheless currently gave modest financial help to the concerts in the Town Hall. Maybe, we thought tolerantly, the dire burden of housing renewal, in which their record was exemplary, had taken all their resources of funds and imagination, and all that now was needed was a revelation, It would be easy to give them that, and we parted that evening with not much doubt that a very small initiative would bring a favourable response and that, rather late in the day, Leeds would be able to offer its citizens and those of the region round it a cultural amenity to parallel those in all the other cities. As someone had to take the 'very small initiative' we decided for form's sake to give ourselves an identity and we became then and there the Campaign for a Leeds Municipal Theatre. Arnold Kettle agreed to become its Chairman; and I, largely because we, the Newlyns, possessed a typewriter (albeit not a typist) agreed to become Secretary. For the first time in my life I was trapped into the activity I most abominated - committee membership - than which only one thing could be worse - being its secretary. But the commitment seemed small and self-contained, and I was not unduly anxious.

How many of us can point to the precise time at which their lives change? I am among those who can: it was on that evening in March. And it was not my life alone, but that of our whole family; and it was not just the pattern of life that changed, but the make-up of my personality, in many ways indisputably for the worse. But on the other hand I gained incomparable blessings: not just the obvious one of working to achieve an objective and succeeding; far more important were the loves and friendships that came from the process - as they had from the Uganda experience. At the last, that is what matters most.

Unexpectedly, events moved very swiftly. We had decided that our first step would be to write a letter to the Yorkshire Post, telling of our initiative and calling for supporters; and at the same time to discover from our local councillors if any ideas were by chance already 'floating around'. A letter was concocted and appeared above my name soon after our meeting.

The immediate result was devastating, to me. I had no experience whatsoever of dealing with the press, and the shock of a telephone interview, with no script as it were, and no self-assuredness, was very disturbing. At the meeting of 'the thirteen' we had, it is true, fully discussed our ideas for the ideal theatre, but we had no written manifesto, and indeed I had had no time as yet to even transfer my hand-written notes on our conclusions to a bad type-script. So I told my first lie to the press: I was at that moment in a conference, I said, and couldn't actually dictate to them the terms of reference of our committee, but I would ring them up, I promised - under pressure - in about half an hour and give them all the details they wanted. Urgently I tried to reach my Chairman, but unsuccessfully. By lucky chance Walter was that day working at home, and together we drafted the following formal policy statement:

**Campaign for a Leeds Municipal Theatre**

*Objective*: a professional theatre, architecturally attractive, with a resident company and good all round facilities, offering good drama at popular prices as a community service.

1. *Professional theatre*: because amateur work, no matter how good, does not attract any but a small closed group.

2. *Resident company*: because, working permanently together, it could produce work of a consistent quality in a planned programme, and working permanently in the same city it would be able to establish a close relationship with its audiences.

3. *Good all round facilities*: because an exciting theatre building could be a focal point for many other activities, and should be used not only for plays, but for concerts, jazz recitals, talks and demonstrations, and should offer amenities such as a coffee bar and restaurant, a bar, a club room for exhibitions and many other activities.

4. *Good drama*: because the people of other cities in England and Europe have shown that good drama, well presented, is what they want, but that the commercial theatre is limited to a narrow concept of box office possibilities.

5. *A community service*: because a community should deliberately set out to provide for its own enjoyment, rather than rely upon the precarious mechanism of commercial profit.

In some ways, fresh as it is from the first dewy days of the dreaming, I think it was never bettered. In its emphasis, which reflected that very first discussion, it is echoed by words written thirty years later, in a programme of the West Yorkshire Playhouse in the 1992 season:

> 'Providing West Yorkshire with quality theatre and a huge range of educational and community projects is part of creating a successful and vital region in which people and ideas flourish'.

The rest of the group were very co-operative in accepting it as a fait accompli when I anxiously phoned them all up *after* the dreadful burning of the boats - the dictating of it over the phone to a Yorkshire Post reporter. We committed it to duplicating paper - green duplicating paper as that was cheaper than white - and it became known as The Green Manifesto. The loftily didactic words at the end of Section 5 had a doctrinaire ring to them that I suspect irritated many in the business world. We were to regret them later, proper though they were. They were less uncompromising than those of Bernard Shaw, that I came upon recently, writing as he was about a century earlier; but they were just as effective in arousing suspicion as his would have been had we used them instead. 'The theatre' he said 'should not be abandoned to exploitation by commercial speculators. The job should be done by the elected representatives of the people, not left to private enterprise. Public enterprise has no more excuse for failing to provide theatre for its locality than to provide libraries and baths...museums and picture galleries'.[5]

It was bad enough putting on the act of self-assuredness and telling that first lie. The second lie was statistical, and gave me very much greater anxiety. How many supporters had we got? Thirteen sounded so few. It *was* few. So I multiplied it by ten and rounded it up a bit and said about 150 had already indicated intense interest. That made an impression, so soon after the first meeting, and it was quoted in the press item. In the urgent calls I made to the group I begged them all to go forth without delay and enrol ten supporters at once. They did.

That was how the Supporters' Organisation began. Built, as the phrase has it, on a lie. But, was it so different from the distortions and exaggerations that are common practice in professional public relations and publicity? I think probably not. What was different was that in this case the practitioner was not professional, and possessed a respect for truth; I was truly shocked at myself for the ease at with which I had been economical with it - or rather over-generous with it - and I suffered hours of guilt and fear of being found out. But it paid off: not only did I soon have a very nice card index of about one hundred names, but that initial press coverage brought in key people, willing to serve actively, who would not otherwise have been reached as they were not among the immediate friends of the core group.

The new City Librarian, Godfrey Thomson, was one - he came from Manchester City Library, where he had been responsible for the administration of the little Library Theatre, once the home of Joan Littlewood's company. Another was Arnold Reuben, a businessman, who had been at Oxford after the war and had been infected by the wave of new theatre practitioners up at that time: he stayed with the campaign to the end, and beyond. There was Ruby Pearce, a member of the wealthy Lyons family by birth and by marriage connected with one of the most important Labour Party figures in the city: she it was, let it now be known, who, anonymously, signed the first cheque for the Campaign - of £100 for the expenses of duplicating paper and stamps when it became obvious that we were to be 'in business'. Alec Baron and Charles Gardiner, of whom I have already written, were brought in by contact with other members of the core group. And John Wood, who was brought in by Ann Severs, joined us at that stage, a Moliere scholar recently retired from adult education, whose life-long passion for the theatre had led to many friendships with distinguished figures in the theatre, such as Tyrone Guthrie and Stephen Joseph. These were contacts that were to be of great importance to us; but of greater importance was John *per se*, whose quixotic, irrascible nature added a spice of danger to relationships and of excitement at meetings, but whose knowledge, wisdom and expertise were among our greatest strengths. His was a dour sceptical nature: I encountered it for the first time on our doorstep, where he stood briefly after we had exchanged one or two letters about the prospects of the Campaign, looking at me with suspicion and no sign of pleasure, until curtly he said 'All right - I'll join you - I just came to see what you were like. You seem all right to me'. Suspicious as I am of compliments, I have held that meagre response close to my heart.

Three other members of the first, wider, group that met brought varied gifts to us. First among them was Bill Oliver, the Deputy Editor of the Yorkshire Post, and its art critic; he brought to us not only the vast value and prestige of his position and expertise in the press, but his dear and gentle nature that so often in the years to come brought a salve of tranquillity to the frenetic states of mind that arose from our frenetic lives. Then there was Tom Costello, who was Deputy Warden of the Swarthmore Centre in Leeds - a young man among a somewhat middle-aged group, and with dynamic energy which he put to use as our Publicity Officer. Finally and unbelievably there was William Shakespeare. He was the nominated representative of the Trades Council, whom we early invited to join us. He never played an active part in much of our campaigning, but his name alone gave an authority to our circulated material. I often wondered if people who did not know that the name had stood above an optician's premises in Leeds for quite a long time thought we were being facetious, or even hubristic, in listing him among our committee members. In fact, it was possibly a sense of aptness together with a sense of humour that had caused the Trades Council to choose him of all people. He did in fact come originally from Warwickshire and, although we knew the male line of the first William Shakespeare had died out with his only son, Hamnet, we found it pleasing to have him with us, even if a symbol only.

Such a group it was that met, more formally than did the first thirteen, in the Swarthmore Centre one Sunday morning in mid-April: a meeting that really set in motion the Campaign proper. For by now, after a month of exploratory lobbying and meetings with various councillors and officers of the local authority, it seemed clear that our euphoric early hopes of the Council responding at once to our suggestion and entering into exploration of the situation were not to be realised. We had met with complete lack of interest and indeed hostility. With something of a sinking feeling at the enormousness of what we had started, we began to realise that it was we ourselves who were to establish the theatre; and that it would be no easy task to undertake from scratch for a self-appointed group of citizens, none of whom were actually working in the theatre.

It astonishes me now, as I explore the minutes of those first meetings, how little time we lost. Very quickly we dismissed the viability of activating the City Council - except as a supplier of a free site: that at least seemed essential as a starting point. Most members of the committee were actually glad not to be circumscribed by the processes of bureaucracy that co-operation at this stage with the Council would have involved - there was a sense of urgency and an impatience to get on with the job; and many members had had years of experience with, or in the service of, this particular authority, and had no illusions about its cultural dynamism. Our task quickly resolved itself into two main activities: planning the ideal theatre; and engaging the support of the people with a view to raising money for it.

Planning the theatre came first, for only with a concrete plan could we hope for support. So our Theatre Planning Committee came into being and, over a few weeks of exhaustive and exhausting work, intensive study and wide-spread consultation, it created the very first plans for our theatre. It is good to reflect that between the first creation of that tiny group, working in a limbo, and the main auditorium of the West Yorkshire Playhouse, there is very little difference. A good time before open stages on the Greek model became common, the plans for Leeds Playhouse were just that. It was soundly researched; it was discussed with Stephen Joseph, Tyrone Guthrie and several theatre directors among the provincial theatres; we made visits to theatres all over the country where we thought we could learn; a long meeting took place with the Drama Director of the Arts Council, who came up to us with words of hope and encouragement and the observation, when we asked why he hadn't taken any previous initiatives in Leeds, that 'I was waiting for you to take them'. There were long, long hours of discussion and argument; a young architect, Martin Taylor, joined us to put ideals and visions into measurements....What fascination and delight it brought, this process of planning from scratch, to the members who for years had pondered on theatre design - particularly Alec and John, who were the inspiration of the Theatre Planning Committee. For me this was quite a new field: I had never really given a positive thought to the *housing* of drama - and as it happens my two experiences outside the conventional amateur scene had been in travelling theatre; it was for me a very educative process.

The other area of expertise to be mastered was that of finance - not just of capital costs but of running costs: how much did a theatre cost to run a year; how much could it expect in revenue; how many people were needed in an audience catchment area to provide an adequate revenue at the box office; of what order of magnitude would be the expectation of subsidy and who would it

*The Greek model: Epidaurus Theatre*

*The model of the auditorium*

come from? Walter, as the committee's economist, undertook an analysis of the economics of theatre within a notional catchment area; no such study had been made before, but the Arts Council welcomed our approach and supplied all the data that they had assembled from the accounts of all the working theatres receiving their subsidies.

When these two studies were completed, by September, the first Leeds Theatre Campaign miracle emerged: the optimum number of seats for the perfect theatre of the type we decided to go for was 750; and the optimum number of seats to ensure a working box-office income from a population the size of Leeds and its region, on the basis of all current data, was almost precisely 750!

While this part of the work and study and planning was going on other processes continued. There was the business of testing the temperature in the business community with a view to fund-raising: this was undertaken by our members who had business contacts and acumen. There was the tedious necessity of continued discourse with the City Council: with the City Engineer in our search for sites; with the Music and Arts Committee which had, with interesting timing that seemed far from coincidental, begun to refer to 'building a concert hall' - a project that would we bound, we felt, to direct attention away from the theatre project; but we had, in all courtesy, to remain in discourse with that committee which was the one most closely affected by our initiative. There was the courtesy process of engaging the concern of our MP's. And of course we wanted to start attracting support from the arts world generally - writers, actors, artists with any local connections in particular. That fell to be my job, and very agreeable it was; the responses were encouraging, confirmatory and supportive.

Perhaps the most endearing of all the good and famous who rallied to our cause was Sybil Thorndike. Two or three of us were received by her in her hotel while she was playing in a less-than-memorable piece at the Grand, in which her husband, Lewis Casson, also took part. Dame Sybil herself was, even in her old age, strikingly beautiful, with an inner radiance that seemed to flow out in kindness and involvement and youthful excitement. 'Oh, if only Lewis and I were younger,' she said, 'we would come and start it for you'. I am sure they would. Lewis, who had hardly spoken until then, agreed decisively when she appealed to him. It was very moving: those two were amongst the real pioneers of repertory theatre, members of the very first company at the Gaiety Theatre in Manchester that was founded by the rich, generous and dedicated Annie Horniman. They had first met there; Sybil played her first great roles there; they married there, worked together there and in 1911 Lewis became the second Director of the theatre. They knew all about starting theatres of the sort we wanted. Sybil once wrote of Annie Horniman, 'I often wonder whether the people of the city appreciate what she's doing - one wonders if pioneer work is ever appreciated'.[6] Sybil understood our feelings, as pioneers, so well, and seemed to identify with them. She remained a friend of the Campaign throughout; and she always sent a message when we asked for one, including one for the night the Playhouse finally opened; and she always wrote by hand - except, as it happened, the precious personal one she wrote me when it was all over, in which she apologised for having to dictate on account of a broken arm. That note did me the honour of assuming her own indefatigability, for among other things in it she said she hoped I would go on to another commitment.

Our meeting with her ended with courtesies from us about the play and the performances. 'Dears', she said, 'it is *not* a good play. One of the troubles is that each act is so like the others that I can't for the life of me remember at any one time which one we're doing'. Perhaps it didn't matter so long as she was in it.

And then there was the 'whispering campaign'. This sinister force was invented by, of all people, Sir Roger Stevens, Vice Chancellor of the University, soon after he agreed in July (with endearing glee) to become our Chairman, in place of Arnold Kettle who felt a change of image at the top would be a good thing. The term really seemed to belong to the world of underground plottings and machinations rather than to a public campaign, or to the ambassadorial circles to which Sir Roger had belonged before becoming a Vice Chancellor; we were all reduced to convulsions of laughter when he suggested it. But it was a splendid proposal, and the name somehow gave identity and form to the untidy process of talking to anybody and everybody in order to spread the word - which is what we were all doing. Indeed, it started off in my mind an idea for a more systematic formalising of our approaches to the public, but that had to wait until we had completed our homework, for we knew that, above all and first and foremost, we had to create public confidence in us.

All through this period of three, four months, there was also the business of the press. There was a curious paradox here: the Deputy Editor of the Yorkshire Post was a key member of our movement; and the Drama Critic, Desmond Pratt, was its bitterest enemy. It was one of the heaviest burdens the campaign had to bear, right up to the night the Playhouse opened, this dedicated opposition from a journalist with considerable power to rubbish us. Partly because Pratt genuinely loved the Grand Theatre and genuinely believed that we threatened it, partly because he sourly and simply despised our non-professional status and the fact that we were self-established, he cast his lot against us; year after year he would seize every opportunity, it seemed, to pour doubt upon our objectives, our progress and our competence; and he succeeded, I truly believe, in hindering the process of gaining support from many people and institutions in the region who might earlier have been more generous. So that was a major commitment - Pratt-watching and Pratt-handling - getting an immediate response into the Yorkshire Post the minute we picked up a slighting reference or a damning comment. Many are the midnight dashes to the letter box, then in Albion Street, that I have made to make sure that an antidote to some poison of his was injected without delay. On the other hand, the Evening Post was supportive from the outset and its drama critic, Ronnie Wilkinson, was throughout a very good friend to the Campaign; he gave us many columns of good informative coverage, as well as intelligent and well-informed comment.

So life in that summer of 1964 was very busy - to me more than a little reminiscent of the early days of the Uganda Pilgrim Players, but much more many-sided. The feverish rounds of meetings and discussions, the visits to other theatres, letter-writing, producing minutes of the various committees and sub-committees, and keeping in touch with everybody in order to co-ordinate activities took over more of my time than there was to spare. The most immediate effect for me was a decision not to complete the MA - that year at any rate. It was disappointing; but I had at least managed to complete the academic part of the course, and would now be prevented from undertaking the practical work, which would have taken me to Spain. The other thing that happened to me was the discovery of the middle of the night. There was so much to do in the day: the phone was ringing constantly, people were continuously coming to the house, there were meetings and interviews and appointments. And there was ordinary life, with the children and their lives to maintain, undamaged if possible. So the long, quiet writing periods had to take place when everyone else was asleep. And how I lamented my incompetence on the typewriter! I think with deep gratitude of the many dear friends who took pity on me, and one after the other undertook to do decent copies of the things that had to be typed properly. They all did it free: apart from Ruby's £100 we had, so far, no income; and our Treasurer's statements make interesting reading, for they recurrently showed an almost intact £100, in spite of all the money spent by everyone on phone calls, stamps, car and train journeys to places all over the country. The explanation was, of course, that nobody charged for anything they did or expended.

This is a good moment to reflect on voluntary effort and to record the incalculable debt owed in many spheres to volunteers who do things out of commitment. In particular, the sixties were still a time when wives-and-mums tended to be full-timers at that job. Many, like myself, had made a deliberate decision to remain so, in spite of personal and financial constraints, until the children were much older. We liked to meet our own children from school, to have a family tea-table when they got home, and to be available ourselves for crises or involvements; and we regarded the job as in no way unworthy of abilities that, in many of us, had been the product of higher education. So, as little by little more time became available, as batch after batch of the children went off to full-time primary school, many of us found time to spare, though not enough, yet, for a full-time job. A very great deal of the basic work of the Theatre Campaign was done by women in that position - a fund of service that I suspect exists rather less now. There were of course others, men and women, in the Campaign who managed to serve hard and fully in spite of full-time jobs: Barbara continued to be a full-time teacher; Alec Baron ran a business; Walter and Arnold were full-time academics; the Vice Chancellor headed a university; Charles Gardiner ran a school; Godfrey Thompson ran a city Library service. But there was a fever amongst us then that made us all, part-timers and full-timers, sweat hard in the campaign service.

By September a final detailed plan for the theatre was complete, together with architect's sketches and costings: the total estimated capital cost was £220,000. At the same time the economic analysis (the first of its kind in this field at the time, and subsequently used by the Arts Council and drawn upon by planning groups in a number of places, including one in Australia) had made detailed estimates of both the capital and recurrent financial implications for our notional catchment area. Now was the time to go out on a wide front to the public, and to intensify pressure on the local authority to provide a free site. There had, over the previous three months, been a number of 'communiqués' sent out to the names on the card index so infamously started. It had already grown quite a lot, at the expense to us all of reputations of obsessiveness. The time had not yet come, it is true, when people actually ran away when they saw us coming (which did actually happen on a memorable occasion later on, when it was the Secretary General of the Arts Council who hastened down a corridor to escape us) but our friends found our conversational orbits somewhat reduced.

So now we had to try to get outside the circuit of personal contact and set up communication routes on a mass scale. In a society everyone is in or touched by some part of the social networks; and through the networks you can reach a large number of people. Some quiet, happy, undisturbed hours with reference books in the library yielded an amazing number of organisations, encompassing, I felt, every single person living in the region; and in September we actually launched our first comprehensive piece of publicity - a duplicated statement (for which we at last drew on the £100) delivered by hand to offices of organisations all over the city and the region, ranging from the West Riding Education Department to the Federation of Townswomen's Guilds, from the Association of Nursery Group Organisations to the West Yorkshire Association of Architects, from Women's Institutes to the Trades Council. The results of this were extremely encouraging: we had a lot of direct responses, newspaper coverage, suggestions, offers of help, requests for talks - this last leading to our setting up a talks panel and a few of us finding another commitment to add to our timetables. Slowly the card index grew. I loved every name on it and knew many of the people behind the names: they were very close to my heart, the people on that first register of names; when now sometimes I meet one of them I am transported back, just by the sound of the name, to an urgent hectic time full of the delights of sharing an objective and of fellow feeling with people completely outside my closed and private world. I was in touch at last with Leeds the city, no longer ensconced in the ivory tower of the University.

With this launch of communication through organisations, it still was more important, in my view, that the whispering campaign should be started, for it was based on the concept of one-to-one 'conversion'. The idea was that a certain number of people acting as 'cell-cores' would undertake to obtain contact with and support from a given number of new people, who would themselves then undertake to replicate the process. The scheme would impose a limited task on an ever-growing number of people, each of whom would be able to feel a sense of accomplishment without an ongoing commitment to campaigning. I produced a mind-boggling statistic showing the result of exponential growth; and it was agreed by the Campaign Committee that we should undertake this scheme, in which it seemed statistically possible that the entire population of Great Britain could soon be engaged. We decided to call the operation *The Direct Contact Scheme* and to produce a Brief, which would be the basis of indoctrination. The scale of the operation clearly required the exclusive concern of one person, particularly in respect of the preparation of the Brief; and this was when one of the now-long-forgotten giant tasks of the campaign was undertaken, single-handed, by someone who had not so far thought to do more than give support and help and encouragement on a quite manageable scale: Ann Squires, one of the younger members of the group, by profession a scientist. At that time, with three little girls, she was at the stage of being a full-time wife-and-mum. She was a dear friend of mine.

How generous were one's friends in responding to impossible requests to do unmanageable jobs! Ann undertook to write, 'by yesterday' as impatient editors put it, a booklet on a subject about which, when she started, she knew next to nothing. A fine mind, committed to excellence, however, can apply to any undertaking the discipline and expertise that it applies to its specialism. Ann produced a booklet, entitled *A New Theatre*, which can still act as a reference work for people who want to know about regional theatre at that time, and about theatre in Leeds past and future; a booklet written in a tone that combines the precision of the scientist with the high idealism of the true and concerned citizen. Apart from the facts about the Campaign, its proposals and plans, it contains a section on the economic analysis - and another section containing detailed accounts and descriptions of nine other theatres - eight of them in Britain in cities comparable to Leeds and one of them a German city, Dortmund, to bring attention to the contrast with German attitudes to supporting the arts. Ann then went on to design the format, the layout and the cover. It was to be very simple; and as we could not afford printing it had to be possible for us to produce it ourselves; in those days there were no word-processors and no desk-top publication techniques: the duplicator was the sole alternative to printing and photo-stating. The Brief was ready for reproduction by the beginning of 1965.

Just at that moment was issued a Government White Paper that filled us all with hope and excitement. Jennie Lee had recently been appointed Minister for the Arts; and her first action was the publication of this White Paper, which was a great call for the encouragement and support by Government of the arts, and in particular for the popularising of them. Written in a style that glowed with the fervour and socialist idealism that were Jennie Lee's own, it contained so much that we were working for that we almost felt she had written it for us. So the production of our Brief was delayed a little, while an abstract of the White paper was prepared, and it was with the following passage quoted in full that our Brief ended:

> 98. Some local authorities will need a good deal of persuading before they are convinced that the money it is in their power to spend on arts and amenities is money well spent and deserving a much higher priority than hitherto. But it can be done. All new social services have to fight long and hard before they establish themselves. Only yesterday it was the fight for a free health service. The day before it was the struggle to win education for all.
>
> 99. Today a searching reappraisal of the whole situation in relation to cultural standards and opportunities is in progress. More and more people begin to appreciate that the exclusion of so many for so long from the best of our cultural heritage can

become as damaging to the privileged minority as to the under privileged majority. We walk the same streets, breathe the same air, are exposed to the same sights and sounds.

100. Nor can we ignore the growing revolt, especially among the young, against the drabness, uniformity and joylessness of much of the social furniture we have inherited from the industrial revolution. This can be directed, if we so wish, into making Britain a gayer and more cultivated country.

101. It is fitting that the present Government should seek to encourage all who are furthering these aims. The proposals outlined in this White Paper, though no more than the first steps in the direction of a fully comprehensive policy for the arts, demonstrate the Government's concern that immediate progress should be made.[7]

There could, we felt, hardly have been a more propitious time to launch our Direct Contact Scheme than this; we were part of a nation-wide revolution. The actual process of reproducing the Brief was, like so many of our major accomplishments, a sort of mad pantomime act. Still without any regular source of income, and with only some of the £100 left, we were always dependant on voluntary labour and scrounged facilities; we bought only our materials, and a lot of those were often begged for, or offered to us at ludicrously low prices by sympathetic firms, such as Austick's, who had turned out that green duplicating paper for us. Producing 2,000 copies of a forty page document was a daunting task. However, there happened to be a happy conjunction of circumstances in that our Godfrey Thompson, being City Librarian, had a huge office in the library building, a marvellously kind and intrepid secretary, an electric duplicator, a keen delight in living dangerously, and a conveniently flexible conscience.

I do not remember who typed the waxes - not me, for sure: the most tolerant of committee members would have opposed that -

but they were taken to Godfrey's office, as were the stacks of duplicating paper. His secretary set in motion and supervised the duplicator, and 80,000 sheets of quarto text were slowly piled up neatly behind the entrance door to Godfrey's inner sanctum, where, as it happened, there was simultaneously a meeting of the Library Committee, the members of which, councillors all, passed unknowing the great pile of unauthorised paperwork. Getting it away was another problem and involved parking on a site at the door reserved for Chief Constable while we made journey after journey to load up, drive off, and return for more; on only one stop-over did the Chief Constable himself appear; but he seemed unoffended and content to park behind us on a double yellow line. The duplicated pages were taken to a room in the University Department of Economics where there was a very big seminar table; use of the room for its proper purposes was temporarily suspended; forty separate piles of paper were ranged round the table; and we had one of our frequent 'working parties' at which volunteers sustained by alcohol and dedication did the circuit, presenting their batched up pages to the clipper at the end.

This sort of mini-drama is a *sine qua non* of campaigning, and all who have campaigned for anything have tales to tell of triumph over the impossible, and of the fun of being up to the neck in it with a crowd of other people. At that stage in the life of this campaign it was still immense fun - we had not yet grown old and bruised by disappointment. The whole operation remains one of the highlights of the campaign for me, and I still feel immensely proud of that Brief and the dedicated teamwork that supported Ann's production of it. She had by now taken over complete control of the Supporters' Organisation which was to be the result of the Direct Contact Scheme. We wanted not only a growing public awareness but a recognised subscription-paying core membership rather than a card index of sympathisers. This, with the help of two or three other people, including Barbara Barber, Ann got off the ground within the next three months; by the direct contact method we recruited a firm body of some 2,000 people, which, though not on the dazzling scale my first euphoric estimates had led us to expect, remained the core of the campaign for the next five years; through this body we distributed the Brief, which was also used along with the Economic Analysis, as our basic information material. The idea of the 'cells' worked well, and the groups thus brought together by the original 'core-cells' found many other ways as ongoing groups of helping the campaign; a lot of friendships were made as people joined this engrossing new interest, shared with others. Copies of the Brief went also to everybody who seemed likely to make good use of them - officials, councillors, businessmen. It was taken by each of us on the Talks Panel, another accelerating activity. And none of us went anywhere without a few copies ready to pull out - at dinner parties, board meetings, outside school gates, in the doctor's waiting room ...

We had a visual aid too, for use in talks: Martin Taylor, who had put the Theatre Planning Committee's ideas into architectural form, made a small model, and this was copied by a group of woodwork pupils in Charles Gardiner's school; so we had three little models, all painted red for no good reason except, I suppose, that someone gave us some red paint, and these travelled around Yorkshire to a variety of venues. One of them was used by Ainsley's the baker's, as a model for a huge cake, also red, for a party at which we celebrated the first anniversary of the meeting of the thirteen. It seemed appropriate that we should actually eat our theatre, because it was by now an integral part of us all anyway.

During the last months of the first year we had planned for a February date at which to launch a Public Appeal, and we had actually booked the Town Hall for it. We had hoped that by then the growing pressure upon the Council would have persuaded them into allocating a free site - an act that was absolutely essential for the viability of our scheme. Land prices put completely out of the question the possibility of our purchasing; and in any case the building needed to be included in the City's plans for all its amenities. It seemed a small enough contribution for the local authority to make as its response to the growing calls for them to spend on subsidising the arts. Our demand for the site was our sole demand: no contribution to the capital cost was assumed by us - and our sceptics said that in any case such assumptions would have been vain ones; in any case we were optimistic about raising funds from a city as prosperous and wealthy as Leeds, with a good record of patronage of the other arts.

But at the beginning of 1965 we were seduced into changing our tactics by two things. One of them was a series of meetings with Council officials at which we were given much more positive indication of the Council's interest in the building of a concert hall, to which, it was now apparently suggested, a theatre should be added, thus providing Leeds with a fine new arts complex. It is impossible to say why this proposition should have been conceived at this precise point in our campaign history. The sceptics among us believed it was in part a device to distract attention from our growing influence and authority; but it would seem to have been a cumbersome way to do so. Perhaps the Campaign's progress had acted as a spur to the music lobby, been a beaconbearer against the inertia and philistinism of our Council. Complaints about the absence of a decent concert hall were a recurrent item of public debate, but no organised popular attempts had ever been made to mobilise pressure and resources. But there had long been strong support for music amongst Leeds people, and considerable criticism had been levied at the Council for its refusal to maintain financial support for the Yorkshire Symphony Orchestra a few years earlier, which had resulted in the demise of the orchestra. Concerts at the Town Hall were now subsidised by the Council and it was likely that plans to improve music facilities would gain ready support from the people. There was a powerful and prestigious sector in the music world in the city, and this was represented in the newly-stirring initiative by Lord Harewood, and by Jack Lyons, one of Leeds' wealthier citizens and patrons; both were referred to as being in consultation with the Council,

Playhouse. One of these first friends was Tony Richardson, Director of the Belgrade Theatre in Coventry, and he gave us an inspiring account of the work and achievements of that first of all the regional theatres. There was a representative from Equity, a well-known actor called Duncan McCrae, a fiery incisive speaker, who, speaking for the profession, reinforced our belief in the importance of drama in the community. And then there was Keith Waterhouse. Keith was by then a well-known and successful writer, of plays and novels and journalism, but he was also a Leeds man; he had grown up in Hunslet, and he was one of the group of fine creative artists that the region boasted about. He was also a witty and compelling speaker, in a truly Yorkshire down-beat way. He was a great success that night - 'A city without a theatre is a city without a heart' was one of the most telling of his statements. He was to remain a true, valued and valuable friend and solid supporter of the campaign right to the very end. He took quickly to his heart the Pratt-factor; he had himself started his writing career some years earlier as a journalist in Leeds; and through the years of the Theatre Campaign he was to deliver, again and again, in writing and in speeches, devastating swipes at Pratt.

The May meeting was one of those lovely occasions when a whole lot of people who think alike get together and confirm each other in their thoughts. The modest objective of the meeting was, indeed, just that: up till then we, the campaigners, had been voices on the phone, faces in the papers, signatures on duplicated letters; and they, the supporters, were names on card indexes. About 250 people came, and it was an evening that brought courage and comfort and hope to us and gave confidence to them. It also raised a little money, activated distribution of leaflets which we had by now had printed, gathered a number of ideas and produced new names for help-giving. In addition there was good press coverage. The only specific impetus it gave to the progress of the Campaign was the authority of 250 people behind a message of censure on the Council for its protracted delay in showing its hand about the concert hall plans and hence about a site for us. This was forwarded to the Council, and may well have been instrumental in putting into motion the slow slow process whereby the Council set up a Tripartite Committee to explore ways and means for building for the city that splendid arts complex. That was in 1965. Now, a quarter of a century later, Leeds still has no concert hall. That it does have its theatre and has had it for most of that quarter century is the miracle not only of the sustained activity of the campaigners, but of their endurance; for they survived, before the campaign really got under way, a dreary period of more than two years of false expectations, dashed hopes, tedious bureaucratic processes and, it often seemed, a devious intention to thwart them.

At this point a dramatic upheaval took place in the lives of the Newlyns which caused us to be absent during those very years. In July the whole family returned to Uganda, for a period of two years this time, leaving behind the frustrations and the excitement of the work in the Theatre Campaign; leaving them, as John Wood sourly said in farewell, with the small matter of raising a quarter of a million pounds. It had not, of course, and sadly, actually come to that yet, and didn't for another four years,; but it *was* rather unfair abandoning theatre matters at home in a doldrum, and heading off for a two-year spell in which theatre matters, as it turned out, were to be engrossingly interesting, very demanding and extremely productive; and which again led me back to my mediaeval obsession.

But the Campaign was well established by now, and very nobly served by a team of planners, workers and organisers who sustained the hopes and interest of the Supporters' Organisation, and maintained a clear profile in the city; there were discussion groups, a Forum, visits to other theatres; the talks programme continued; the press campaign of letters and interviews went on; news letters were sent out, though they make sad reading, always having to report that there was nothing to report. Moves continued, to form a joint committee to bring together the Council, the Theatre Campaign and the music lobby. The campaign was in a cleft stick: to stand aside from this initiative would be misguided and would look bad; the initiative might indeed lead to something; but there were clearly problems in contemplating a joint home. With these other powerful interests likely to take over control, how would the independence of the theatre be assured; the artistic policy protected from pressure and interference? On the other hand, would there be any hope of gaining a site from the Council if participation in this initiative were refused. Agonised debate took place, and it was agreed that we should join the Tripartite Committee. In fact it hadn't met by the spring of 1966. And when it did meet its one action was to name and designate a site for the joint building - a good one, in fact, where the old fire station used to be, alongside the Town Hall. I remember getting a cable in Uganda which simply, marvellously, said 'Site allocated. Congratulations'. But the congratulations were premature; a site on a map was all the Tripartite Committee ever achieved. And when we returned to Leeds in June of 1967, the situation was almost precisely the one we had left behind, although there was a lot more scepticism and weariness.

In the meantime....

# 5

# Between The Scenes

Six years before, we had left a colony approaching independence. The Uganda we returned to had been for three years an independent state. It had suffered no violence in the change-over-period; there had been little jostling for power, and there had been no white settlers to pacify, or eject, as there had been in Kenya. The land belonged to peasant farmers, except in Buganda, where it was owned by a few wealthy families, such as that of my friend Olive Kagwa's husband - the family which traditionally held the post of Chief Minister, or Katikiro, to the hereditary king of Buganda who was called the Kabaka; in its turn, his kingdom was one of the richest and most developed of those making up the country of Uganda. The major owners of industry and the sugar estates were the Asians, citizens of Uganda who had for long been a part of Uganda society, and there was a handful of extremely wealthy Asian families. But most of the Asians were in fact far from wealthy, although trade in the country was dominated by them: retail shops, from big stores in the larger towns to tiny 'general shops' in the villages, were predominantly owned by Asian families, many of whom had a standard of living that compared ill with that of the more prosperous African farmers.

The economy of Uganda was almost a model for a developing country; its affairs were flourishing, and a mildly socialist Prime Minister had, it seemed, established a fairly stable society. It had always been a very beautiful place, on the equator but high up, and its climate was, except for an area in the north, quite as idyllic for people as it was for agriculture - even for whites, for it was rather like a perpetual English summer of the best sort, with long, warm, sunny spells, but plenty of mostly moderate rain scattered throughout the year. The land always looked green and well-watered, the crops flourished, and the gardens of even the humblest farmers in the bush were often rich in flowers, like an English garden. The educational standards were good - a high proportion of all the children went to primary school, and there was a rapid growth in the availability of secondary schools. The University of Makerere was of excellent standing academically, as well as being a sort of paradise within a paradise domestically, and it was here, this time, that we were to live, working within the University and not the Government, based in Kampala not Entebbe. Walter was for two years to direct economic research in the East African Institute of Social and Economic Research; and it seemed to me, when we arrived at our house on the campus, with its huge garden and orange trees and a banana tree and a passion fruit growing all over one wall, and one kind, friendly, mature woman house-servant already established - and with moreover all the congenial society of a University to enjoy - that the next two years were exactly what I had been waiting for: a rest, after six demanding family years with four children with no more than three and a half years between them, and with the Theatre Campaign thrown in; a relaxed, peaceful life, in a place where I already had many friends, most of them from the Uganda Pilgrim Players, and many of them, now, in senior government posts in their own country's administration; a two-year summer in cotton dresses and a swim suit; perhaps a little teaching - perhaps making good the loss of the practical part of my language teaching course, which I had been unable to complete; a relaxed life, with help in the house, with an amazing range of fruits and vegetables, all the rich dairy produce of Kenya, and local coffee beans of the highest quality; the life, in fact, of an old-style 'colonial wife' but blessedly in a society that no longer suffered the inequalities and injustices of a colonial system. For once, I thought, I will not get entangled in theatre matters.

But 'there's a divinity that shapes our ends, rough-hew them how we will'. Within the University of Makerere, in 1964, a travelling theatre had been set up. It had just completed its first tour, with a repertoire of no less than eleven plays and forty-two venues, in which they reckoned to have played to 17,000 people. In the way that things happen in a small community, it was not long before I was invited to participate; and it was, of course, irresistible. Quite soon I discovered that a few of the students involved had, at school, seen and remembered performances by the Uganda Pilgrim Players, six years before; it was good to feel that some of the seeds we had sown had germinated and contributed, perhaps, to this second travelling theatre. But there were many far more important influences, the main one being the beginning of indigenous writing. It started later here than in Nigeria, where Wole Soyinka was already recognised as possibly Africa's greatest writer and had since 1960 been staging his own plays with a company formed by him; his work was a compelling influence on writing throughout the continent. The Kenyan, Ngugi wa Thiong'o - who had also been at Leeds, working under Arnold Kettle's supervision - had written the first play to come from East Africa, although in English, in 1962; the first full-length Ugandan play, in Luganda, was performed in 1963.

By 1965 a number of one-act plays had appeared, and the Makerere Travelling Theatre's repertoire of plays in both English and the vernaculars included three by student members of the theatre, and four more by local writers. One of these, Elvanira Zirimu, was already a friend of mine, for she and her husband had just spent some years in Leeds; Pio Zirimu had been doing the language MA at the same time as I was, while Van (as she was known) had done a BA course ( the Finals for which she had taken in a maternity hospital, where she actually wrote one of the papers while in labour). They knew all about the Leeds Theatre Campaign; and although they were not actually to return to Uganda until our second year there it was another crossing thread that thickened the web. There was still not a lot of work of Ugandan origin being performed in the National Theatre; but the University had an English Department which gave great emphasis to drama, and it was this that had been the birthplace of the travelling theatre. I thought with a certain sadness of the discouragement I had actually received from here in the days when I was working on the idea of the Uganda Pilgrim Players, but it was obvious that different people and different attitudes were at work; perhaps - who knows - the eventual success of that early venture had overcome doubts and even given some incentive to this new one.

My commitment with the travelling theatre was a very comfortable one - producing one play in the repertoire for the next tour. I was in no way involved in the organisation, which was very well administered; there were funds available, an established circuit, good support from the Ministry of Education and, above all, a company of extremely talented though variously experienced young actors with great enthusiasm. So, for me with no administrative work, only a play to produce, it was a most happy prospect.

Quite soon I was allocated my play, which turned out to be *The Proposal*, by Anton Chekhov, and a trio of actors, Tim Wangusa, Rose Mbowa and Noah Sentongo. It was quite clear form the start that these three were a very remarkable group, and when at our first read-through I said 'Let's adapt it to Uganda' they fell in with the idea and the undertaking with immediate delight. And so we rewrote Chekhov at the same time as rehearsing it; it was a sustained exercise in creative theatre. The result was very successful, and the performances given by those three were amongst the best I have ever seen by amateurs. The play worked well in its changed social context; and the actors were clearly able to identify more deeply with the characters, having in some measure created them in their new form.

Moreover, the style and idiom, created by the actors who were to speak them, had a vitality and fluency that an adaptation made in a study would never have achieved.

This involvement with the Makerere Travelling Theatre was both inspiring and happy. The best talents of the country were engaged in a creative process of primary importance to the entire population; this was no ivory tower elitist pastime: there was a strong sense of mission in all the members of the theatre, of whom at first I only knew well the cast of my own play. The full group contained a considerable number of extremely talented men and women who had been privileged in their educational opportunities and who were now concerned, exactly as we were in Leeds, to bring to all their people the enlightment and stimulus and delight that they had found in drama. I felt a huge sense of identity with them, for they and we Leeds campaigners, in different cultures with different histories, were in fact committed to an identical mission. It was clear that the work of the Uganda Pilgrim Players had been of minor significance, but that was of no consequence now. The right way had been found to fill the gap in the country's cultural life of which we had been so aware a decade ago, and it was successfully achieving what we had seen as a possibility then. In every way what they were doing now was superior to our early efforts: the enterprise was totally based on African talents; local languages were being used; a range of plays was being presented, which maintained a careful balance between the local and the imported. The organisation was exemplary and the range of venues was very wide. Moreover, the time was ripe: the emergence of creative writers provided the material, and the existence of the theatre provided a vehicle for the writers. Ironically it seemed that a major theatre campaign had succeeded here, while back in Leeds ... I felt envious, but at the same time it was good to be associated with success; and of course it was an entirely delightful activity for me personally, bringing friendship as well as a feeling of usefulness and involvement.[1]

*Makere Travelling Theatre. Two performances in a leprosorium. Top: Chekhov's 'The Proposal'; below an original work by Angelos Okello.*

*A mime play at Jinja*

*An audience at Mbarara*

*The Proposal* went off on its summer vacation tour, from April 1966, and I saw very few of its performances (which turned out to be extremely popular with audiences everywhere) because by now I had got another undertaking on my hands. So much for my two years of restful life. I had been asked by the Headmaster of a secondary school in Kampala to 'do some drama' with some of his senior pupils. The school was a large one, and the pupils were a mixture of Africans and Asians, predominantly boys. The assignment was a daunting one, involving three hundred third year students (whose ages ranged perhaps from 15 to 18) in twelve classes for a period of about seven weeks; the work was to be a part of the curriculum rather than simply an extra-curricular activity, so it was to involve entire classes as distinct from groups of enthusiasts. No drama had been done at the school before, except as an extension of literature study.

I cannot pretend that it was a sudden moment of illumination that decided me to turn again to the Mystery plays: I confess that I spend a lot of my life looking for opportunities to do them. But it is truly the case that no other established work offers such obvious potential as a group project involving a large number of people with a great range of talents - a sequence of short plays linked by a common theme. So that is what I proposed as the form that my half-term's work should take: a mini Mystery Cycle. The plays, after all, were written by amateurs and acted by the ordinary populace: in other words, they were 'people's drama' and were therefore ideal material for our purpose which was a 'popular' group production. Moreover, they have a unique appeal for young actors and audiences anywhere; they are strong, concise and forthright; their comedy is broad and distinguished by a total absence of unctuous reverence for even the most hallowed subjects; the characters are boldly drawn and realised not only in contemporary terms but in fundamental ones; the satire is directed at timeless and universal subjects - politicians, government, taxation, nagging wives and grumbling servants, foolish academics, bad tempers and low cunning and all the other things that make people everywhere at all times familiar and tragic and funny.

I selected eight plays from the four major extant cycles, on the basis of their dramatic merit, the relevance of their content to 'here and now', and of their place in the cycle of man's history - trying to include as great a range of dramatic type as possible, from broad farce to high drama. I translated them into modern English and local idiom; and, like all good popular texts, they proved in rehearsal most amenable to modification. Part of the fun of the work was interpreting with a modern and local slant; in some cases this was just a matter of place names and references, of current jokes, but in others it consisted in emphasis on parallels with modern and relevant situations.

By choice, as well as of necessity (the school had no school hall) we planned an open air production under a large mango tree in the garden, and used a few tables and benches to provide a raised acting area with different levels; in fact, most of the production was acted on a fan-shaped ground area, with the audience surrounding it (over-running it at times, too, in the way they had in the Uganda Pilgrim Players' production). Entrances were through the audience, but God always appeared in each play through a huge curtain which we slung form the mango tree; the prompters sat with the audience, effects came from behind and within the audience, and the choir and musicians sat in the audience area as well. In other words, the whole project was planned to involve everyone as much as possible all the time. In each group the pupils who were not acting main parts or doing jobs were formed either into crowd groups within the play, or crowds within the audience - sometimes the one merged into the other.

Music for the whole production was drawn from every source: Hindu conch and gongs heralded the entrances of God; an orchestra of Indian instruments played interlude and atmosphere music; we used both Kiganda and western drums, a trumpet (played by the Headmaster) was used for one very important entrance, and in one interlude we had some Kiganda dancing, which was immensely popular. There was a choir, which in fact did more work than any other of the music groups, for, led and trained by a pupil, it sang throughout - Negro spirituals, Kiganda songs, Christian carols and our own version of Beethoven's *Ode to Joy*.

The total budget for the production was £25, so we set out from the beginning to improvise rather than spend. The ingenuity of the pupils seemed endless, as was their enthusiasm - the best example of the former being, undoubtedly, the construction of one of the two great scenic symbols of the acting area: it was the symbol for The World, and they devised a free-standing perfectly round framework by pulling up some little-needed school railings and bending them round the mango tree to achieve the perfect circle, which was then fixed securely into the ground at one side of the acting area. All our properties and the individual settings for each play were simple and impressionistic rather than naturalistic, except for a fine ark in the Noah play; and we did use (for me not for the first - or last - time) a live goat. One hundred characters were costumed, and the costumes were planned and designed by a member of staff in collaboration with the pupils of each group, who were then responsible for effecting them; they were borrowed, improvised or made in the needlework class. They were not designed on the basis of historical accuracy, or even of consistency, but of dramatic and visual effect: some plays were in modern dress - the Pilate play, for example, which is a sinister study of political shiftlessness, true for all times, our own included.

The Gods in all the plays wore identical robes, but each had a grand cloak of a different colour, symbolising the appropriate mood and his relationship with the world in that play; the 'robes', incidentally, were in fact one and the same robe throughout, for economy's sake, which made for some problems, as some Gods were tall and broad and some were slight and short, and they all had to change swiftly between plays. The catholicity of our approach to costuming produced some delicious inconsistencies such as that between Herod ( the school football champion) in screaming pink satin, and his army, a nasty little rabble of soldiers in modern Ugandan army uniform - an inconsistency that achieved the peak of farce during the mock official army-inspection which got worked in as a bit of business. In later days I often had a vision of that fat, crimson-robed Herod, played so well as a loud-mouthed, bullying vicious character by a football champion of great sweetness of nature, seeming to foreshadow the terrible figure of Amin, who was to devastate Uganda not many years later; he too was a huge and lurid shape, but the evil in his face was real.

The seriousness with which those pupils involved themselves in the project is something I shall never forget; nor the devoted co-operation of the staff. There was of course the small group of teachers who were deeply involved and worked with tireless energy and astounding versatility; but beyond them was a whole staff that for six weeks taught gallantly against a background of uninhibited rehearsings in the garden - rehearsings involving drums and riotous crowd scenes; oh, how the sound carried! Each group of pupils had an assistant producer, a pupil (in every case having his first experience of producing, and in many cases revealing real talent), who would take extra rehearsals when I was with another group. There were some afternoons when as many as four groups came back specially, (they were normally morning pupils only, as the school premises could only accommodate half the school population at a time and so two shifts were run) and then the noise in the garden was deafening. During the last week, when we had all three hundred concentrated in and around the acting area, school life became so difficult that school was cancelled for two mornings; the play was all.

Three performances were given and audiences comprised the rest of the school, numbers of friends and relatives, observers form other schools, and various dignitaries from the Education Ministry, including one Inspector who discovered, to his glee, that the familiarity of the style of production, if not its scale, was attributable to the features it had in common with one he had

*Rehearsing the Mystery Cycle*

*The Noah Play*

*Herod inspects the troops*

*Pharaoh*

*Cain*

seen eight years before given by - a travelling group! As ill luck would have it we had, in the middle of the dry season, three wet days, and although the performances went on undeterred, problems resulted - one of them concerning that same grand crimson robe of Herod's. He, in a rage of very convincing wild temper (also, I feel, prefiguring Idi Amin) would throw himself full length on the ground and bellow loudly; the splendid robe - really the show-piece of the wardrobe mistresses - had to be laundered every night to remove the mud. But the weather was as little regarded as no doubt it had been in the streets of the cities in the middle ages in England, where the weather was as unpredictable as is the weather of Uganda. The Noah play at least benefitted from divinely provided atmospherics.

When I assess the project in terms of one of the themes of this book, the contribution of amateur drama to the cultural equipment of a society, I hesitate to make great claims for it. For the participants it was as valuable as any other large-scale collaborative effort; and it gave some valuable experience of acting and producing to young people who might have acquired it in no other way and who might, as a result of it, think about going on to work in theatre later on - or, at the least, form part of an appreciative audience for other people's work. The actual performances did little, I think, to bring theatre to many people outside the world of school - to the 'man in the street'. The Makerere Theatre had the key to that, firstly by dint of its peripatetic nature, and secondly because it was at the same time acting as a vehicle for local writers and therefore more likely to be speaking in the voice of 'the man in the street'.

It could also speak in the language of 'the man in the street' too, rather than, or as well as, in the language of the educated. Although English continued to be the language of government, of administration and of higher education, it would be the language of the vernaculars that would speak home. However, one of the most interesting features of the Makerere theatre's first tour was that they found that the most popular plays in their big repertoire were in fact the plays in English. Now this may have been, as they suggested, that the plays in English were also the best plays, while the vernacular plays were the first works of new writers and so, not surprisingly, inferior in both content and craftsmanship. But the fact remains - a good play will surmount language as well as cultural barriers. There is no doubt in my mind that, for the school project in which I had engaged, the overall excellence of the material, and its suitability, justified its use.

There are three ways in which I judged this work to have possibly made a contribution to the developing of an indigenous theatre tradition in Uganda. One was the co-operative nature of the production and the confidence it fostered in the pupils who emerged as the gifted ones - especially the directors; their involvement as individuals in a great shared piece of theatre gave them unique opportunities to try out their newly-discovered skills in a community context in which responsibility was shared, and in which they therefore felt able to take risks and to experiment. Then, as a result of the scale of the production, involving so many students in one production, interest was instilled in a lot of people at one go, who might go out into adult lives with a sense of familiarity with the experience of theatre. Finally, I saw the undertaking as a parallel of the scholastic drama of the 15th and 16th centuries in England; for while the Mystery Cycles in mediaeval England were the province of the ordinary people both in terms of performance and enjoyment, the other thread that went into the fabric of English drama was the scholars' drama, performed by, for example, the 'Gentlemen of Grays inn': imitations of Seneca, translations and imitations of Greek and Latin - foreign - plays, for minority audiences of nobles and royalty. That drama was the product of an educated élite: perhaps what we had done in Old Kampala School could be regarded as the input of the educated élite, although in this case the imported material happened to come itself from a popular root and might the more easily provide a model or an inspiration.

For me personally, of course, the whole enterprise was unmitigatedly joyous. I had waited a long time - over a quarter of a century - to mount a full-scale production of these mediaeval plays that had so profoundly moved and inspired me, and that had been so curiously neglected and under-valued for so long. Not only had I had to come a long way to do it; the chance had come at a point in my double life in theatre matters when the other side, the Leeds campaign, was at its most depressing and static; I felt unfairly blessed.

The years 1965 to 1967 were precisely, in Leeds, the very years when the long inaction took place. We were in regular contact, and not only by letter (and cable on that misleadingly exciting occasion of the site allocation). Arnold Kettle, still the active Chairman, Sir Roger Stevens having been elevated to President, arrived in his other capacity of English academic, to act as external examiner to the three Universities in east Africa. He stayed with us of course, and insofar as Leeds affairs were concerned, our escapist idyll was not undisturbed; but all seemed rather remote; we felt deeply and fully tied up in all the theatre matters in Uganda. It was not only in the travelling theatre that things were happening. Theatre generally was in a most exciting and promising state of change and development, and we were much involved. The first Ugandan director of the National Theatre was appointed - a brilliant and eccentric poet called Okot p'Bitek, under whose influence a great deal of self-questioning went on about many of the same issues that were also, in fact, at the heart of the Leeds campaign: the role of theatre in society; the role of the National theatre - this western-style building, expensive to run, with which the colonial government had saddled the country; public patronage and government subsidy; the desirability of founding a permanent resident company in the capital, and the place of the amateurs in the move towards it; the problems of the plays to perform - local, or imported; adapted? the much bigger issue of getting drama to the rural population outside Kampala, beyond the city dwellers and the educated élite; all these issues were eagerly and intensely discussed whenever people got together in private houses or in the National Theatre itself.

European-style plays and productions still predominated in the National Theatre, but increasingly in translation into Luganda, or adapted to a local context. I saw Hamlet in Luganda, and a Tartuffe too - difficult for me to understand, but a welcome development. Under p'Bitek's direction a lot more Ugandan music and dance was performed in the Theatre. One interesting company was set up - on an unpaid basis - by our friend Van Zirimu, with the objective of creating drama based on local folk story and legend. Another was established by one of the Travelling theatre members, Robert Serumaga, and this travelled widely, some time later on, performing his own plays and experimenting with a form that used music, sound, movement and dance. The theatre was truly alive in Uganda.

Well practised by the year in Leeds I engaged in several press campaigns, in the sending of Memoranda to ministers to stimulate government support, and in some interesting press controversies about adaptation of Western drama - an issue that had come greatly to interest and concern me. I undertook one more piece of direction for the Travelling Theatre: a Strindberg, *The Bond* - an unlikely subject for adaptation; but the interested and accomplished collaboration of a most talented cast enabled us to explore the play in local terms. It was not taken on tour, but performed in the conventional theatre-hall on the University campus, and was useful as an exercise in adaptation rather than as an influence on Ugandan writing.

All this activity resulted in a life busy with friendships as well as work. Again our house was filled with people for a lot of the time. Once, it was dominated by a less than amiable guest - one of the many goats in my life, who was being cared for between performances of the Shepherd's Play that I slotted in with a group of children including our own. Poor little goat - it hated being on loan from a local farmer and kept in solitude in our garden: it cried all night and brought us much opprobrium from our neighbours. I think they felt that a fitting judgement had fallen upon us when that one of our daughters who was to play the Angel fell out of a tree and broke an arm. However, she was patched up in time to present possibly the only Angel ever to appear on high with an arm in plaster. Perhaps it was meant to suggest a war-cry for our return to Leeds: 'Carry on Regardless'

For the return to Leeds came upon us. Two years was the extent of the secondment time, for times were changing in a way that could only be welcomed: the secondment of ex-patriates to senior posts in the academic and research fields was becoming as much a thing of the past as had already the government by a foreign colonial power. But we had been so blessed in those two years, I by the varied involvement in theatre, and Walter by the fruitfulness of his spell as Director of Research, and as an economist with specialist skills. He had been deeply concerned in the affairs of the monetary system of East Africa, had been on advisory missions to other countries in the continent, and had been the only European member of the Board of the first National Bank of Uganda. He had written two books - the royalties of one of which he donated to the National Theatre into perpetuity as a token of our joint feeling of identification with things theatrical in Uganda. This, incidentally, resulted in a flamboyant display of delight and gratitude from the wonderful p'Bitek, who arrived unannounced one day at our house, accompanied by reporters and photographers, and proceeded to make a great press item out of it - unwelcome to Walter, but all grist to the mill of theatre concern.

For the children, too, it had been an idyll. A great garden, within an enclosed but very extensive campus, made a huge adventure playground within which existed little woods, trees to climb, friends in large numbers, and freedom and security; and there was a swimming pool which became the centre of family life, where we used to picnic every day at school dinner time. We travelled to most parts of East Africa: to game parks, to the beautiful lake and mountain regions of the south west, to the coast where white sands edged by coconut trees stretched beside the Indian Ocean. They enjoyed the constant coming and going of people in the house, and they formed at the most important age a view of life within which racial differences were not just irrelevant, but unperceived.

So, as our plane flew out, and we waved for the last time to the host of friends who had come to say goodbye, we were all in tears. But none of us knew then that the tears should have been for Uganda, not for ourselves; that within four years the country would fall under the mindless oppression of a maniacal and ruthless dictator, that many of the people we cared for would be numbered amongst the countless victims of that oppression, and that the progress of this promising land would be halted by years of destruction and war, ravaged by disease and poverty, and reduced to economic stagnation. All we knew on that tearful occasion was that we were leaving a country and people that we loved.

During the two years the Leeds Theatre Campaign had been dwarfed by the concerns of theatre in Uganda; but in fact the dual involvements were mutually supportive. Heading back to pick up the threads of the work in Leeds, I knew that I had gained inspiration from the convictions and the endeavours and the achievements of the Ugandan people I had worked with, who in so many ways were confronting identical challenges to those we faced in Leeds. Insofar as my thread in the web has strength and continuity, it comes in no small measure from Uganda. It was many years before I was able to trace in the web the threads that had crossed and recrossed mine in Uganda. The story will be told, but later, for now I must rejoin the main story of this book, at the point when, a week after getting home to Leeds we sat once again around a campaign committee table.

# 6

# The Action Develops In Leeds

By June 1976, when we went to our first meeting of the Theatre Campaign Committee for two years, even the most resilient of the campaigners had abandoned expectations of action and progress from the Tripartite Committee. At the best, (which involved actually believing in the Council's good intent) the suggested site for a combined concert hall and theatre - an Arts Centre - would not become available until 1970, and building could not possibly start until some time after that. Who could tell what would happen in the meantime to the impetus of the theatre campaign and, more important, to what extent the campaign would retain its independence and its effective control over the design of the theatre, let alone over the ultimate policy? It was in October of 1966 that Alec Baron had made a proposal that seemed to take the campaign back to one of its starting points: the one that had been rejected out of hand in the early days. We should, he proposed, 'obtain some land for a short period at a nominal rent....and erect....a temporary building of a new and exciting design to contain an arena-type theatre'.

The idea of starting with a temporary building, or even of converting an existing building, had been fully discussed at the outset, but dismissed because we judged then that attracting money for a modest, possibly undistinguished, building would be more difficult than exciting interest in a permanent, attractive 'bespoke' building, and that this was particularly the case for us in that there was not an already-established, operating professional theatre company. Had there been such a company, with a reputation and an audience already created, the raising of funds to provide it with a modest home would have been a straightforward undertaking; donors would have been motivated by their wish to support a going concern whose worth they would already have measured. Joan Littlewood had a company and a national reputation before she found a permanent home in Stratford East and the funds to get established there; Stephen Joseph was a working director with a distinguished reputation before he took over a building in Scarborough with local and public support. In both these cases it was the name of the director and the quality of the company's work that inspired confidence in sponsors, and made audience building a viable proposition: it was therefore of considerably less consequence that in both instances the building or its location were less than inspiring or ideal. But our view had long been that in the total absence of a company, an audience and a building - any substance, as it were - we had to start with the building to enable us to engage a director who would do all the rest. It was a vicious circle: we were very much in the position of the traveller who, on asking directions to somewhere, was given the unhelpful answer 'Well , if I were you I wouldn't start from here'. Our start *had* to be from here: the venture in collaboration with the City Council offered no firm prospects of achievement; we had to make the best of it and get on with the job on our own.

Following the 'Baron initiative' of 1966, a search for 'some land' in private ownership at a 'nominal rent' had proved completely fruitless. There remained the possibility of a short-term rental of a Council site not immediately to be developed.

This was a less costly option to a donated free site for the Council to consider as a means of validating their stated intention for the future: an *easy* option. During the summer and autumn of 1967 several attempts were made by the campaign to have discussions about such a proposition. But it seemed that the now-familiar Fabius Cunctator methods of dealing with a 'nuisance' were adopted. The advised technique for effecting a meeting to discuss an issue was to obtain the ear and interest of the Leader of the Council - that is, the Leader of the party then in power. Delay after delay in simply arranging a meeting with us was justified (privately) by obscure references to reasons that could not be divulged at the present time. The long history of Leeds Theatre Campaign offers many disturbing examples of a contemptuous disregard for the appeals by a group of citizens for a hearing by their elected government. It seemed then that the democratic processes in local government are ineffectual in the face of determined opposition, or even prejudice and lack of interest, from the power groups within it; that the secret of effective action is the interest and commitment of a councillor who controls such a power group. We of the Theatre Campaign had no special appeal for the power group of the time - no wealthy patron, no noble title amongst us; and no on councillor emerged to champion our infant cause, concerned as it was for the common good.

Indeed, it seems in retrospect that many of the set-backs that were to follow one another were engineered in order to deter us; but so mysterious are the ways of caucus-control in local government that the truth is very hard to get at. Today the Leeds City Council is proud of its association with the Playhouse, a jewel in the city's crown - a success; and rightly proud of its generosity towards it. But it is fitting to remember that this resulted only in part from the ultimate success of the venture that struggled to success in the teeth of many obstacles: even the success, in itself, might not have been enough; it is really to the adoption of the cause by a particular, dedicated individual in the power group of the time, Councillor Bernard Atha, that the Playhouse owes its fine building and its financial support.

One other line of action had been explored: that of acquiring an existing building susceptible of conversion. A number of buildings had been considered, including the Corn Exchange and some disused cinemas - of which at one time the city possessed more than forty. But none was suitable even if available at a possible market price, and certainly none was available for a reasonable rental.

The Chairman's last ditch request for the Tripartite Committee to meet again received the response that neither the Council nor the music lobby could 'see any purpose in calling a meeting in the near future': another example of the Council's power to frustrate even our rights as members of that committee.

That is how it was when we Newlyns tearfully left behind all the positive activities in Uganda, and came back to Leeds; and very depressing it seemed. But it is when the lowest point is reached that the climb upwards can begin: indeed, from the lowest point there is only one direction to take, apart from self-destruction, and at no point did most of the core campaigners ever dream of that. Changes of emphasis and objective planning were necessary to create a new momentum, and the very effort of planning for that provided a dynamic for the spirits and the confidence of the campaign. We determined to re-align our sights and plan a two-stage strategy: while continuing to foster the public's expectation of an eventual purpose-built theatre as a part of the City's planned arts complex, we would re-formulate the Baron proposal for an interim building, and renew the efforts to find one to convert, publicising our intentions and appealing for help in carrying this out. The financial support needed for that would be considerably less than for a temporary purpose-built structure such as Alec had envisaged, and would possibly offer more readily and more quickly the facilities that would attract a good director. For the essential feature of the new strategy was that we were to establish a company in readiness for the final theatre; we hoped this way of trying to break the deadlock would have sufficient appeal to the public and the Arts Council to enable us to raise the funds, given that the final objective, Stage Two, was kept clearly in the public view. It furthermore seemed fairly likely that the building of an audience where at present none existed would increase the pressure upon the Council to make effective their stated intention to build the arts complex.

Thus, at that first meeting in June, was the dreary two-year hiatus brought to an end; whatever might result from the new assault it would not be the dejection that comes from inactivity. We all prepared ourselves for a very busy time, and this started with us taking stock of our organisation and the best way to utilise the varied and valuable talents within it. There had been few losses from the core campaigners; John Wood, in fact was the only one who, jaundiced and disillusioned by the stalemate, had withdrawn - although to the sidelines only, for he remained at our service. But one major loss was sustained at exactly the moment that the new initiative was launched: that of Arnold Kettle. His visit earlier in the year to East Africa had resulted in his seduction by the attractions of the challenges there. We didn't actually cross in mid-air, but he went off soon after our return, to the Chair of English in the University of Dar es Salaam, where he stayed for three years and from which he came back to the Chair of English in the Open University; so Arnold was lost to us. He had reluctantly, but unstintingly, served as the Campaign's chairman from the beginning, taking back the job when Sir Roger Stevens found the day-to-day commitment too much for him. He combined intellectual clarity with vision and commitment and was a skilled and patient chairman and negotiator. His commitment was rooted in the deep compassion of a communist, and the blessings of his chairmanship put to shame the critics who whispered that the campaign had a left-wing ideology that did it damage; in any case, different critics shouted rather than whispered that, on the contrary, we were élitist and bourgeois. Our team, including as it did Arnold, Sir Roger, Dick Knowles and several well-known businessmen, really demonstrated the truth about us: we were widely representative of all convictions and interests in the city. For me personally Arnold's departure at just the point when I came back into the work was a grievous loss, although there was a great compensation in a new partnership with a new chairman, Bernard Sandler, who was a respected businessman, Deputy Chairman of United Draperies.

I think it is true to say that Bernard, who took on the job when really no one liked the look of it, was actually just exactly the man we needed; certainly the partnership that he and I established was as near perfect as any partnership could be. It operated on mutual dependence, was enhanced by mutual affection and respect, and seemed to bring the best out of us both; we never, to my memory, had cross words; he never, to my memory failed in a promise or an undertaking; I hope I did not either. He had an amazing resilience, an obstinate refusal to accept defeat. His most-used phrase was 'No problem, no problem' - about both trivial undertakings and the most daunting of tasks. But at the time, in June 1967, Bernard was known to me only as a good campaigner; whereas Arnold was one of my oldest friends, and working with him had been so easy. His wife, Margot, oddly, was working in association with Walter on a project in the University, and the two households were so frequently intercommunicating that private telephone lines and partner-swopping schemes were talked of! Arnold is lost to us now for ever; and, remembered as he is for his academic distinction, he is not by all remembered for the part he played in those early days of the theatre campaign. Let the debt owed him be now acknowledged.

There were gains as well as losses: during the previous few months several new people with skills and expertise that were to be of immense value to the campaign had joined. There was Martin Banham, recently appointed to be the first Fellow in Drama in the University, where, with no Drama Department yet established, and based on the little Theatre Workshop that had been almost surreptitiously brought into existence by Frederick

May, he embarked on a programme of drama work that eventually led to the establishment of one of the most distinguished Drama Departments in the country, and where he subsequently came to occupy the Chair. He had, as it happened, gained a great deal of his practical expertise in Nigeria, and his devoted commitment to the Leeds campaign was no doubt strengthened, as was ours, by that wider vista of theatre as an important social force. His colleague in the Drama Workshop, also newly appointed there, was Trevor Faulkner, a theatre technician of great knowledge and skill, and he too joined the team: his work, given unstintingly, with the Theatre Planning Committee was to grow more and more important, both in the planning stages, and then, in happier times, in the designing and installing times. There was Alfred Bradley, the Drama Director of BBC North; before joining the BBC he had had many years experience in drama in education, and his experience and vision had a great influence on the policy planning in the days when the theatre was actually coming into being; but at the time of which I am writing now, when the campaign was being re-vitalised, he brought to the group two marvellous benefits: one was his personality - lively, funny, generous and kind, with the least malicious wit I had ever known and an inimitable capacity for making people feel respected; the other was a direct contact with the creative life of the region, where he had a unique reputation for being the discoverer and the encourager of many talented artists who, like Alan Aykbourne, claim that their first real boost came from him. Then there was Bill Houghton Evans, an architect with a deep, ideological commitment to the objectives of the campaign and ... but more, much more, of Bill later.

The advent of these new people brought not only their specific talents, but fresh supplies of ideas and confidence and determination; and we once again re-structured our organisation, which had grown somewhat unwieldy. We established a Campaign Council of which everyone who was active in any field of the work was a member; and an Executive Committee and four specialist committees to work independently on theatre planning, financial matters, the membership organisation and publicity. The publicity team, which had been entirely non-experienced in the work until now, was at last augmented by two members with professional expertise: one was Ian Morrison of the University's Press Office, and the other was John Kirwen, the chief of a publicity and public relations firm in the city; both of these were to transform our handling of that most important of tasks.

Thus re-formed, we set about implementing the new strategy: intensifying the search for a building to convert to a temporary theatre; trying to get a high-quality director to start a company in whatever resulted from the search for a building; pursuing relentlessly our assault upon the local authority and the Arts Council, to maintain our right to assistance from them both; and - an act of faith though not of urgency - the setting up of a Theatre Trust, which, with charitable status, would become the body legally responsible for whatever enterprise we were able to undertake.

Another of those extraordinary hectic periods ensued which, in retrospect, seemed to consist of a hundred times more days than were in fact involved. All sections of the organisation were feverishly at work, and we all had to keep in touch with each other. The intercommunication was one of my jobs, and once again our house became the hub of the operation. I was, of course, again not able to take up a professional job, for it was clearly essential to have one full-timer to co-ordinate things, and to be available at all times. I enjoyed it immensely, in fact, although the frequency of committee meetings, appointments, phone conversations, press interviews and talks engagements left little time for everyday life. But the children were all full-time at school, and I tried to establish the convention within the campaign that I was not on call after four o'clock until late evening, so that by and large their lives were only as much affected, at this stage, as they would have been if I had been in conventional employment. In actual fact, of course, the campaign spilled over into evenings and weekends, and I could only hope that the excitement of it all would also spill over and make them feel involved; perhaps the most detrimental thing for them was that I was in the grip of an obsession and to this day I have been unable to determine whether this was damaging in any specific way to their development.

There were certainly memorable occasions when the obsession took over and fearsome scenes were caused by the children's frustrations and my weary impatience. But I have to comfort myself with the belief that, given the natures of all those involved, something would have caused the same scenes even if not the campaign: family life is a jungle, anyway. But often it was possible to engage their help on large-scale clerical tasks; and we continued to make our regular theatre visits, which became more and more enjoyable as they grew more receptive and critical. To our great delight one of our dear Ugandan friends came to Leeds University the year after we returned - Tim Wangusa from the Makerere Travelling Theatre, and we all felt less cut off from the happy life in Africa; Tim used to join us on many of our theatre trips, and the return-journey discussion sessions gained a great deal from this additional critical mind.

I recall from that time a series of journeys: to Nottingham, to see John Neville, who was to leave the splendid Playhouse there in a blaze of publicity after a devastating clash between Director and Board, and who was actually contemplating coming to us; to London, to see the Arts Council at various stages; to various dreary old buildings around the city to look at potential conversions. I recall a round of meetings, minute-writings, and news letters. I recall the interminable phone calls, with exciting prospects and dampened hopes, mad suggestions, requests for talks, messages of encouragement; and the thrilling moment when Neville phoned to say he *would* come to us if we were actually able to acquire a building to convert.

More cinemas, more chapels were all being considered; the two architects, Martin Taylor and now Bill Houghton Evans, drew up feasibility studies time and time again. The names of those buildings drift up to me from the fusty smell of old minutes

- fifteen of them in all; among them the Clock, the Capitol, the Carlton, the Gaiety, the Dominion, the Shaftesbury - all those cinemas, in various parts of the city, all disused; a Unitarian chapel; a warehouse in Hunslet; a disused factory - actually offered by Hepworth's the clothiers, for many of the buildings were suggested as a result of our new publicity drive which had given great prominence to our regenerated activity. We must have looked at every existing large building available for sale in the city. Many, such as the Hunslet warehouse, were not suitable for reasons of location and inaccessibility; some, like the Brunswick Chapel, would have cost too much to convert; one cinema, suitably sited on Roundhay Road, was very dilapidated and had very limited parking potential. Even a cinema in Bradford was suggested, and this precipitated deep discussion as to the viability of starting Leeds Playhouse in Bradford, the Executive Committee being split on the issue of parochialism versus non-parochialism! The former view predominated. Negotiations were actually entered into in respect of two very suitable cinemas, the Dominion and the Shaftesbury. In both cases they were eventually withdrawn from sale: the Dominion later went to a Bingo developer, although during our negotiations we had received assurances that such change of use would never be granted planning permission; in the case of the Shaftesbury no reason was ever given to us for its sudden withdrawal by the owner, and this was the worst disappointment of all; the feasibility study for it had shown that it had considerable promise, and in many ways was ideal for our purpose; furthermore it was this specific project to which Neville had been attracted. By the end of September it began to look once again deeply discouraging, but we went on steadily, some of the planning committee spending quite a lot of time prowling around the city looking for disused buildings.

Amazingly, there was no evidence of disillusion setting in; this was possibly due in part to the fact that no one had time to give to contemplating failure; but, once again, it is possible to see the hope and intensity of determination in the campaign as a manifestation of the spirit of the sixties, and particularly of the inspiration from the new status and achievements in the arts. Certainly writing for the theatre at this time was at full flood: Harold Pinter, David Rudkin, David Mercer, Joe Orton, Peter Nichols, Tom Stoppard, Alan Bennett were all at their peak; and in the regions specifically there was an upsurge of creative writing: Stan Barstow, Henry Livings, Willis Hall, David Halliwell, Keith Waterhouse, Alan Plater, John Braine - not all playwrights but all part of the creative regeneration in the regions. Jennie Lee's *Policy of the Arts* was exerting influence and bearing fruit. The Lee / Lord Goodman / Lawrence Olivier axis began to make a reality at last of a one hundred year old plan for a National Theatre - not to reach its final home until 1976, but actually established as a company in 1963. The growth of theatre in the regions, and the widening of the scope of the work done in them was taking place from Newcastle to Exeter, from Bolton to Watford; and more names were added to the list of directors with progressive and imaginative vision of what theatre should do - Stuart Burge, John Dexter, Robin Phillips, Philip Hedley. In Yorkshire the Yorkshire Arts Association was being formed to join the network of Arts Associations that had already started in other parts of the country. The prime movers in this were Raymond Clarke, the secretary of the Yorkshire Council for Social Services, and Lord Feversham (he who became famous for controlling meetings with a referee's whistle); Raymond took evidence from us in a review of the state of the arts in the region, and promptly joined the campaign and became one of its wisest counsellors. It was a time of real social excitement and although 'bliss' was not how I would describe it, it certainly was stimulating to be alive - even if no longer young. There was an electric energy in the times that charged the batteries of many in our campaign, and I suspect that in any other time there might have been lacking the tireless energy and devotion that was displayed by them, sustaining them through long periods of frustration. We used to look beyond our seemingly abortive activities and take hope from others' successes.

We grew to understand that there was a specific lumpishness in our city fathers (of all political creeds) and in our wealthy classes, the genesis of which was hard to understand, but the undermining of which we felt to be not only necessary to our success but a good object in itself. Much of our publicity consisted at this time of accounts of other cities' achievements, and we seized every opportunity in the press, on radio and any public occasion - to the extent of virtually hi-jacking them - to keep the Theatre Campaign at the forefront of public awareness. There was a regional conference in York on the progress of the Arts Associations, which was subjected to an unscheduled harangue from us. There was a civilised evening when a Brains Trust run by Fannie Waterman, one of the creators of the Leeds Piano Competition, was, with her generous connivance, dominated by questions about theatres rather than about music - which resulted in more publicity for us. We missed no opportunity for plugging our cause, and were given magnanimous support by many distinguished and well-known people - Keith Waterhouse, Stan Barstowe, John Neville, Colin George, to name a few.

And suddenly it happened. Almost without warning emerged a viable proposition; it came to us from our closest friend - the University; a proposition that met virtually all our requirements - with one exception: it was a site within the University precinct. The campaign had always stressed the need for a central site, one not only easy of access from the city, but one that would create and display a popular image; and the concept of a people's theatre that would break down prejudices and class attitudes towards theatre was difficult to reconcile with the idea of a site in the University. But now that our immediate objective was 'to bridge the gap and to increase the pressure on the Council to implement its plans (for an Arts Centre in the city centre) by creating a well-established audience and a flourishing company'[1] we were ready to reconcile ourselves to the only disadvantage that could be seen in the plan put forward by the University. The precise proposal was this:

> 'The University would be prepared to allow us a rent-free site for a minimum of ten years, upon which would be erected a building identical with and adjacent to (the existing) Sports Hall ... The cost of the building and its equipping would be ours, but the University would undertake to buy the building at the end of our tenure at current replacement cost'.[2]

The University's motive in offering the opportunity was not just philanthropic. Although there was a great body of support for the campaign amongst the staff, there was also a substantial body of scepticism and disapproval. But it so happened that the University had rather a difficult problem of its own to which a solution was proposed that would also benefit the Theatre Campaign. In the hey-day of university expansion one of the elements in the replanning of Leeds was the erection of two Sports Halls. The site was decided upon, and necessitated a large-scale clearance of an area of low-cost working class housing which had surrounded the University. This had been going according to plan, and one sports hall had been erected, when suddenly a period of financial retrenchment necessitated suspending the building of the second sports hall. The University had a not surprising sense of guilt at the premature demolition of housing; and Sir Roger Stevens, and his resident architect, concocted a scheme that would not only benefit the Theatre Campaign (and hence the city as a whole - surely a sufficient justification in itself) but would settle the conscience of the University planners, and also undermine the disapprobation of the theatre-sceptics in its ranks. Unable to use the great empty cleared site, they would see the dual value of lending it to the Theatre Campaign. The shrewd and subtle Sir Roger must have extracted great delight from an idea that resolved at one blow so many problems with which he was directly involved.

So that was how the idea of a 'theatre circle in a square' originated. Alec Baron, in his unpublished memoires, describes the campaign's reaction to the proposal.

Bill Houghton Evans and I immediately went to see the Sports Hall. It was a large, high, rectangular open building with no ancillaries. After careful thought we felt that if we divided the space into three on the ground and also its height, it would be tight, but we might just manage. On the stage side, the stage would occupy the ground floor, the first floor would be dressing rooms and green room, and the top floor would be the wardrobe. On the other side the ground floor would be the foyer, the first floor would be the bar and the top floor would be the control box and projection room (for I insisted from the beginning that we must have a cinema capability for late night and Sunday screenings). The theatre would run diagonally in the centre sections. We reported back to the Campaign Committee that we could make it work.

The proposal was received with enthusiasm by everyone working in the campaign. An outline plan was drawn with amazing speed, and a cost analysis likewise, indicating that the cost would be of the order of £135,000. The Arts Council's approval was sought, the local authority informed and our modest claims to their support re-asserted; and negotiations were initiated with the Council of the University. In the meantime our press publicity went on, refuelled by the now concrete opportunity. A splendid speech was made at this time by our constant friend, John Neville, at an Arts Festival in Bradford, calling upon the people of Leeds to demand action from their local authority who were 'dragging their feet' - a call to which one of the campaign supporters who heard him reacted by writing to me to suggest we got up a public petition, calling, simply, for Council action. By now we were ready to try anything and everything, and we took up this idea and fell immediately to implementing it. Within a short time we had sent out 10,000 petition forms, which simply urged '... the City Council of Leeds, in co-operation with other councils concerned, to help establish as quickly as possible a professional repertory theatre in Leeds'. We sent out the forms through our networks, and organised two public signature-collecting days. We aimed at 10,000 signatures.

This was another time of frenzy - and delight; the feeling of *doing* something fired us all with renewed energy. I come upon a letter in my hand to Alec Baron, scrawled, undated, but of this time:

> Alec - the last personal words I shall have time to utter! can one really believe that we are near achievement? the tensions are awful, but I suppose that's because they're optimistic rather than depressed ones ... Signatures up to five and a half thousand today - not bad. We'll make it, I think. Amazing people are signing. Bank managers (I've sent to ALL banks in Leeds). Matrons in hospitals (all hospitals in Leeds and districts have had it). I'm sure Pratt is wrong.

(The old ghost haunted still, and Pratt was hard at work to make mock of us).

Not only were those 'amazing' bank managers and hospital matrons signing; so was Henry Moore, who actually wrote, unasked, a hand-written letter of support; Phyllis Bentley was the first signature actually to be received by us; Wilson Knight, Herbert Read, Diana Rigg ... there were many many more people of great distinction in addition to the hundreds of citizens of the region as well as the city whose signatures were received by post. We had two fruitful days on the streets in the city, on two bitter February days, at a number of key spots such as the market; and people queued to sign. We kept getting requests for more forms; by now, although we still lacked a campaign office and still ran the campaign from our homes, the committee had indulged in a little hand-operated duplicator, so that we had no longer to scrounge the use of that facility for all our documents. It had been installed in the cellar of our house, and now it really came into its own. Our four daughters were put to forced labour (much enjoyed, I may say) on the production of petition forms; and as fast as we got them out the signed ones poured in -

brought in batches, signatures carefully counted, by the gallant campaigners who had stood in the cold bitter wind collecting them. When finally we got back, from all sources, the forms we had dispensed, we found we had 21,000 signatures - twice as many as our target.

A few days later, on March 5th, a group of five people - the maximum number allowed - from among us, including Mrs Burton, the lady who had made the suggestion in the first place, carried the great batches of petition forms to the Civic Hall in Leeds and presented them to the full Council; the convention is that five minutes only is allowed for any accompanying speech, and we chose for this occasion Charles Gardiner, who delivered our 'oration' perfectly timed in ringing tones; the old familiar (to us) arguments were made about the need for this cultural amenity in our city, and the responsibility that lay upon the Council to contribute to its establishment. The great piles of petition forms were collected up by an official, and we departed; the gallery had been packed with our supporters, and one of my daughters reminds me that all four of them had taken the afternoon off from school to be there!. We did not expect a dramatic response to this representation, nor did we get one but it was the only chance we had ever had to communicate direct with our elected local government, and it may be that some of the councillors who were still unaware of the campaign, or unclear about its purpose, became a little more informed. It is the fact that this is the only available way for the public to make its voice heard direct by its governing body; with a good number of citizens to back us we had at last entered into official records; and we gained again a lot of publicity.

Now began a really purposeful period. John Kirwen, our publicity expert, who directed a publicity business, very generously made available to us a room in his premises in Park Square, in the centre of the city, and this enabled us to have a prestigious address, a campaign telephone number, and room to expand; we were able to centralise all our records, have a base for storage of material, a room for meetings and accommodation for a part-time typist; that was the change that made the biggest contribution to my own private well-being, for I no longer had to struggle with a skill for which I was completely untrained, nor to beg and wheedle help from whoever might happen to have some spare time, the necessary expertise and the facilities.

Even before the agreement with the University was approved by the University Council, and signed, the detailed planning of the actual theatre was going ahead. The theatre that was eventually built in Leeds was designed by a committee, a group of unpaid experts, none of whom was actually working in a theatre, but all of whom had great knowledge and clear vision, and amongst whom there was an architect who believed that nothing was impossible. That it should in the event have proved so successful a design, and been so approved by all who worked in it for twenty years, that it was replicated precisely in the main auditorium of the permanent theatre that eventually replaced it, is the most remarkable tribute to that small group of planners - Alec Baron, Bill Houghton Evans, Trevor Faulkner and Martin Banham; and to the even smaller group which included John Wood, that had, in the first days of the campaign in 1964, conceived a vision of the auditorium that was far in advance of current theatre design.

The Appeal now was planned in detail. In our oration at the presentation of the petition we had made, for the first time, a specific money request to the Council - for a capital sum of £25,000: this represented at that time a third of a penny rate - a small sum in the context of the sixpenny rate permitted (but underspent by Leeds) for 'cultural activities' - and a once-for-all expenditure. It was, furthermore, a modest demand compared with our earlier demand for a free site. In the light of the firm undertaking of substantial support from the Arts Council, and of the modesty of the overall costs compared with those in most other cities where theatres had been established, it seemed unlikely that the demand would be rejected. The support of the City Council was vitally necessary to give a kick-start to the whole of the appeal; big donors - from whom, in so wealthy a city, we expected considerable generosity - would be stimulated by the evidence of official support and the status it would give to the project as a partly civic one; and once the big sums were established at the top of a donations list, the rest would follow from the general public by means of the wide-ranging appeal schemes we were already planning.

Although no response whatsoever came from the Council we held a Supporters' meeting in the greatest of high spirits - in the existing sports hall - as accurate a visual aid as one could hope for! Stan Barstow was our star guest speaker on that occasion, and a large number of excited supporters turned up, privileged to have a pre-view of site and plans. At that meeting on March 31 1968 the Playhouse Club was established: the first breath of real life in a real theatre in Leeds; it still exists, though under a different name. We had hoped to raise a good sum of money at that meeting, but the response was less encouraging than we had expected, as was the initial approach to the closer circle of campaigners, and the solid base for a public appeal, timed to start two months later, did not materialise. Indeed, by the time the appeal was actually launched we had only some £5,000 in promises, exclusively from amongst our own small group of campaigners. All those with any experience of fund-raising were shaking their heads sadly, for they were convinced that only if you had the big sums to start with would you succeed at other levels. Clearly this too was to be different, harder, in Leeds. But nevertheless the confidence inspired by that first meeting of supporters in the replica of the building that was to become their theatre was a spur and inspiration.

A public meeting in the Town Hall was to be the centre-piece of the appeal scheme, this to be complemented by a very carefully-structured personal direct appeal over Sir Roger's signature to all sectors in the city's and county's society from which we might expect substantial single donations. The public meeting was designed to give the impetus to the whole exercise, which in our new euphoric mood we announced was to lead to a start on building in September of that same year, the beginning

# THE LEEDS THEATRE CAMPAIGN WILL ANSWER TO A MOCK PUBLIC INDICTMENT

That the Leeds Theatre Campaign contrary to the public interest has, over the past four years, conducted a conspiracy, which threatens to succeed, for the purpose of establishing a

## PROFESSIONAL REPERTORY THEATRE IN LEEDS

## FOR THE DEFENCE

APPEARING IN PERSON

PETER O'TOOLE
JOHN NEVILLE
RICHARD HOGGART
HENRY LIVINGS
KEITH WATERHOUSE

Recorded Evidence and Testimonials from

HENRY MOORE
SIR HERBERT READ
PHYLLIS BENTLEY
Prof. BONAMY DOBRÉE
DAME SYBIL THORNDYKE

## TOWN HALL 3 P.M. SUNDAY MAY 5th

Members of the public are cordially invited to come to this celebration of the launching of the Public Appeal for

***THE LEEDS PLAYHOUSE***

*The handbill distributed*

*The Town Hall Meeting*

of rehearsals on August 10 and Opening Night on September 29 1969. How carefully, to the day, we planned it!

The great Town Hall meeting, on May 5 1968, was for a lot of people one of the most extraordinary events in the city for many a year. It was planned to take the form of a mock trial, with the Theatre Campaign in the dock, facing a charge brought by two 'inquisitors' of 'conducting a conspiracy over the last four years contrary to the public interest for the purpose of establishing a repertory theatre in Leeds'. The city was saturated with publicity - 10,000 hand-bills, 5,000 car stickers, a display in the library, coverage by all the media - press, radio and television, and directly by means of a radio car with loud hailers. And the star quality of our platform was sufficient attraction in itself: Peter O'Toole, Keith Waterhouse and Richard Hoggart - all born and bred in Leeds - and John Neville, perhaps the best-known regional theatre director in the country, and a great actor. Together the four comprised a representative group of those concerned with the arts - a director, a writer, actors and a scholar-essayist. They were billed as the principal witnesses called for the defence of the accused: the accused were representatives of various aspects of our work - theatre planning, educational work, economics, and organisation. Our format was so designed as to give a credible context to a variety of statements from the distinguished speakers, as well as giving us the opportunity to bring forth all the objections and criticisms to which we had been subjected over the years - and then refute them.

Certainly no campaigner involved in that occasion will ever forget it. It was the first time in four years that we actually confronted the public head on. The whole thing turned into a great celebration, a marvellous, heart-lifting theatrical festivity. The Town Hall, which holds 1,250 people, was packed to capacity long before starting time, and 200 were turned away. We had a large number of important 'observers' by invitation, who sat ranged behind the two sets of front row people on the platform - the accused and the defence witnesses - observers representing various interests: Phyllis Bentley, Henry Livings, Stan Barstow, the Bishop of Wakefield; the Chief Education Officer of Leeds; a senior representative of the West Riding Education Department; there were several West Riding County councillors, but of all the Leeds Council, to which a mass invitation had been extended, there was but one; there were representatives from youth organisations, from the women's organisations, from the Chamber of Commerce. It was a massed bank of observers providing a living background to the conduct of the trial.

The trial itself was conducted tongue-in-cheek with irony and great flourish by Charles Gardiner, and by Derek Holroyd - Director of the University Television Centre and on of our core campaigners. Both of them were grand, impressive figures, with fine, ringing voices and a splendid mock-theatrical barrister manner. Our accused were attributed with the lowest and vilest intentions, and in their defence speeches managed to present the public with every aspect of the value of theatre to society, the excellence of the theatre we proposed, the integrity of its financial planning, the essential contribution it would make to the education of the children and the health of the society as a whole. And then the defence witnesses did their part. John Neville made a short terse attack on the contemptible lack of support from the local authority; he bore witness to the high value of a theatre that belongs at the heart of a community, and the achievements of the one he knew best, Nottingham Playhouse; he was economical, spare even, but passion, integrity and conviction so shone out that he made a deep and serious impression and received a great and warm ovation. Keith Waterhouse was greeted with a roar of applause before he even started to speak - a greeting of real Yorkshire warmth for one of our 'own'. He was born and grew up in Hunslet, and his first job, he told us, was as 'fourth assistant drama critic on the Yorkshire Evening Post'. He had already entered into the campaign's work with real generosity, and he specialised in the Pratt-bashing sector, with all the deadly effectiveness of his down-beat wit. In his level, phlegmatic voice, solid with good, thick Leeds vowels, he summed up the Pratt-orchestrated opposition as meaning

> 'The people of Leeds are too thick and stupid to warrant having a theatre built for them. They have too recently crawled out of the clay to be ready for the same things as the people of....'

- and the long familiar string of city and town names followed. On Pratt's more moderate recent statement doubting the 'advisability of such a plan at the moment', Keith wickedly commented 'He doesn't give an alternative date'. 'It isn't really essential that Leeds should be anything more than a gigantic factory site: provided, of course, that you happen to own one of the factories', he said, before going on to list the other things that aren't essential, such as libraries, and art galleries, and museums, and Olympic swimming pools (Leeds had recently built one of these, which later in the decade was to figure in a scandal about an error, or a cheat, involving the flawed architect, Poulson). A masterly handling of the huge audience brought the house down with a great roar of laughter: no need to press these points with such an audience, he realised; it would be rather like 'praising the benefits of sex to the crew of an American destroyer'.

The Town Hall was by now a place of jubilation and celebration; throughout the proceedings the Inquisitors read out, between the set pieces, messages sent for the occasion: from Sybil Thorndyke, from Herbert Read, from Henry Moore, from Judi Dench, Diana Rigg, from Phyllis Bentley and Stan Barstow - both the last two rising to be greeted in person from their places on the platform; from Jennie Lee, and Bonamie Dobree and Lewis Casson. Two other defence witnesses were yet to be heard - both also men of Leeds. Richard Hoggart first: author and scholar best known for his work *The Uses of Literacy*, and currently Director of the Centre for Contemporary Cultural Studies at Birmingham University. Succinct, plain-spoken, reasoned - with a disarming high note to his warm, level voice that every now and again gave a quite extraordinary punch to a particular argument. He spoke with high authority about culture and working class communities. It wasn't a matter of 'bringing culture to Leeds', he said 'for the snotty-nosed kids of the back streets', but of 'allowing an outlet in Leeds for the creative energy that is potentially there'. The recent years had 'thrown up, nobody quite knows why, a new kind of audience for the theatre....broken the old culture-vulture European high bourgeois pattern of theatre-going'. And 'British drama now is the most engaged, imaginatively and intellectually alive, form of literature that we have - more than the novel, more than poetry'. This theatre would have 'an irrigating effect right through the life of the city'. And it had to be subsidised: theatre was no longer middle-class, middle-brow, middle-aged and 'able to look after itself'. To be within the reach of the young and low-paid it must be subsidised, for the cost of running theatres was too high to be met by ticket-purchase except at exorbitant prices.

More messages followed, and then the final witness for the defence rose in all his glamour and glory to a roof-raising ovation: Peter O'Toole; an unpredictable, somehow manic, beguiling character; he had been driven up from London at break-neck speed and arrived breathless and latish for the lunch we had had for all our special people beforehand; and no one knew what to expect; but just his being there was enough - one of the great stars of our day, who also had started life as reporter in Leeds, and an amateur actor at the Civic; a giant of a figure, looking all loose about the limbs and magnificent. For a little time he played with the listeners and juggled a bit with some funny non-sequiturs, tossed in some quips about the dark things behind the whole campaign, before with extreme skill and artistry coming on to an impassioned defence of theatre as an art that 'allowed a man to be more than himself and to escape his consignment to solitary confinement for life; that enabled him to find bridges to the lives of other men; and that brought experience to all and light to dark places; that enabled him to say, after sharing in the gigantic make-believe of the theatre "We have lived a little more; we have not escaped" '.

It was quite extraordinarily moving. Perhaps he just was a very, very good actor; but somehow, I think, we all felt that we were being given a look into a restless, bleak, tormented soul that knew more about the agonies of loneliness and longing than most of us, and for whom the theatre was a life-line to an existence that was more endurable.

The formal defence could have done no more after that even if there had still been more to do. As Derek Holroyd cried, bringing the 'trial' to a conclusion, 'This prosecution case was no good from the beginning'. The mood now became almost solemn, almost evengelical; and it was with immense skill that Derek, abandoning his guise as Inquisitor, brought out the heart of the meeting's purpose: 'something to do with the quality of life in this city and this country' - and then swung into a great cry for help: 'Who that is here will help us to do this? Is there anybody here who will help?'

It was quite splendid. Unforgettable for all the people who were there that afternoon; and immensely theatrical, too, which seemed right. We ended with the Youth Orchestra of the city playing a trumpet concerto, and with a sort of mock auction money-gathering, conducted by Henry Livings, in which he tried to talk in some donations - in much the same style, all those years ago, that we are now familiar with in Comic Relief. In fact, not a lot of money was gathered in, but the raising of interest and excitement and confidence was perhaps of as great value at that stage. There was only one thing that didn't go according to the detailed planning with which the whole event was mounted; I find a cryptic note in the Minutes of one of our more hilarious committee meetings at which things were organised; it reads:

> For Finale: release of dove into hall; pigeon acceptable alternative.
> <u>Action</u>: Pigeon - W.T.N. (A.B. first to seek dove)

I have, all these years later, to assume that Alec Baron's search for a dove proved vain, and that Walter T Newlyn failed likewise to capture a pigeon. Or, perhaps, that he simply couldn't face that last task. For the 'finale' was more orthodox. The crowds lingered for quite a time, seeming reluctant to leave what had been so dramatic an event - and of course gathering autographs from the famous. Various small-scale money-raising schemes were put into operation, and I still have one or two paper 'bricks' ready-signed by John Neville that remained amongst the few unsold at £1 a brick.

Our new information leaflet and appeal pamphlet both carried at the bottom the words, adapted from a Chinese proverb:

> If God sends you two pennies
> Spend one on bread and one on flowers.

This was our response to the perennial criticism that was most difficult to counter: that better housing had a greater claim to public resources than a theatre. But a less compressed claim for our objective was in the words of Sir Herbert Read, who, very shortly before his death, had written from his home in East Yorkshire; and these words were on the front of the programme for the Town Hall meeting - a modestly duplicated affair as fitted the style in which we had, perforce, so far conducted the campaign:

> Drama is an art of the people, for the people. It is a direct expression of the life of the people. Every great city should support a theatre where drama can be freed from commercial shackles and flourish in freedom. Such a theatre would create its own dramatists, its own school of actors, its own participating audience. A civic theatre is more than a place of entertainment: it is a symbol of civic maturity, of civic pride'.

I think a great many citizens went home that day, from the great hall that had been built in the days of very great civic pride, with the wish that the new object of their pride might really materialise.

May 5 was a day of triumph and delight. It decisively established the campaign in a position in the city to be taken seriously, at last; it was a success, as an artistic production as well as with audiences - a measure, perhaps, in people's view, of our competence for the undertaking we were engaged on. It was psychologically a major tonic and dynamic for the weary campaigners. The triumph was short-lived, and many more infusions of tonic and dynamism were needed before the end was reached; ominous clouds had already begun, only a week before the meeting, to darken the horizon. But it was a good day to mark what was, in truth, a turning point.

# 7

# The Long Entr'acte

In the background of any campaign run by voluntary effort is a large supporting cast. In the background of the theatre campaign was a large chorus of children playing an active part; and in the front row of the chorus were the campaigners' own young people. Most of the core campaigners had sizeable families, and as quite young children can be seduced into thinking the most tiresome repetitive jobs are great fun if they are shared with grown-ups, there was a very handy supply of labour onto which to off-load the most irksome of these. It is perhaps only now, as mature years are attained by the fifteen to twenty young people who were involuntarily involved in the obsession that gripped their parents, that the effects on them of those demanding years can be assessed. How many of them, I sometimes wonder, have strange, neurotic aversions to, say, the slightly rough, slightly porous texture of that characteristic, now obsolete, duplicating paper, or to the folding of campaign leaflets for any of the concerns that currently occupy them? Are there middle-aged Barbers who utter strange cries when stapling pages together; are there Barons in high places who grow pale when asked 'to sign' something; are there others than the one (at least) of the Newlyns who is pathologically averse to the telephone; and how many secret vows were made by that little crowd that they would never, never, never ask any of their children to help put pins in badges, minutes in envelopes, or leaflets in doors?

Apart from the direct services they rendered - and they are too numerous for any of us to list - they all had to adjust to the fever-atmosphere of the house-obsession. It is not so easy to be light-hearted about this, for there can be real hardship for children at the mercy of a parental obsession. There is obviously the loss of much of the time that would otherwise be theirs; and although, as I have already written, I tried to arrange commitments so that they took least toll of my 'family time', I still have small doubt that some educational problems that two of our daughters suffered in the last two years of the campaign were the direct result of their being sold short on maternal time; paternal time, too: our problem was that *both* parents were in it up to the neck. On the other hand, in our case, only one of the pair was also carrying out a full-time professional job. I am still amazed at the amount of time that was found by most of the core workers. How they managed to teach, head departments and schools, prepare courses, run businesses, design buildings, as well as to 'help build Leeds Playhouse' is difficult to understand: except that they too perforce cut down on their 'family time'.

But on the other hand the young did have a lot of fun and excitement: fielding phone calls from Diana Rigg is really worth a lot; getting a privileged opportunity to have Peter O'Toole sign your brick-token offsets a lot of sacrifices. And in any case, it must be good for youngsters to see commitment at work, to see adults working flat out for no pay, for an ideal, for a cause, whether it is for CND or a hospice or a flower-arranging society or for a theatre campaign. Thus I comforted myself at the time, and afterwards; as, I am sure, did my fellow-campaigners.

In the next ranks of the 'press-ganged' were many hundreds of children in the schools of Leeds. Masterminded by our two Trust Governors who were also teachers, and supported by a number of gallant staff in many schools, a mighty fund-raising campaign was launched which brought steadily over the next two years quite astonishing sums of money raised in small amounts in all sorts of ways. Certain key schools with which the Trust had direct links played regularly an active role: making banners and placards and models; servicing public occasions, supplying manual labour for chair shifting and door-manning; distributing leaflets; delivering letters by hand to save postage; and providing a host of distribution outlets for the pencils and the Christmas cards and the bookmarks (designed by one of them) that steadily went on bringing in the pennies. Of course, all this involvement, which had the support of practically every Head Teacher in the city and county, and certainly the blessing of the two Chief Education Officers, was a certain way of arousing the interest of the young in the theatre-to-be. It would be nice to know how many of the audiences of today feel they have a personal stake in the West Yorkshire Playhouse Campaign because of the many small things they did for the parent Playhouse Campaign; and how much the free publicity stemming from the impact of their activities on their families still helps to fill the theatre.

So the success of a great effort such as the theatre campaign is as much attributable to those off-stage and back-stage as to those at the centre; and one hopes that the benefits of involvement in a shared cause outnumber the ill-effects of time lost to other things. What is more difficult to feel easy about is the extent to which an obsession affects the nature and personality and behaviour of the obsessed. Again, I can speak with certainty only for myself. I know that my character and personality did change under the stresses, in face of the challenges and as a result of the needs. I became dictatorial, impatient, demanding; I expected everyone always to give top priority to the next set of demands from the campaign. And yet - sharing as they did the same battle-field - so did they. We all changed and we changed each other. There were few interpersonal crises that were not resolved; though, oh yes, there were a few, and terrible they were: when nerves cracked and endurance was used up, and people spoke, in desperate terms, of their tether-ends; there were many misunderstandings - ill-chosen words setting in motion quite unintended repercussions that were difficult to forgive. And we all, but especially I, made bad misjudgements. There was one raging row very early on in the campaign that echoed down the corridors of a certain public office. There was many a tactless error that caused damage and wasted time in the repairing; and there were many, many pages of night-written apology and explanation that went, with affection albeit, between us all.

But such is the nature of obsession. And those who stayed the course garnered deep friendships; even, at the worst, that form of wary concern for each other that members of a family have. One way and another, we were irrevocably tied up in each other. When now, twenty five years on, we who are left meet, perhaps after long separations, we find on the instant that our friendships are undiminished by years and distance, and we fall at once into the idiom of people who have known each other well, and are a part of each other. I can point to no greater recompense, for years of work in a shared undertaking that offers no personal gain, than that of deep, true friendships; on a purely personal level even the worth of the cause in which one shared, and even the attaining of it, are of less importance. At the last, nothing matters as much as relationships with other people.

For those of us who were directly involved in contact with supporters and the public there was the bonus of more ephemeral but often deep and interesting relationships. I tried to go on as I had started - knowing everyone who was in our records. But success and numbers defeated me eventually, although I think that the team of core workers as a whole kept a very personal set of links with a wide range of individuals. I often think that it was one of the bases of our success in mobilising public feeling: as important, I sometimes think, as more conventional public relations - and far more sincere. If people know themselves to be personally known and respected, no matter how little they are able to offer, they identify more fully, their commitment is greater, and, in pragmatic terms, may bear more fruit. 'Direct Contact' - that name we gave to the whispering campaign - really does consolidate support. Of course, the direct contact with 'key' people, through whom could be effected communication with what I used to call 'the networks', paid very large dividends, again not to the campaign alone, but also to those of us who established and enjoyed the contacts. It brought a great widening of our personal horizons, and, in Peter O'Toole's words, 'gave us bridges to other men's lives'. It is another way in which, no matter how little had come of the campaign, I should for ever have been grateful - for that widening and enrichment of my own life.

It might have been expected that with the subsiding of the excitement of the 'Twon Hall' meeting (as it came to be known, on account of my invariable and recurrent typing error), we would settle into a steady course of progress towards our so-carefully-scheduled deadlines. But the reality was sadly different from that. It is true that many nice things happened. We had our office: it had a 'good' address, too - in Park Square, a nice, respectable and substantial old square mainly inhabited by solicitors and dentists and other such respectable practitioners. We had our typist, and we had our telephone - those two factors being the ones that most transformed my own life. A handsome new emblem graced all our material; and our new letter-headed paper gave us, I am sure, a better 'image'. The funds we now had at our disposal, limited as they were, and guarded with Scrooge-like rigour by our Treasurer, enabled us to upgrade our material - leaflets, handbills, donation forms now began to make us look very much more like a going concern. We still lived on a shoe-string, but this was not evident to the public; the gloss on the paper made a better impression than the matt of the duplicating paper, though the content was the same. The illusion of success was deemed by the experts in public relations to be necessary to inspire confidence in potential donors.

The campaign organisation was once again restructured, for in the summer of 1968 Leeds Theatre Trust formally came into existence. The Trust consisted of the original Theatre Committee, the small core group, seven of whom were named as Governors, the rest as ordinary members - a division that was of no consequence except legally (specifying who, for example, would go to prison for our crimes) - for the work went on as before, with a share-out of functions into the original committees but with the addition now of an Appeal Committee onto which were co-opted the few active workers among our supporters who were also businessmen. Meetings took place with devastating frequency, and we really might have been well-advised to move into communal residence. Incorporated into the Campaign Council were any supporters who were prepared to take on a specific area of work-organisation. Finally, there was the Playhouse Club, with its own organisation headed by Barbara Barber, whose special concern it had always been, and who continued to be its Chairman until - and after - it became Friends of the West Yorkshire Playhouse; a sustained, unbroken history of service that out-ran all others, for Barbara was one of 'the thirteen' of 1964. The Club had its own independent finances and its own programme of fund-raising and public relations, and long after, even, the building of Leeds Playhouse it continued to raise funds for various ways of supporting the theatre.

There was regular communication between all these bodies and a less frequent send-out to the entire Supporters' organisation which now included donors. Our many re-structurings (on which we expended a lot of thinking time) always blessedly seemed to be accompanied by - even precipitated by - the advent of new people prepared to help and filled with ideas. Some stayed the course, to the end, others couldn't, some didn't - and one or two we wished wouldn't. Money trickled in steadily and quite comfortingly. But it was small-scale, for the kick-start of Council support did not materialise, and we were certain that without that it would be very unlikely that the business sector would join in. At this point such an intention on the part of the Council seemed to be as little likely as ever, for a bolt from the blue had been launched in the week before the Town Hall meeting. The City Council, with inimitable timing, had in fact embarked on an enterprise that was so unheralded and turned out to be so damaging to the campaign as to raise serious suspicions about the motives underlying it.

An eight week summer season of 'plays, comedies and farces' was projected by John Beaumont, Managing Director of the Grand Theatre, to be presented by a so-called Leeds Festival of Drama

Company. A week before the Town Hall meeting it had been announced with a flurry of press coverage that the City Council was to back it financially with guarantees against loss. In other words the Council was for the first time ever prepared to subsidise drama in the city - but at the Grand. No word of this had been revealed to us, which at the least seemed an act of the gravest discourtesy in view of all the implications for us - and in view of the fact that it was, in fact, announced almost exactly to coincide with our Town Hall meeting. Promise was made of high quality work; much was made, especially by Pratt, of the Leeds origin of one of the directors of the production company, of it having a Leeds as well as a London office, and of the purpose of the enterprise, which was to 'found an annual festival of drama for the North of England....at which as much emphasis as possible (would be) given to educational considerations and the encouragement of local authors and plays'.[1]

These were claims that looked suspiciously like bare-faced purloining of campaign material, but if genuine, they could only be welcomed. Less was made, especially by Pratt, of the difficulties John Beaumont found during the summer months of keeping open a 1,500 seater Victorian theatre and guaranteeing employment for his permanent staff of seventy. At the time of these announcements, coinciding as they did with our absorption in the Town Hall meeting, the full implications escaped us. They were later to be made explicit by a statement to the press by the Chairman of the Council Finance committee: the Council intended to regard this festival as a trial run for the Playhouse, to see whether public response to a season at the Grand, subsidised by the council, justified consideration being given to subsidising the Playhouse. The logic is of course non-existent: in the first place the Theatre Trust had not sought subsidy from the Council - it had sought a contribution to the capital cost, and our estimates gave clear indication that we did not expect a revenue subsidy; in the second place, nothing could be less comparable with the work of a resident company working throughout the year in the city than this collection of separate production companies spending each a week in the city; there was nothing in this season that was in any way different from the usual run of shows that the Grand had always put on - except for the status given it by this official support. The deviousness screams out from official statements: 'The theatre campaign members, in their petition to the City Council, had said it contained 20,000 signatures ... if every one of those 20,000 people bought a ticket each for this summer season there would be no call on the corporation' (to make good a potential loss).[2]

The Leeds Festival of Drama, which was in fact a portmanteau name for a collection of six productions of extreme mediocrity, put on a string of plays of even greater mediocrity,[3] with the exception of Shaw's *Candida*. The casts of each play were self-contained - one indeed was straight from the West End, with its London cast - and there was no semblance of the ensemble work that at the least might have been expected from a 'Festival company'. The educational considerations seemed to have been overlooked; the nature of the plays was predominantly trivial when not downright bad. Each production played to diminishing audiences. It was June, July and August: most theatre directors know the facts about summer play-going habits in the best of circumstances, and close for a short period. In so arbitrary an enterprise the mere addition of a blessing from the City Council was not likely to buy in audiences.

Poor audiences, and the extent to which the Council would finally need to pay up on its guarantee, were predicted by the campaign experts, in articles in the press and in a letter to the Council. Exactly as they were warned, the full £7,500 guarantee was forfeit, the total loss being £15,000. But the Grand had been helped through its dead season; and perhaps the Council felt it had gained evidence to use against the Theatre Campaign.

For now, of course, when the facts emerged in September at the end of the 'Festival', the inevitable conclusions were drawn by Council and Pratt. The Trust sent a closely reasoned statement to the Council and to the press; and yet another stormy press controversy ensued, in which yet again our old friends like Keith

Waterhouse and Stan Barstow nobly weighed in. Keith's contribution, once again, was a campaign manifesto in itself:

> 'The repertory theatre has the role of a benevolent spider. It spins a web embracing schools, factories, working men's clubs and homes where the TV has not been switched off since 1948....it entertains. It infuriates. It stimulates. It stages brilliant successes and disastrous failures. Sometimes it loses money....our capacity to enjoy is rusty. We have forgotten what we are supposed to be doing ....All this will become apparent to Mr Pratt, the prudent aldermen and others when Leeds eventually has, as it will have, the repertory theatre that is its right and due'.

And - inimitable man - he ended with a typical piece of lunatic sarcasm that, as so often in his writing, struck a keener blow than did all the reason and the facts: 'In the meantime I am happy to see that the city has become celebrated for staging the world's first international gargling contest'.[4] Now just how did he find so ludicrous a piece of information with which to identify the city's cultural priorities?

Sometimes in the throes of dejection, frustration and rage, we derived from such sallies a relief and delight that were perhaps out of proportion to their effect on the course of the campaign; but that is comedy's purpose in life - deflation, mockery, relief. Keith was a master of this art. He was also one of the Governors of the Trust from the early days, and he served the campaign throughout. He was living in London at that time, but I never remember him not responding to requests, usually feverish and with no warning, to do what he did so uniquely well - use words: in articles, in letters to the press, in speeches at a variety of functions - speeches in that Yorkshire monotone from which he craftily excluded any promise of excitement in order the more totally to catch his listeners off-guard with the wicked thrust of his irony, his wit and his ability to ridicule. What delight he gave us as he advanced the cause!

Indeed, this is another abiding memory of all the years working for the campaign: the encouragement of the 'professionals', whose

but he continued to be unsympathetic towards the use of the Sports Hall, and he persisted in his challenge to Bill's costings - a massive breach of propriety which was proved by the facts in due course of time to be completely misdirected, as we knew it would be.

This untimely intervention not only caused us additional anxiety, but extended the delay in finalising the written agreement with the University. However, the knot was finally untied by Sir Roger Stevens, who, although no longer chairing our day-to-day campaign meetings, was himself working hard at the work he had undertaken, mainly concerned with the appeal, and was as committed to the Sports Hall scheme as we all were. 'Don't worry,' he told us. 'We shall put the theatre in the Sports Hall. Leave Chamberlin to me'. One would like to know what happened: we only knew the result, which was that Chamberlin acquiesced. Both are no longer alive; both were persistent, both somewhat imperious; both were charmers but with iron at the core. It will always be for me a personal regret that this was one meeting at which I was not present. I was always rather touched that Chamberlin seemed to bear no grudge, and every year until he died he used to send to me personally one of his very splendid Christmas cards; was it, I wondered, a way of saying that he accepted that we had won a righteous victory?

The comedy of that summer of 1968 was yet to reach its climax. While the 'Chamberlin factor' was delaying a finalisation of the agreement with the University, with the result that it was impossible to get completion before the onset of the long vacation and the slowing down of all administrative activities, there came to the Trust no less than two invitations to establish the Playhouse in two completely different sites. It hardly seemed credible: all those years of searching and now we had a surfeit of tangible possibilities. Once again we entered a period of inter-communication of the most complex nature - and necessitating great secrecy: groups were delegated to investigate and negotiate, to report back and compare, while another group continued working on the terms of an agreement with the University; and all the time, of course, fund-raising and campaigning continued on the basis of the scheme already presented to the public.

One of the new possibilities was of a share in a large commercial development in the city centre, on the site of the old Queen's Hall. It had many attractions, but it finally foundered on the proposed financial basis which was that the Trust would be a rent-payer for the theatre. Although the Arts Council was prepared to contribute towards capital costs and, after establishment, to make revenue grants, it was not in a position to earmark into perpetuity the money needed for rent; and we were not in a position to enter into such a position without support.

The other possibility was of a site adjacent to Yorkshire Television, on Kirkstall Road, and clearly one that would have brought benefits to YTV in the form of a supply of artistic talent close at hand - a benefit which seemed to make sense of the impression I was given, when I first received (by telephone) the offer from a senior executive, that the site would be free although the building cost would be the Trust's. But somewhere along the line a terrible misunderstanding had occurred. In the course of an 'exploratory meeting' held in some style at the Queen's Hotel, with sizeable negotiating teams on both sides and the campaign members formally dressed (as was not usual), occurred one of those frozen moments of suspended breath, when truths emerge, and the shocking nature of both the truths and the erroneous assumptions is revealed - a moment of deep hush, suspended hand-gesture and fixed eye-gaze - a moment that should be written into a play by some better writer than those present at that occasion - an Ibsen, for example. From the Chairman of YTV emanated an icy displeasure: it was clear that the unguarded reference made by one of the Trust's delegation - too soon; irrelevant; audacious; who knows? - to this freeness of the site and its concomitant attractiveness to us, was not welcome.

It was also clear that one of three things had gone awry: one was that I had got it wrong over the telephone in the first place (which seemed improbable), and that I had introduced a concept into the situation that was anathema to a profit-making enterprise and evoked only contempt for the enterprise with which I was concerned; another was that the executive who approached me at the outset had been inadequately informed when he intimated so advantageous a proposition - perhaps even revealing unguardedly his own preference; the third was that the executive had been premature in revealing it to me and that the Chairman was furious (a) with the executive for having revealed it to me and (b) with us for bringing it into the light of day at this embarrassing moment. The negotiating teams parted somewhat stiffly, all expectation of freeness disclaimed, and nothing more was heard of that proposition. I often wondered about those three scenarios, and I never learnt the truth. But - well, it wasn't a good site, anyway, and certainly wouldn't have been worth paying for. And as it was no longer the only egg in the basket, we allowed ourselves to reflect upon the drama of the 'moment critique' with considerable relish.

It may seem that it was perverse of the Trust not to have contented itself with the bird in hand but instead to have continued chasing others through the bush. In fact, that is not quite what did happen - no chasing took place, for in both instances we were approached - a measure of our changing status. We responded because several of us really did regret that we had been forced to settle for a site where the theatre would inevitably be stamped with a University image. Everything in our ideology was incompatible with elitism; we had stressed firmly the objective of getting the theatre out to the people, breaking barriers of prejudice rooted in class - 'getting through to South Leeds' was how we expressed it. Of course this was only Stage I; it was only to fill the gap until the city built Stage II. We pursued the University site proposal, which was concrete, on the grounds that we were more likely to promote Stage II if we established a going concern and proved its value and its popularity; we hoped we could do that even if the social barriers remained unbroken. In any case, the real heart of the matter was to get and retain a director who would undertake the barrier-breaking and would be prepared to regard his remit as including a large evangelising element, involving taking the work out in some form or another, or preparing special schemes for bringing in audiences from the South Leeds sector. The Green Manifesto lay upon our hearts, and when there came, unasked, before the agreement with the University was finally signed, what seemed like chances of honouring the proposals in that manifesto, they could not be resisted.

Our misgivings about a University site were to some extent shown to be well founded during the actual life-time of Stage I, Leeds Playhouse. It was regularly referred to by outsiders as 'that University theatre' or 'the theatre in the University'. It was even erroneously, and irritatingly, included, for example, in Rowell and Jackson's *The Repertory Movement*, among the theatres that operated in a building generously given by a University,[5] the singular nature of our actual financial self-dependence being totally misunderstood; and certainly there was little evidence over twenty years of a shift in social bias in Playhouse audiences. Only a sustained positive policy tantamount to continued campaigning could have offset the disadvantages of the image. There was very little 'outgoing' in the policy of Leeds Playhouse after its second year, except in the work of its Theatre in Education company, although it had been a plank of the policy at the beginning. It had to wait for Stage II, for the West Yorkshire Playhouse, before it finally began to implement the ideals of the Green Manifesto. This is not to belittle its artistic achievements, and perhaps the hopes were unrealistic; but the fact was that in 1968 if we could have found another (non-University) site, we would have taken it. As it was, we were finally left with this plan that had in fact many features that recommended it.

By November 1968, long past the date scheduled for building to start, the negotiations were nearing completion. As the moment for signing drew near we could no longer hide from ourselves the terrible financial realities. The total result of the campaigning at that stage was a cash balance of £3,500; in promises and covenants there were some £16,000. The Arts Council contribution could be claimed only on a pound-for-pound basis, and promises would not qualify. The University required, before signing an agreement, that we show our ability to complete, at the worst, the building of the shell - the only part of the enterprise with which they were concerned. This was estimated to cost £50,000 - far, far more than the total of promises, expectations, grants and pennies that we had; and until we had the agreement completed, no progress could be achieved, visibly, that would begin to establish confidence and attract a faster flow of funds from the public. The only hope was that the City Council would respond to the request first made in February for a once-and-for-all grant of £25,000.

Once again the campaign's future was in the hands of the local authority that had persistently shown so little will to share this project with us. Typically, the immediate response to an urgent request for the £25,000 was that it was considered at a Finance Meeting in November and a decision was deferred until January. The Council, it was claimed, was not prepared to risk subsidising our capital expenditure without yet more evidence about our estimated running costs that would free them from any fear of subsequent responsibility for our activities. Yet again the familiar facts were mustered and presented; yet again the supporters were mobilised to write to their councillors, to send letters to the press. Once again the Drama Director of the Arts Council knuckled in with his support - with letters and facts and exhortations to the Council: Jo Hodgkinson, a man of long-suffering patience, unshakeable calm, and great amiability, who had seen a few struggles like ours in Leeds but few so bitter, and who remained throughout the years imperturbable, resourceful and a constant support to us.

So 1968 ended with Leeds Playhouse exactly where it was at the beginning of the year: on a set of architect's drawings. But the campaigners were not unchanged. Depressed and despondent they might grow, often and again; but the die had been cast - too much had been accomplished, too many expectations roused, and too many people in the city had trustingly given their modest donations and their confidence. There could be no turning back, although the way forward was fraught with uncertainty and risk.

There was something more: a profound sense of outrage that brought out of many of us a bulldog determination to win. It was all so mindlessly unreasonable, this persistent prevarication by our elected local government. In the absence of honest confrontation and frank reasonable discussion there abounded hints and suspicions of vested interest and prejudice, of fact-hiding and the secret pursuit of personal objectives. Too much anger and energy can be expended in pondering such unprovable possibilities, and in a democratic society it is wrong that affairs of public concern should be conducted in such a wasteful way. This conviction hardened the Trust's utter determination to achieve its object, and whatever had been the object of that group at that time - were it an old people's home, a theatre, a refuge for aged donkeys or a public lavatory - I am sure we would have persisted for the sake of the principle.

Each of us had different sources of strength. Mine came from a habit of battling that I had learnt in the brass foundry in Metrovicks, long ago, and that had fired my energy as a social worker in many battles for the rights and needs of clients in that work. Others in the group had different sources of strength - some purely that of dedication to the theatre; but I have to say that at this point in *my* journey through the network of intercommunicating paths to the final landmark, I harnessed general forces of dynamic that came not from convictions about theatre but from convictions about life.

David Halliwell's funny and touching play, 'Little Malcolm and his Struggle against the Eunuchs' was first seen in 1965, and was often produced in the years following. Foolish, mad even, as may have been the finally defeated hero of the play about the endeavours of an individual against the forces of conventional bureaucratic control, some of his early cries to action could well have been ours: 'It's an outrage against the cultural aspirations of Mankind'; 'They hand us nothing but contempt'; 'They should be down on their knees begging, begging to help....' And finally - most apt of all - 'We can't let the buggers keep us down'.

No, we couldn't.

# 8

# Climax: The Last Chance

Leeds City Council today has a fine record of support for the arts. It played the main part in the final act of the Playhouse drama, when, in 1990, Stage II - the West Yorkshire Playhouse - finally came into being. But by then the city was part of a much bigger authority. It is also the fact that it had benefited by a fabulous amount from the availability of surplus funds, when the West Yorkshire County Council was wound up in one of the local government re-organisations that took place during the eighties. But this should not detract from the fact that its priorities had so changed that it was prepared to become a major patron of the arts by its massive contribution to the building costs of the new theatre, and by its continued revenue grants. It also took over the ownership of the Grand Theatre, rehabilitated it, and eventually established it as the permanent home of Opera North - enabling the great old building to come into its own again. The Council's support for ethnic activities and festivals, for amateur theatre and the continuing maintenance of the Civic Theatre as a centre for a great range of non-commercial activities, its financing of the Henry

Moore Sculpture Gallery - all these have transformed the city culturally.

It is difficult to understand why there was such iron corporate resistance to the giving of the relatively small input they were being asked to make in 1968. Of course, Leeds had, since the war, been committed to a gigantic programme of re-housing - whole areas of appalling slums - where Richard Hoggart grew up and of which he wrote in *The Uses of Literacy.* We did not deny that priority had to be given to housing needs which troubled us as much as all caring citizens. But we also believed that cultural regeneration was as important as environmental progress; we shared Jennie Lee's belief that too many had been excluded for too long from the best of our cultural heritage. We knew that the words with which Keith Waterhouse had summed it up at our very first supporters' meeting were the truth: 'A city without a theatre is a city without a heart'. We wanted the penny for flowers as well as the penny for bread.

We had drawn in our campaign upon the writings and views and experience of so many leaders of thought, had activated from the grass roots a swell of such pressure, and it seemed inexplicable that none of this impacted upon the corporate will of our elected Council. Individual councillors in considerable numbers spoke in support - councillors from all parties. We had recruited a Conservative, Paddy Crotty, Chairman of the Education Committee, to be a Governor of the Trust; the Labour Party had long ago formally passed a resolution welcoming the campaign's objective; Michael Meadowcroft, leader of the Liberals, had joined the campaign and worked tirelessly as our advocate. But the ways of local government are such that civic support depends upon the stance of the caucus of the party in power - a small handful of people with strong personal convictions and interests. Support was now being withheld by the Conservative caucus as it happens, but the die-hard, rather reactionary, Labour party often made tactless public pronouncements of damning adverseness to our cause, and could equally well have taken a similar stance to the Conservative one if they had been in power. Ronald Wilkinson, the drama critic of the Yorkshire Evening Post - one of our staunchest supporters - wrote that there still existed in the minds of many opponents

> 'an image of the Leeds Theatre Trust as a bunch of earnest, starry-eyed enthusiasts, deliberately left-wing, talking hot air about culture and regarding profit as a dirty word'.[1]

Certainly it was true that we stressed the need for theatre to be subsidised, to be free from market pressures so that artistic risks could be taken and so that seat prices were within the reach of all. But how a view of the Trust such as Ronnie suspected to exist could still persist was hard to understand. Quite apart from the evidence available of identical policies in every other city like Leeds, we were backed by people of irreproachable repute: such as all the Leeds MP's and many from the West Riding and other Yorkshire regions; by the Yorkshire Arts Association; by the Arts Council; by the Leeds Chamber of Commerce; by the two Chief Education Officers; and by the Bishop of Wakefield (who had joined the Campaign Council soon after the Town Hall meeting). And one wonders how Sir Roger Stevens, once British Ambassador to Iran, felt at being tagged a 'starry-eyed, hot-air talker' - or even an 'honestly intentioned inspired fanatic', to use another of Ronnie's colourful phrases. Clearly the explicit phrase in the Green Manifesto, 'the precarious mechanism of private profit' had set a-quiver the sensitive antennae of the cautious Tory businessmen and the suspicious die-hards in the Labour party. But that they should still be quivering after so many years of careful explanation was difficult to comprehend.

The fact is, of course, that any impasse is set in a particular context of a contemporary complex of factors, and to break it an understanding is needed of all the component parts. In this instance it was impossible to disentangle the interests and the vested interests, the truths and the distortions, which persisted beyond the point described at the end of Chapter VII. Out of the yellowing press cuttings and the pages of crumbling duplicating paper - Trust minutes, letters, reports - leaps a narrative of rage, frustration and desperation that finally led the Trust to take a mighty gamble, which it won. The episode now to be recounted is typical of the history of this campaign from the outset, and it exposes better than any other the razor's edge upon which the prospects for Leeds Playhouse rested. It is necessary to go back a little to the summer of 1968 and to the controversial Leeds Festival of Drama.

The claims that had been made for the company that ran the Festival, financially guaranteed by the Council, were that it was a non-profit-making company: (Was profit a dirty word to it?) mounting plays of the highest standard, with emphasis given to educational considerations and the encouragement of local authors and players. In other words, the policy seemed to have much in common with that of the Playhouse. As we have seen, the failure of the season - attributable in reality to poor quality plays, a transient set of casts, the summer period, an entirely ad hoc relationship with the city and its people, and a complete absence of any of the 'policy' referred to - was used by the Council as proof that a repertory theatre was unnecessary, doomed to failure, and a potential recurrent expense to the funding bodies. On November 22, the deferring of our renewed application for £25,000 until a date in January 1969, seemed just another instance of foot-dragging - endurable as all the others had been, but deeply distressing in the light of our inability to sign the contract with the University and get on with the job, thus, in turn, effecting a stimulus to donations. That there was a more sinister explanation burst upon us one day before the City Finance Committee meeting of 10 January 1969.

It came in the form of an announcement in the Yorkshire Post by John Beaumont, the Grand Theatre's managing director, of the imminent failure of the Grand, which could only be averted if it were to be taken over by the Council. 'After many years of partial concealment the truth about the theatre in Yorkshire has come out with a bang. Unless Leeds Corporation is prepared to take over the city's Grand Theatre, the latter may have to close', was the first paragraph of the leader in the Yorkshire Evening Post of 9 January.

And then came the punch line: 'Mr John Beaumont makes the shock announcement with consummate timing. For tomorrow Leeds Finance Committee will decide whether to recommend a grant towards a new repertory theatre for the city'.

The Trust and the campaigners were completely shattered. And of course the outcome of the City Finance Committee's meeting was a foregone conclusion: a decision was deferred 'indefinitely'.

Now the full implications of the Council support for the summer Festival became clear. It had been expected to fail; and its failure was to be exploited, and was exploited, to cast doubt on the viability of the Playhouse. A good softening-up job had been done in public relations, arousing public sentiment for a well-loved building, establishing the belief that Leeds could not support one theatre let alone two, and opening the way to a conclusion that whatever was to be made available for theatre in the city should be spent on the Grand.

The two local papers were inundated with correspondence on the issue and, of course, on the campaign as well. It seemed that Leeds was becoming the most theatre-conscious city in the land: an ironic contrast with the image drawn of it by Keith Waterhouse in an article which had appeared in the Yorkshire Evening Post the very day before the Beaumont announcement. He referred to it as having 'one distinction. It is the last city in Britain, and possibly in Europe, without a repertory theatre of its own'.[2]

Amongst the letters was one from John Beaumont, disclaiming the intention 'of embarrassing Leeds Theatre Campaign's application to the city council'.[3] It subsequently emerged that the announcement (with its 'purely coincidental' timing) had been made without the approval of the Board of the Grand; and some few days later, in what I now guess (for want of a written transcript or tape recording) must have been a pretty fiery conversation with our long-standing opponent, Desmond Pratt, I learnt that...but let me quote here from the Newsletter that went out on 10 February to the Campaign Council:

That the timing of the announcement was deliberate cannot be doubted. Mr Beaumont at first was quoted as saying that he had timed it to come before the Finance Committee decided about our grant so that the whole position of the theatre in Leeds could be looked at; he subsequently withdrew this statement. Desmond Pratt told me over the phone that (a) the timing of the announcement was entirely his, Pratt's decision, and he had only just got wind of the position at the Grand; (b) that he had taken steps to stop the Yorkshire Post reporters running the line of the Evening Post that it was Beaumont's decision; (c) that when he made the announcement, he had no idea our application was to be considered the following day. This is fantastic, in the light of the sentence at the end of his front page splash on Thursday January 9th, which specifically refers to the decision being expected! but there it is ... that's what Pratt said to me on the phone, though he might possibly not remember, or deny it! he also, incidentally, asked me during that conversation if we had a site yet!

It was impossible to thread our way through the facts and the lies and the half-truths - the web of intrigue spun by the coalition of Pratt and Beaumont (who were very old friends) and the Board of the Grand, some of whom were members of the Council. The Trust here and now decided that it would not attempt to. We had had enough. The iron had finally entered our soul. Our patience was exhausted. It was then that we took the gamble: we decided to give an ultimatum and a dead-line to the Council; and if our application for £25,000 were not granted by the date of the deadline, we would stop. All the money received would be returned. The campaign would end. But we would blazen the news from end to end of the country through every medium to which we had access, and put utterly to shame the City Council of Leeds.

In such terms was written a long, cool, lordly letter to the Town Clerk, giving the council a date - that of the next meeting of the Trust four weeks ahead. We conceded no link between the campaign's affairs and those of the Grand and stated categorically that unless we received a grant of £25,000, announced immediately, the campaign would be terminated. The nature of the Council's responsibility for this was spelled out. The letter was copied to the Arts Council, and the gist of it was circulated to all members of the Campaign Council and to the press. But the letter itself was hand-delivered in a manner that belied the coolness of the time. It was, to be precise, thrown at the feet of the Deputy Town Clerk in an unplanned confrontation that took place in the corridors of power, the poor man chancing to emerge from his office as I approached it. The irate, unpremeditated gesture was caused by his incredulity and his placatory attempts to dissuade us from implementing the measures we would be taking if our ultimatum were disregarded. The Deputy Town Clerk was a wily, clever man, with a dry sense of humour and a deceptively relaxed, diplomatic manner; I had long had a rather entertaining relationship with him, in which we played the games of manoeuvre and tactic with mutual suspicion and mutual respect. But no tact could counter the fury of an enraged woman taking her stand at the last ditch; he was shocked by the facts as much as by the histrionic, but had little time to be placatory as I left in a whirl. But I remember with gratitude that we remained friends - and he became a keen theatre-goer.

About four weeks were to pass before the deadline we had set. It was a wretched time, for the Trust nerves had been too long over-strained to be able to endure much more. But we busied ourselves with media involvement, Pratt-watching, and the servicing of already initiated appeals. There was no point in, and no enthusiasm for, initiating new ones and the wider circle, that of the members of the Campaign Council, had by now succumbed to a sense of failure, so that even the smaller scale activities - the coffee mornings, the bring and buy sales, and even the talks programme, ran down. The surprising thing was that there still persisted, at the core of the Trust, an inability to believe in any other outcome than success. Although there was some ambivalence as well; if the gamble were lost, there would at least be the compensation of freedom from this wearisome endeavour without responsibility for its failure.

But it seemed that the dramatic action we had taken was in fact well-judged, and that the time was right for it. Clearly the public embarrassment caused by the crafty but ill-fated revelation by Pratt and Beaumont threw doubt on the good faith of the Council as well as on that of the Board of the Grand; although suspicion may have been unjustified, it may be that the long build-up of public interest in the Playhouse, reinforced by public sympathy over this new contretemps, pushed the Council into feeling it needed to act at last. Perhaps, even, the Council did not relish the prospect of the denigratory publicity that it knew would follow a further rejection of us. Or perhaps, on this occasion, a very strong pressure was exerted on our behalf by the Arts Council - also, no doubt, prepared to make one last-ditch effort to bring Leeds into line. As so often, the precise sequence of causation was unknown to us and, to us, it was of no consequence. What mattered was that when the Trust met on 'deadline day' it had received sufficient evidence that the battle was won for it even to condone a further slight delay in the process of formal authorisation.

The Finance Committee had met immediately after receiving the ultimatum, in a special session at which the Arts Council was present - whether by invitation or through its own intervention we did not learn. A new element had come into the situation which imposed an additional demand on the Council and made it impossible for them to meet our deadline. But we received outright assurance that one half of the sum we asked for had been put into the estimates for the coming financial year, and therefore would be available in April of this very year; the second half of the £25,000 would be in the estimates for the following financial year. This undertaking could not be made formally until after a meeting that we were invited to attend on 17 March between the Trust, the Finance Committee and the Arts Council.

The need for this meeting was an important shift in Arts Council revenue funding policy, about which we now learnt for the first time. Revenue subsidy from the Arts Council was henceforth to be dependent upon some recurrent contribution from the local authority concerned; hitherto it had been granted without condition.

Obviously this was a new policy designed to make sure that local authorities did not drag their feet and leave central funds to make good their niggardliness - a very proper and welcome change, but one that put us into an uncomfortable position. Much stress had been laid by us on the very fact that our request for Council subsidy was for a once-for-all grant; minimal though we knew this contribution to be, and less than was reasonable, we had such a low opinion of our Council's concern for the theatre that we had no intention of asking for recurrent support - although, of course, changing their attitude was one of our longer term targets. It was something of a miracle that this change, which would have caused us deep embarrassment at any other time, coincided with the crisis over the capital grant: the Arts Council entering into the centre of our arena on account of that crisis, had the unenviable task of adding to the demands upon a reluctant Council.

In response to the invitation to attend the meeting on March 17, a second letter now went to the Town Clerk - the most satisfying that was ever mulled over and perfected by us in one of our longest and most euphoric of Trust meetings. It maintained our cool and lordly tone; we agreed to withhold temporarily the threatened withdrawal from the scheme, being moved, as we said, by the speed with which the Council had shown its desire to respond and the proximity of the date for the meeting; but we stipulated as one of the conditions of our agreeing to meet that when (not 'if') the Council support was authorised it would be given full and immediate publicity, so that (as we put it) the damage the campaign had suffered might be repaired. We further stipulated that a statement should be made about the Grand, to dispel alarm that it might be preparing to launch an appeal for private and business funds. Finally we made a condition that the Council would subsequently be fully prepared to participate officially in all our fund-raising activities.

A long meeting took place on March 17, at which for the first time we sat in conference with representatives of our elected government, their officials, and officers of the Arts Council, to examine the financing of Leeds Playhouse. It had taken five years to bring this about. What a lot could have been achieved in those lost years! But it was no time for regrets or for recriminations, for at the meeting, which was in a sense historic, it was established that Leeds Playhouse should receive a recurrent subsidy from the Council, as well as the contribution towards the building cost. It was clear at that meeting that the Arts Council had already brought its full weight to bear upon Leeds City Council after they learnt of our ultimatum. Although the revenue subsidy was to be only £5,000 a year, it was nevertheless a complete break through. The principle was established of shared responsibility. In the event, the Council's involvement grew greater and greater as the years went by, until, with the establishment of the West Yorkshire Playhouse - Stage II, the Council became a major donor and a major source of recurrent subsidy.

Five years, from March 12 1964 to March 17 1969, to achieve the single most necessary contribution to the establishment of a repertory theatre for the city! Leeds had indeed been left behind in the lost years; not only had the building of new theatres gone on in places which had not had them before; but in many places, like Sheffield and Birmingham and Leicester plans were now in hand for replacing the extant theatre buildings with new ones at costs greater by a factor of five, or more, than the modest cost of Leeds' first Playhouse. In Exeter, Plymouth and all the rest, the theatres had long been in receipt of the support and respect of their local authorities that we had only just started to get. But at last Leeds was to join them: though with a scheme remarkable not only for a first class design but for a financial modesty that many, like Chamberlin, believed unrealistic; even, like our inconsistent critic, Desmond Pratt, not worthy of Leeds, (although Pratt proposed no alternative)! Twenty years later no such doubts were remembered; twenty years of satisfaction in those who had used it (both audiences and actors) had justified the plunge the Council took in becoming involved with it, on 17 March 1969.

The sluggishness of Leeds City Council could have been attributable to many factors: a confluence of particular personalites, conflicts of interest, the pressure of the city's social problems, sheer bloody-mindedness. Or did it reflect some quality of indifference, or hopelessness, that was born of the city's heritage from the industrial revolution and was indigenous to the native population? There are many threads in the web of a city: in the complex, mysterious identity that makes one love it and hate it and remember it and call it 'home', and that makes one want to serve it and help it to improve. Certain it is that Leeds changed radically in the years to come, as did its Council's attitude to the part it had to play in the cultural and artistic life of its people. How much those changes were the product of external influences operating in the country as a whole - greater population mobility, increasing material prosperity, the dynamic impact of ethnic communities - and how much they were the result of the very developments, such as Leeds Playhouse, which the Council resisted so doggedly, is a part of the mystery.

# 9

# Finale: The Razor's Edge

'Spring is here. The thaw begins'. So opened the first letter that went out to the Playhouse Club in April. This new tone sang out from all our communications as the campaign was reactivated, for everything had, once again, ground to a hal: the many branches of the appeal; the negotiations with the University; the detailed work on the design and planning. The club members, the campaign workers who constituted the Campaign Council, and the public - all had once again to be inspired with confidence and roused to action. But there was a great difference: 'We are no longer battling against the indifference or hostility of our elected City Council, but working with them for a truly "Civic Playhouse" '. So continued the Playhouse Club letter.

What was it that had kept the core group together, almost intact, able to surface again and again, and breathe more life into the unwieldy campaign organisation? Without the unitedness of that little group there is little doubt that the campaign would have foundered. Many campaigns have the same history, in which it is the 'bonding' that provides a foundation for sustained effort. Shared conviction is the force that initiates a joint undertaking.

Thereafter, if the undertaking goes ahead, there emerges a microcosmic society within which, if the group is blessed, are established bonds forged by fellow feeling and a deep sense of responsibility and obligation to each other; competitiveness does not operate; dependability and confident reliance on it are taken for granted; and strong emotional ties develop, which are both a consequence of the sense of coherence and a strength that contributes to its maintenance.

The unusual thing about the theatre campaign core group was that it was predominantly middle-aged; most members were senior personalities in their professions, with the consequent rival claims upon time, thought and emotional energy. But rarely, I am sure, can there have emanated from recurrent intense meetings of great frequency and length such a feeling of mutual affection. It was tempered, of course: there were Jovian clashes of will, deep differences of opinion, frequent irritations caused by personality qualities and vulnerabilities, and the stress of life on a razor's edge. But these seemed at the last to engender insight and tolerance, not friction. My abiding memory of all the years - bad, good, hopeful, despairing - is of generous mutual respect, and a growing feeling of mutual dependence. Perhaps the fact that it was a middle-aged group was actually a part of the secret: being, as we were, a group of happily married people, we were free to cultivate great affection for each other that was profound but relaxed. And perhaps if a campaigning group looked for a reward for its efforts and sacrifices, it could find no better one than the deep joy of friendships. 'Remarkable and sustained comradeship' is how the Governors themselves expressed it in a message in the Souvenir Brochure. Well, in T S Eliot's words, 'That is another way of putting it'. Most of us treasured the sense of magic that had enabled us to tolerate as well as inflict outbursts, accept and exploit weaknesses in each other, honour and admire strengths, and rest secure in mutual affection. It was upon this blessed store that in April 1969 we drew for the job of reactivating the campaign.

For the Trust the first priority was, of course, getting the building in hand. The agreement with the University was drawn up; and although once again there were always delays and difficulties that, unknown to the public, kept us on the razor's edge, it was finally completed in time. There was a civilised, urbane quality to all the negotiations with the University officers, and especially the Bursar, whose personal habit of restrained language achieved its apotheosis when, being asked, 'And what if they start the building and then the money runs out?', replied 'Then our confidence will have been misplaced'.

One of the things that needed the University's approval was the designation of the architect. The Trust had no doubt whatsoever that it wished to appoint Bill Houghton Evans, and the University accepted his name with complete readiness and confidence. Not only was he an experienced and talented architect, a Senior Lecturer in the University's Civil Engineering Department and also a partner in a private practice; but he had worked unstintingly as a member of the Theatre Planning Committee and had by now accumulated a wealth of knowledge and ideas about theatre design, which was not a field in which a great deal of innovatory work had at that stage been accomplished in Britain. He was a marvellous colleague: totally committed, always positive, never defeated, always ready to scrap plans or adapt them as new ideas or new constraints impacted. The theatre design that emerged from this 'miracle of teamwork by a committee of experts'[1] was to be

> a theatre of involvement: one where audience and actors meet eyeball to eyeball; one where active participation takes over from passive contemplation, where the real drama of life is intensified and lived again. We wanted, in fact, a Greek theatre. And since no-one has yet managed to improve upon their original, we had to find a way of fitting a stage with its half-moon of tiers into a 90 feet x 40 feet box.[2]

There was an additional condition: the agreement was for ten years, and the plan was for the shell to revert to the University and be used for its original intended purpose as a sports hall at the end of the period. So the shell had to be constructed in such a way as

*Bill Houghton Evans,*
*the architect*

*The Auditorium*

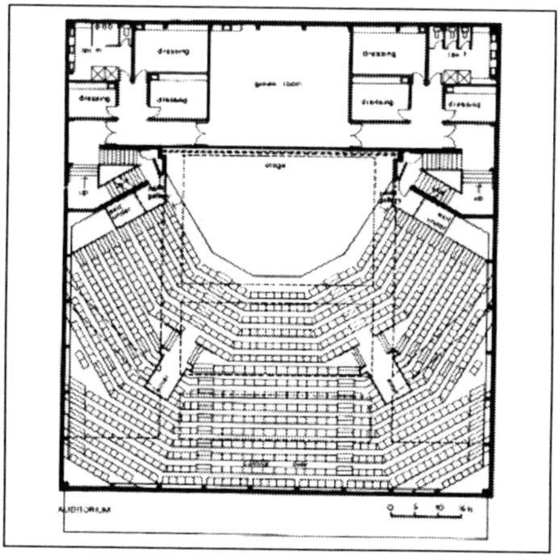


*Ground Plan*

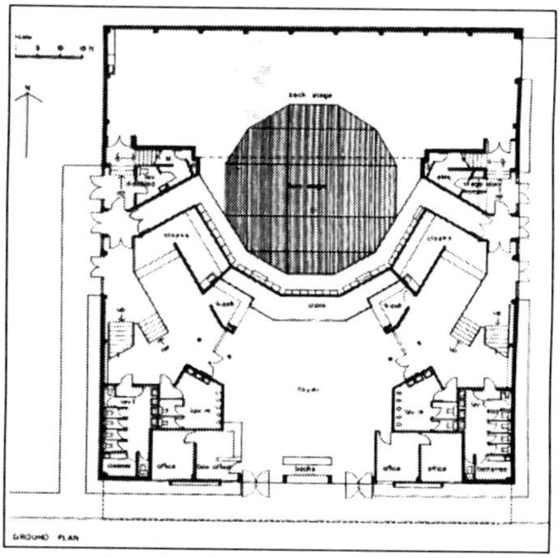


*Section*

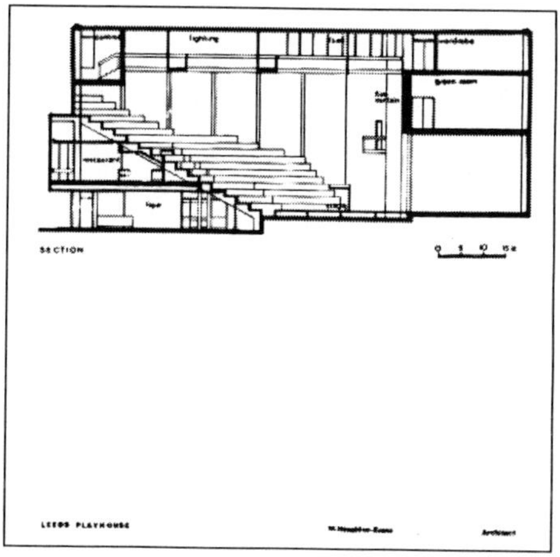

*Architects drawing*

to serve the purpose of the theatre, but be convertible to that of the sports hall: the whole building had to be

> quickly and cheaply put together in such a way that its interior could be removed to a fresh site with the minimum of waste when the time came. Rather like being presented with a packing crate, and asked to design the contents to suit. On the face of it, a crazy way of proceeding.[3]

'In the event', as Bill put it in his nonchalant way, 'it proved simple enough.

> The saving grace was in the height. By carrying floors right up into the rafters, we were able backstage to get in not only a lofty scene dock, but also two floors of dressing rooms and stores. By raking the auditorium as steeply as possible, we were able to slip foyers underneath. We cheated a little - the upper foyer protrudes from the shell. But this (and everything unwanted in the future sports hall...) can be changed with little more than a spanner and a nail-wrench. Our ground floor, to gain headroom and avoid expense, keeps close to the existing slope of the ground. But it can form the base of later tennis courts and indoor football pitches. Our steel frame is not lined with planking: it had to have incombustible cladding, since ours is a multi-storey building. But holes are already drilled to receive future boards. Our clerestory could just as easily have been a solid wall - a theatre hardly needs natural light at all. But the opaque panels now in place are easily replaced by glass.
>
> Given a free hand, we could probably have avoided some initial expense in providing for the longer term. But it was in the spirit of the undertaking that our temporary building should not in any sense be a write-off. Ours is a first-stage venture in a long-term endeavour. Out of this Playhouse will grow the next, and at the end of its ten-year lease, much of enduring value in the fabric will remain and be recovered.
>
> Materially as well as spiritually, our Playhouse is designed as a long-term investment for the citizens of Leeds.[4]

The professional implications of this extraordinary commission, of which the completed result is so described, are clear: while designing a theatre usually offers, in Bill's own words, the most exciting opportunity for 'one-off' architecture, 'eloquently expressing the varied and bustling life of the place' - using the fly-tower, foyer, auditorium, 'to relieve the flat rectilinear monotony our towns seemed doomed to become', there was no such delight in the designing of this theatre; and the architect would be able to expect little conventional prestige associated with striking external appearance and style. Few architects would also accept the stringent constraint imposed by the 'box' limits. But Bill said that

> Since all choice concerning the total form was removed, we were free to concentrate on the best internal arrangement. The paradox is that, if now the restriction of the shell were to be removed, we should be hard put to it to find a more satisfactory solution.[5]

This was entirely typical of the mixture of pragmatism, ingenuity and humour that characterised this man - whom we now commissioned to build the Playhouse.

The promise now to the public was that the theatre would open in the winter of 1970/71. For that, building needed to start within three months of the re-launch. In the event, the basic drawings were produced in three weeks, and the theatre opened in September 1970. The schedule was even more unrealistic than the one that Chamberlin had doubted. But it was achieved, for Bill swept into action the very second the agreement was signed - and long before we had the money.

The rest of the organisation was now plunged into an intensive period of fund-raising. Apart from the major grants from the local authority and the Arts Council, the sources to be tapped consisted of funding foundations, large enterprises such as Yorkshire Television (who were, by a clause in their franchise, charged to lay aside some funds for the support of the arts in Yorkshire), the banks, the industrial and business sectors and the general public. This last was the responsibility of the Campaign Council, which now set in motion a long-term programme of big events and a large number of small fund-raising occasions. The Playhouse Club, with its stalwart core of old-time supporters, engaged in a continuous round of small events, which brought in a steady stream of money. The schools campaign grew and grew, and in schools at all levels activities were undertaken in the name of the Playhouse Appeal.

Then there were the 'organisations'. There were quite a lot of these, which had the characteristic of linking in one network a number of smaller groups, such as the Women's Institutes, or the Leeds Chamber of Commerce. Best known to me was the Federation of Townswomen's Guilds: I had from the beginning maintained close links with the Yorkshire Federation; had given talks to many individual Guilds, and found there a really strong body of support. One of my happiest memories of that phase of the campaign was an evening spent with the Leeds Federation some time late in 1969. By then we had a long list of items that could be earmarked as paid for by specific donations, and the Federation's very considerable donation was matched by the cost of two alternative items. At the very happy engagement when the cheque was handed to me I offered the choice: a set of double doors, or a gentlemen's urinal. They chose, by unanimous vote amidst great hilarity, the double doors; and until the old Playhouse closed in 1990, their acknowledgement plaque could be seen in the foyer on doors into the left-hand lobby - seen by many more people than if they had made the alternative choice!

A valuable by-product of a public appeal is that it keeps alive the interest of the public in the objective. An appeal for a theatre, in a city lacking a theatre-going tradition, had the additional objective of advance audience-building: so, no matter how small the sum of money involved, every contribution, whether from the Young Chamber of Commerce or from an infant school, was doubly important, and the happiest months I had in the campaign were those spent in receiving in person, or acknowledging in personal letters, the money that was given. This was, for me, the real 'community' part of the job, as it was for the others in the team whose main job it was - a marvellous team: fanatic, single-minded, brimming with ideas, and indefatigable. Between them they managed not only the running of their own individual areas of work, but the participating in and servicing of many of the one-off occasions. At one time there was a display caravan (a personal possession, brought temporarily into campaign service) which travelled around a number of venues, from the Garden of Rest in front of the City Library, to Roundhay Park. Poor caravan - it was ill-fated on its first venture out on campaign business: it was damaged by a bus on the corner of a busy road, in the morning rush hour. Innocent, but self-conscious, we were chastised by the policeman on duty, who said, 'You must be mad, bringing this out at rush-hour'. We were due at the Garden of Rest at 9 am, and said plaintively, 'What else could we do?' and 'Look what it is for....' indicating, somewhat unnecessarily, the generous display of Playhouse material covering the whole surface of the van. We hoped that, in compensation for the delay and the damage, we perhaps achieved some unplanned publicity effect among the streams of waiting drivers. I cannot remember if we asked the policeman for a donation on the spot, but we may well have done ...

There were many functions run by other organisations, too, at which a campaign stall was set up by an intrepid team that travelled, like mediaeval peddlers, to wherever they could 'set up shop': to charity bazaars, to the Leeds Flower Show, to dances and balls whenever we could get ourselves accepted. We ourselves held dances, and another Town Hall event, though of less glitter than the first. And we organised a 200 Club, the immensely complicated structure of which, handled by one Eddie Whitham, I never understood, but which brought in a lot of money and the prize of a car to the lucky winner, who was only one chance ahead of - us! It was all great fun, generating a lot of pleasure in the events themselves, but not producing vast sums of money. These, however, were the means by which a very great number of people were brought to feel that they were involved in the theatre, quite apart from giving to it.

A 'seat appeal' was set in hand - a very attractive form of donation-making, for it enables the owner to have, into perpetuity, the satisfaction of knowing his name is attached to a seat in the theatre. Alfred Bradley and Keith Waterhouse jointly directed a special appeal of this sort to the profession - who might, after all, be securing their own futures by helping to fund seats. Benefit performances and productions were given, too: there were many by amateur groups, amongst them a few that had in earlier days been suspicious and unsympathetic; but there were three that were professional, by artists of great distinction. The first was in the Civic Theatre in November, a splendid performance by Henry Livings and Alex Glasgow of their marvellous miscellany from the North, *The Northern Drift* - one of the fruits of Alfred Bradley's years on Radio North, when so many northern writers found an outlet to a wider audience. In December Michael Horden did a one-man show, also at the Civic - a programme of readings from a variety of sources. He was an old friend of one of our earliest members, a sweet-natured, endearing man, gentle, kind, very funny and very modest. His evening brought a large audience and a lot of money. Soon after this, there was a concert given in the Great Hall at Leeds University for us by the distinguished harpsichordist, Alan Cuxton. Every one of these benefit performances gave us publicity as well as prestige, quite apart from the financial benefit to us and the delight to audiences.

Of all the funding organisations to which detailed applications had been made, laboriously mobilised into the form required by each, the only bite came from the Gulbenkian Fund. A response at all was surprising, for at that time the Fund was directing its grants primarily to the cultural amenities in universities. I made a not-too-hopeful dash to London to keep an appointment with the London representative, who gave me quite unexpected hope but with a time delay that dampened it slightly: the Grants Committee would sit the following week, and then not again for another year. 'So', said the representative, 'you should make your application by the end of the year, and we can perhaps do something for you for next year'. And then he added, 'unless....no, it's impossible to get an application in by next week'. Everything is possible when needs must, and I was sure we could manage it by next week, if he would be prepared to accept it. He was a little overwhelmed, for I dare say he worked at a different pace from ours and hardly believed that we could prepare the very full and technical brief in so short a time. But I knew the working ways of our architect and our finance expert, who would be the only ones involved; and when I got back they both went into the darkness for 24 hours. Three days after my first meeting with the representative in London, four days before the Gulbenkian Grants committee met, there arrived on the representative's desk a complete set of drawings with all items specified and costed, and a complete statement of our financial state and needs. We had no idea what to expect, but nothing could be lost. The most likely outcome was that our application would be deferred as a late-comer. But our friend in London processed it on a wave of sympathy and enthusiasm, and to our unimaginable delight we were granted the immense sum of £17,500 - the largest single sum to come to the campaign, apart from the grant from the Arts Council.

It was August by the time this happened. We had received tenders and were ready, if we had the money, to start building. And again we were balanced on a razor's edge - for we did not have the money. The major source from which we had expected a surge of donations now that the city had decided to come into the scheme seemed to be dry. Business and industry did not start to yield anything like the support we had expected. This seemed to be another feature of Leeds that made it so wayward, so unlike most other cities of its size and nature. There was no one single big businessman prepared to give a starter donation that would inspire or shame others into contributing. The biggest sum promised at this stage of the campaign was £1,000, of which there were a few expected, and those predominantly from our own campaigners who were in business, not from the wider business circle. It is true that by the time we were able to launch our Business Appeal, delayed as it had been until we had the clear backing of the local authority, a period of financial stringency had just begun; we had missed the bus; the years of expansion were coming to an end, and the whole business world was less prosperous and optimistic. Our Appeal Committee had worked hard since the re-launch, but with such minimal success that at the very moment when we needed to sign a building contract in order to complete the job on schedule we simply did not have the necessary liquid funds. The granting of the mighty sum from the Gulbenkian was an inspiration, but it was in fact ear-marked for all the lighting installation, and so could not be drawn upon for building; but it was given great publicity in the hope of encouraging the others. A complex of negotiations about the timing of our grants put us into the precarious position of being able to take the risk. And on 20 September 1969, a building contract was actually signed: the single most frightening moment, for me, at least, in the entire campaign.

The firm whose tender we had accepted was an example of the good fortune that occasionally came our way. It was Robert R. Roberts, an old, small, family firm of Leeds. Alec Baron, in his unpublished autobiography, says of Roberts, 'They produced the lowest tender but I have a sneaking feeling that they were out of pocket'. Whether this is true or not can perhaps not be known, but what we do know is that the firm did a magnificent job, in eleven months. If they were out of pocket, then theirs was the biggest and most generous donation from the business world of Leeds.

The contract-signing was immediately followed by a public ceremony for the laying of the foundation stone - and, true to promise, the City played its part and the stone was laid by the Lord Mayor. It was a very informal occasion on the great space, rather wind-swept, beside the Sport Hall that was to gain a twin. I remember noticing Lord and Lady Harewood standing in the small crowd that had gathered. He perhaps was feeling a little envious, for no stone had yet been laid for a Concert Hall, and still had not been laid twenty years later when the second stage of the Playhouse, the West Yorkshire Playhouse, was opened.

There was a grand reception given by the Lord Mayor immediately after the stone was laid, and in the evening a celebration in the form of a Folk Concert took place, on the site, in a huge, hired marquee. Jake Thackray was the generous unpaid star of that occasion - another of our debts to the profession. The hearts of those who knew we were on a razor's edge may have been heavy and anxious, but it was a great moment to celebrate; and 'girt with a throng of revellers' we 'held high feast' until the early hours. But for each Governor of the Trust, as for Matthew Arnold's *Mycerinus*, the loud joyful laughter would fade occasionally from the lips

> ....as some pale shape
> Would thrust a hand before the lifted bowl,
> Whispering 'A little space and thou art mine'.

The pale shape, for us, was insolvency, not death. But the die was cast.

That anxiety, and indeed the rest of the story, is familiar to any who have been responsible for the construction of a building dependent on grants and donations. 'Public appeals, raffles, jumble sales and other fund-raising events were the order of the day in numerous towns and cities that planned new theatres during the sixties and early seventies'.[6] The bald words give little hint of the day-by-day obsessive activity that this involves. The Trust now had a reality to appeal for - a physical building, that went up with quite breath-taking speed. It constituted the best visual aid for publicity purposes, while being a constant reminder that there was no turning back.

The year ended with the appointment, eight days before Christmas of 1969, of a Director. Signing a contract had been the most boat-burning event, but this appointment was the most crucial for the future of the Playhouse and the part it would play in the life of the city. For it was at this moment, uniquely, that spirit would be breathed into the body. Choosing a person who would realise to the fullest possible extent the ideals upon which we had based our long endeavour was a task fraught with unseen dangers. Moreover, it so happened that at this time in the history of regional theatre there had been a number of causes célèbres which had

*Bernard signing the Contract*

*The Lord Mayor lays the Foundation Stone*

*The Frame*

*The Auditorium*

*Dianna Rigg inspects progress with Bill Hayes*

*Bill Hayes*

*Alec Baron*

*Roger Chapman*
*Director of Theatre in Education*

*Keith Waterhouse*
*Founder Governor and staunch supporter*

*Dianna Rigg inspects progress with Bill Hayes*

*Bill Hayes*

*Alec Baron*

*Roger Chapman*
*Director of Theatre in Education*

*Keith Waterhouse*
*Founder Governor and staunch supporter*

highlighted the problems inherent in the relationship between a Theatre Trust and an Artistic Director. The problem was likely to be, predominantly, about reconciling the financial needs of artistic policy with revenue constraints, but it could only too easily take the form of an acrimonious conflict of artistic and policy judgements. There is a very good treatment of this subject in Rowell and Jackson's book, *The Repertory Movement.*[7]

It was one about which we were very anxious, for we were new to the game, in every respect: not only were we a team of citizens rather than a group of theatre professionals, but we were, as a governing body for a repertory theatre in Leeds, without a body of experience to hand, upon which to draw for guidance. Nothing like this had ever existed in the city. The Governors of the Trust were, of course, experienced in the administration of a large range of organisations and activities, and they shared a considerable body of general wisdom, understanding of the arts, and strong, disinterested views about the operation of the theatre. We had watched the crises and troubles in other places, and we wished above all to avoid the sort of clashes on policy that had cost the Nottingham Playhouse John Neville. We regretted deeply that by now he himself had become otherwise committed, for we felt sure that we could make a better job of working with him than Nottingham had. Overwhelmed as they were at this time by all the other problems, the Governors sat through many a long evening trying to establish a code of practice and a format that would give free reign to the creative work of the Director while ensuring that financial responsibility, for which they would be answerable to funding bodies and the public, remained with the Governors. The Articles of Association of the Trust had been drawn up in close association with the Arts Council whose job it was to advise and monitor these things. But among the Governors themselves there existed a wide range of interpretation of the terms on which a Director could be appointed: from those who favoured a close involvement with artistic policy in such matters as choice of plays, the duration of contracts with actors, and maintaining or otherwise a true repertory system;[8] to those who favoured giving absolute autonomy to the Director, within the budgetary constraints, once he had been appointed. It was this latter view which finally prevailed, and we finally stated, in an information sheet sent to applicants, the following:

> It is assumed by the Trust that the theatre will work repertoire for 10 to 11 months. The planning of the programme will be entirely the concern of the Artistic Director. The Trust feels strongly that, within the proper operation of its responsibility to manage the general affairs of the theatre, the artistic policy should be determined and executed by the artistic director.

So it was a truly crucial appointment. It needed to be made at this early point, even before the campaign had come to a conclusion, so that the Trust could at last have to hand the experience and expertise of the profession in respect of the final technical modifications within the building, and also in the critical matter of budgeting - for a real programme rather than a hypothetical one. The latter had all been done within the Trust, on the basis of exhaustive research into the great body of data held by the Arts Council, and in ongoing discussions with those actually engaged in operating theatres elsewhere. The spare-time finance Governor looked forward with immense relief to off-loading this massive task eventually onto a full-time administrator - to be appointed later - but in the meantime to be working in terms of real plans for a live theatre. Balanced as ever on the razor's edge, we were able to offer a half-time salary for an immediate appointment, to become full-time at a later date when the work on the first season actually began in full.

The response to our advert for Director was very impressive. To quote again from Alec Baron's autobiography, 'We short-listed and interviewed six whose names I won't mention, but who are today without exception leaders of the theatrical profession'. We appointed Bill Hays, a 'new-style director for a new-style theatre', as the Playhouse Club Newsletter described him. He seemed from the outset to be the man for us. He seemed to gust into our lives with all the confidence, vitality and optimism that were needed not only for the challenging job of starting a theatre in lag-behind Leeds, but of doing it on a shoe-string while financial uncertainties still hung over us. His experience was wide-ranging, from work in small-scale theatres to those in the West End, and for TV; he identified closely with the objectives of the campaign - the need for 'out-reach', for overcoming prejudices and barriers, for appealing to South Leeds. He came of a working class Tyneside background, and his most recent reputation was built on a marvellous production of *Close the Coalhouse Door*, a documentary drama about miners which he and Alan Plater and Alex Glasgow had jointly created and he had directed in Newcastle - a very fine example of a company drama rooted in a community. He was particularly enthusiastic about Theatre in Education; and he had an appetite for risk and adventure to which the precarious state in which we were at the time strangely appealed. He was a man of laughter, but proud, steel-tough, brave and a fanatical worker. With a little navy cap on a head of dark curls, he could be taken for a charming boy: in many ways he was just that - maddening, cocky, obstinate, irrepressible. He had an irreverent disregard for formality, but established a strong, curious bond with Sir Roger Stevens. He threw himself into the job, and gave as much to the Playhouse on his half-salaried appointment as he did when he became fully paid (when he worked not full-time but double-time). He was always around, haunting the building, ready to take on any fund-raising occasion, meeting businessmen, giving talks, while planning his first season - in fact, he caught immediately the spirit of the campaign and worked in it as a campaigner as much as at the professional task.

It was many months before we had the funds to appoint the Administrator to take over the administration and financial work. It was delayed as long as possible, for economy's sake, but Walter Newlyn, who had by ill-chance been doing his own three-year stint as Chairman of the School of Economics in the University at just this time as well as a full-time academic job, was, by mid-summer in 1970 unable to go on any longer, without professional support, planning the financial affairs of the operating theatre - there was still enough to do with the problems of the building fund. We could as yet offer little in salary or incentives, and the first applicants - of very high quality indeed - were lost to other theatres. It was a sudden inspiration of one of the Governors that revealed to us that the most obvious 'candidate' was just conceivably in our midst if he could be induced to consider it: Alec Baron, who had been at the centre of the campaign from the outset, had master-minded the work of the Theatre Planning Committee, was a successful businessman, and a life-long devotee of the theatre, with a fund of knowledge about it equal to no-one's. He was completely flabbergasted when the proposal was made, but he was urged and supported by every member of his family, in spite of the financial sacrifices they knew this move would involve. When he agreed, we knew that we had appointed a man who would serve the Playhouse as he had served the campaign to establish it - with unfailing devotion, unstinting effort and personal sacrifice. His decision to accept brought a revolution in his life, but he said many years later that he had never regretted the decision. He never returned to business. The work in the Playhouse was relentlessly hard, the rewards few apart from the personal satisfactions, but although his term as Administrator of the Playhouse lasted only two years, he spent the rest of his life in theatre affairs. The change that was wrought in his life was possibly the greatest of all the transformations for which our theatre was eventually answerable.

As 1970 came in it was difficult to believe that a building and a company were already in existence - the building itself seeming to grow rapidly indeed. A new office within sight of it came into our hands, and it was good to work with the evidence before our eyes. Press reporting took quite a different form now: a place on the landscape, and a real live Director always ready to talk to press, businessmen, clubs, schools and unions, now validated the campaign's existence; and pictures of Bill Hayes, in, on, or under the skeleton building, in company with Diana Rigg or whoever else would subject themselves to the danger, were now more frequent than letters of doubt and criticism. Pratt-watching became a thing of the past.

A growing stream of small monies vouched for the growing of a sense of involvement in all sectors of Leeds life - except amongst the big businessmen. From them we had hoped for the big donations, but they did not materialise. The appeal work continued grindingly with depressing results. All the governors were mobilised into joining the Appeal Committee and into undertaking personal follow-up meetings. Batch after batch of appeal letters, all personally signed by Sir Roger, went out to firms of all sizes. My own vividest memory of a follow-up was consequent upon the letter sent to the Head Office of Woolworths in Britain. A reply was received from the manager of the branch in the centre of the city, and I made an appointment with him. He took me into his office, opened the petty cash box and proffered me £3. I felt little was lost by refusing it in high dudgeon. The petty sum followed me, in the form of a cheque, sent to the campaign office. It was included prominently in the published lists of named recent donations which we persuaded the press to run.

A very special attempt had been made to engage the involvement of the very biggest firms with the establishment of a Consortium, membership of which necessitated a donation of at least £1,000. A business-style brochure was produced by Walter, called *Background to the Appeal.* (It brought, to us two, reminders of the threads that 'life is perpetually weaving', for it was based on a format used by Walter when he was Economic Adviser to the Ugandan Government, called *Background to the Budget*). It was a detailed analysis of the financial facts, both those concerned with capital costs, and those which were the basis of our revenue and expenditure planning for the theatre in operation. It was sent to all the big firms in Leeds and the region, together with an appeal letter from Sir Roger. The target was twenty-five firms, and the intention was that the Consortium would appoint a Governor to the Trust. By the time the theatre opened the Consortium had only sixteen members, but among those were several whose managing directors became very committed to the Playhouse, and who, over the years gave valuable service to it. But their efforts to get the big donations in 1970 were not rewarded with the results that were needed to save the project from grave trouble. What was needed was a couple of really big patrons - a Barry Jackson, the wealthy man who started Birmingham Rep and directed it - or an Annie Horniman, who was a more traditional patron in that she paid the money but left the directing of the theatre to others. Such individuals did not materialise in Leeds.

This seeming absence of concern for an amenity for the community that comprised the work-forces, the staffs and, to a large extent, the consumers of the industrial enterprises in so large a conurbation, is still difficult to account for, contrasting as it did with the response to similar appeals form the 'merchant kings' of other similar cities. The economic conditions at the time were not really worse than at most other times, although 'hard times' was a phrase much used, as always, in letters of refusal. There was no longer hostility from the conservative press, and from the other media there had rarely been anything but support; a lead had at last been given by the local authority, and the theatre-to-be had the status of civic support.

What was wrong? Could it have been Yorkshire caution and Yorkshire thrift? But Sheffield was Yorkshire too, and a different pattern of giving existed there, for the new Crucible Theatre. One possibility was that our scheme was too modest to inspire respect amongst the big money-makers of our society - hadn't Pratt said something like that in one of his many-pronged assaults upon us? Another possibility was that the really wealthy patrons of Leeds were preoccupied with the music world, which had considerably more prestigious adherent and contacts. Or was there a suspicion, rooted deep in the 'boss' class, of an art that by its very nature would 'provoke and disturb', to use the words of Michael Horden in his message to the theatre when it did open? One explanation may have been that there were few great firms that were still 'family' firms with Leeds roots, in the way that Sheffield still owed a lot of its prosperity to a few great steel firms; some of the biggest employers in Leeds were subsidiariesof national enterprises, and may have lacked a sense of identity with the spirit of the city. Certainly the first firms that did give, that came into the Consortium, and shared the Trust's endeavours on the appeal side, were family firms; but even so there were many firms that had originated in the city or the region that still had family members at the helm, and steadfastly ignored the pleas to give their patronage to an art in the city to which they owed their wealth. Today the concept of business sponsorship of the arts is much more developed, and forms a part of government policy for supporting the arts, with tax concession incentives; but in the sixties there was no such encouragement. Although the West Yorkshire Playhouse of today is generously supported by Yorkshire business and industry, it should be remembered that Leeds Playhouse was far more indebted to nursery schools and youth groups and clubs and societies and a mass of individuals than to the captains of industry.

Week after week as the building went on and the company came into existence, and as the bills came in, the Governors and the members of the Appeal Committee beat their heads against the closed doors of most of Leeds' industrial enterprises. There seemed no way in which a crisis could be averted, at this last minute. In a desperate (and totally private) move I wrote to Lord Goodman, not in his capacity as the Chairman of the Arts Council (which would have been pointless, as we were already well-supported by it) but because I thought he might have personal connections with some of the region's businessmen; and this, I had learnt, was the way to loosen purse-strings - to find an opening through personal contact. I did not know Lord Goodman, but I knew that the campaign of which I was the secretary would be known to him. I wrote in bitterness and despair, describing the condition in Leeds in these terms:

> .....a tradition of tight-fistedness, puritanism, deep conservatism, and a basic lack of concern for the arts in general and theatre in particular; a heritage in part of the Methodist domination of a populace crushed by the industrial revolution. By February 12 our

total undertakings from the industrial sector of Leeds and the region was about £20,000.

The letter contained a revealing list of old Leeds firms and of great businessmen whose wealth had grown from businesses started in Leeds, but that had ignored our appeal.

The response to this letter, of which none of the Governors knew, was immediate; and it displayed an approachability and a capacity for concern that could accept the unconventional approach I had made, and the lack of restraint in which I had written. He was kindness itself and I was invited, almost by return, to go to London to meet him. It was very daunting, for I really hardly knew what I would say, as I had said it all. 'All' was quite a lot - a very very long letter and, for good measure, a book that had recently appeared (coincidentally, by an early member of our campaign); it was a sort of moral fable, inspired by a sense of regional inferiority and bitterness, about a civil rebellion started in York on the grounds of central government neglect and contempt for the cultural needs of the region.[9]

From behind a vast desk in an unimaginably large room in Fleet Street, an astonishingly large man greeted me with the works 'You have sent me a very long letter', and I replied sadly, 'I'm sorry - I don't expect you have had time to read it all'; which was really a bit rude and ungracious. But he had, and he was as perturbed and mystified as we were by the regional non-responsiveness to the Appeal. I hardly expected any specific promises for, new as I was to this game of high-level begging, I knew it operated in a world of 'a word over lunch' and 'the old boy network' in which confidences were kept but it all happened on the basis of personal goodwill. I never discovered if any of the donors of the future had been inspired by a word from Lord Goodman over lunch; there was not a great spurt in the sluggish flow of funds immediately following this maverick meeting. But psychologically it was of very great importance to me personally, for it justified my deep indignation about the niggardliness of Leeds industrialists, made me feel righteous in the need to persist in our continued pressure upon them, and gave me a small fresh spurt of energy, which I think stopped me from despair. All in the campaign were at this time on the razor's edge, and if any one of us had despaired at this point it would have been a serious break in the bonds of inter-dependence. How strange it is that from such small gestures as a kindly parting pat on the shoulder and an exhortation to 'not despair at this stage', should come rejuvenation! 'A little touch of Harry in the night', was one of the secrets of Henry V at Agincourt, so Shakespeare tells us. I have always felt there was a little touch of Goodman in the Playhouse in Leeds, fanciful though that may seem.

The single act of generosity that enabled the building of the Playhouse to be completed, at the eleventh hour, came from the Yorkshire Bank. It happened, as miracles do, at the very last minute. It was at a dinner that was given to the members of the Consortium, of which the Yorkshire Bank had become an early member, and thus a donor of £1,000. It was a convivial occasion, by all accounts, with the Sir Roger, Bill Hayes, Bill Houghton Evans team at its most beguiling, and with a tour of the nearing-completion theatre to end up with. Then the shock was delivered: the building appeal was vastly under-subscribed, and there was, quite simply, a cash-flow crisis of such immediacy that bills could not be paid, and work could not be continued. The Consortium members listened in gloom; they were by now rather more committed to the Playhouse than of old, not just because each of them had given £1,000, but because they had come to care. Two of their members were now Governors, one representing the Consortium itself, the other being a nominee of the Chamber of Commerce, occupying a seat in parallel with that designated for a representative of the Trades Council. But the manager of the Yorkshire Bank, sitting next to Walter, murmured 'Come and see me in the morning; we'll see what we can do'. That next morning he offered overdraft facilities, immediately, on such favourable terms that then, and then only, in mid-August, was there absolute certainty that in mid-September the Playhouse could open. Generous as were the terms, of course, there was a burden of interest and repayment laid upon the Playhouse, and this - the measure of the failure of the Appeal - was to bring problems that might have been diminished if we had been able to open with our capital costs fully met. But to open at all was the miracle. The story - or rather the long, long introduction to the story, of Leeds Playhouse, ended as it had begun: on a razor's edge.

The story itself remains to be told. For most campaigners the introduction and the first pages of the story overlap: for everyone, that is, except for the Secretary to the Trust. Self-knowledge and general observation had long convinced me that the theatre would do well to lose me when it came to birth; and I, for myself, wanted to pick up life where I had left it in 1964. The campaign had become a complete obsession, intensified by the dual commitment of Walter and myself. It had taken over my life full-time, and the lives of our four daughters too; we had all become 'possessed'. The family needed a new dimension - it had also reached the stage when it could benefit from an additional salary! But more important, the hovering image of a domineering woman was the very last thing I wanted our theatre saddled with. So on opening night I left the Trust. It was like being re-born. I said to them when I wrote my letter of resignation 'They climbed Everest because it was there. We've built the Playhouse because it wasn't'. In truth I felt that it was I on the top of Everest, and it was quiet and fresh and peaceful, and the only movement necessary was an easy one, downwards. I felt a bit mean at deserting, for I guessed at hard times to come, and after all I had 'conjured them all up'; but the ones who were left were all better equipped than I was for the new job. I was a campaigner for, not a runner of, a theatre; I was an 'accidental' committee woman - and I doubt if I would have been rash enough to start the thing up if I had known all that it was going to involve. After all, it had only been a pressure group....

So it was a carefree ex-Trust Secretary who joined the audience - on the birthday, by chance, of one of the daughters whose interests had been one of my inspirations - for what was in fact an awful anti-climax: only just short of an outright disaster.

Such an occasion!

> The opening, a month before schedule, of the cheapest purpose-built theatre in the country....is a great feather in the city's cap....

John Raymond wrote in *The Stage*. (Had he by chance got the cap on the wrong head?) He continued:

> Based on a scaled-down model of the fourth century BC theatre at Epidaurus, its ample green-room and wardrobe room, well-fitted dressing rooms and spaceship-style control room for lighting and effects, its steeply raised seating, accommodation for disabled play-goers, and radiation panels designed to throw the sound back to all parts of the auditorium, would seem to make it a resident company's dream.

There was no doubt at all about the good favour in which our lovely building was held; tributes to its design, its astounding inexpensiveness, and the excellence of its equipment, came from all round. But the play with which it had opened was a different matter:

> Bill Hayes....has chosen to open with a specially-written entertainment by Alan Plater (book) and Alex Glasgow (songs), directed by himself. This is the team that made the memorable *Close the Coalhouse Door*, but there is little in common between that show and this, except the sharp left-wing slant....Mr Plater has not been able to find a theme appropriate to Leeds, as the pits were to Newcastle, and has settled for a general blast at the middle and upper classes....

was how the critic of the *Financial Times* reviewed it on 22 September. And John Raymond continued his review in *The Stage* thus:

> Alas, the thinness of Alan Plater's text almost defeated the evening - a patchy, threadless, sometimes witty, but often ham-handed attempt to impale a number of cliché targets....

'A writer' said George Devine 'should have the right to fail'. It was cruel, though, that the only play perhaps that Plater ever wrote that actually bored people should have been our opening production. For that is what it did. It bored people. 'May you delight, disturb, provoke, please, shock and entertain, but never, never bore', wrote Michael Hordern in his opening night good wishes to us.

But it was a riotous production; and Alex Glasgow's songs

> Witty, tangy, lewd or tender, haunting....burrowing satirically into public appearance and reality, went with a sinister, gleeful punch....Delighted with the grace and skill of the production, above all with the cheering nature of the occasion itself, the audience was mostly prepared to overlook the show's lack of satiric substance, treating the whole affair with baffled good humour.

concluded John Raymond generously.

It is true that we in the audience did our best - apart from the MP from a Yorkshire constituency who noisily walked out in the middle of one of the lewd, tangy songs, thus giving the Yorkshire Post its first opportunity for a long time to 'get us'. The two-hour traffic of the stage was colourful, excitingly designed, attacked with gusto and high professionalism by a talented cast - a cast that had already presented, to universal acclaim in Edinburgh and Nottingham, the other play in the opening repertoire - Pirandello's *Henry IV*. But we knew they had a flop on their hands - and worse - that it was a flop that was exploitable by the sceptics for the wrong reasons, for its anti-establishment theme, lacking in real satirical power as it was. How gladly would we have welcomed the risk, even for a theatre whose founders owed gratitude to 'the establishment', of a satirical work that bit deep - that was an artistic success, memorable for being searching and shocking and disturbing! But it was a muted, lost-for-words campaign that celebrated back-stage that night with the company, many of whom shared our views but were to have to live with the piece for several weeks.

We campaigners had long since given up believing in fairy stories; and a 'big hit' success to start with would perhaps have been too much like a fairy story. In fact, the work of that first company, under that first director, did go on to fulfil the expectations of a public that had been given so many promises, and to validate the campaigners' efforts. There was a glamorous official opening later in the year, with a riotously successful irreverent musical, *Oh! Glorious Jubilee*, in the presence of the Prince of Wales. It was bedevilled by adverse factors, as somehow seemed in keeping with the nature of the campaign. It took place during a period of electricity cuts, imposed on a rota basis throughout the city; the royal presence justified an adjustment to the rota so that the theatre had lights; but half the audience, kitting themselves up for a grand do, were doing it in the dark. However, small mercies fall from time to time: the quagmire that constituted the area surrounding the building, for the surfacing of which no money had been available, was, in honour of the one limousine trip to and from the entrance, given a strip of tarmac by the University, and was enjoyed by many people subsequently.

There were several immense successes, sold-out houses; there was a children's play at Christmas - a new play written for us by Ken Campbell - that packed in the children of Leeds for weeks. I shall never forget the emotional phone call from Walter, who had gone down to the theatre for the first performance: 'You have to come down and see it', he cried, 'There are streams of children pouring into our theatre'. There were lively discussions (one with Alan Plater); there was a great Festival of Children's Drama in the first summer. The bar was always full; the actors felt they belonged and were eager to meet the audiences: that first company stayed with us for many productions. It was a gay, tumultuous place. But its fraught life was lived, continuingly, on the razor's edge, and the cherished policy of playing true repertoire proved too expensive to operate and had to be modified. It is the only element in the Green Manifesto that has long proved impossible to achieve, by either Leeds Playhouse, by the West Yorkshire Playhouse, or indeed by most other theatres in the regions.

Perhaps one of the most important achievements was that of the Theatre in Education company. It was established at the very beginning, and in fact was in operation even before the theatre opened. It gained a reputation as one of the best companies in the country, and its work as an education team working through drama has enlarged the sensitivity to and awareness of a great range of serious issues in generations of Leeds children. Its first Director, Roger Chapman, had been very close in aspiration and motivation to Bill Hayes, and they shared a great joyous vision, and worked marvellously together. Roger himself was lost to the seductions of Australia some four years after the Playhouse opened; but his company and its high repute, continuously supported by the Education Department of the City, maintained its high standard of work throughout the whole life of Stage I. It moved into Stage II and was undoubtedly one of the most prized and admired Theatre in Education groups.

Bill Hayes himself stayed at the Playhouse for only two years: all the Trust's care to build into its policy the means to avert the classic and familiar head-on clash between Board and Director came in fact to nothing, and the Leeds affair became another cause célèbre. There were many reasons for it, but this is not the place for an analysis of them, for this is the story of the campaign not the history of the Playhouse. But it is only right to give tribute here to the man who started the Playhouse in the spirit of the campaign that had achieved it. He worked on a shoe-string, inadequately financed by revenue grants, and indirectly disadvantaged by the outstanding debts. His zest and ebullience brought a spirit of excitement and fun to the Playhouse; he worked feverishly hard, lacking as he did the funds to engage assisting directors, but determined to keep the theatre open for as long a season as possible. He and Alec Baron, as a team, worked miracles in those first two years, and to both an enormous debt was owed by all who came to enjoy the theatre, and all who helped to build it.

The full life story of Leeds Playhouse must be told by some other writer at some other time. It is a story that has more in common with other theatres than has the campaign to build it. It pursued for many years a sound, safe policy of offering good quality enjoyment through good quality productions, but with no very adventurous exploration of new and local work, and no extension of the theatre's role as other than a purveyor of plays: no programme of 'out-reach'. But as such it did its modest job well. The ten years lease expired, and still the city had not built the promised permanent home. The University magnanimously hosted the theatre for another ten years, its 'confidence' not 'misplaced' but exploited. A familiar scenario of pressure and bargaining and negotiation was played out; new Governors joined the Trust, new energy came onto the scene and gave a new dynamic to the efforts; and at long last the dream if 1964 was finally realised, in 1990 when the West Yorkshire Playhouse opened on a site in the centre of the city: a great joyous enterprise, which realises in a way that Leeds Playhouse really did not, most of the principal objectives of the Green Manifesto. Not only does it produce, in both auditoria, a great range of drama, including a considerable number of works by new and local writers; it is a hive of activity all day long for the young, the very young and for senior citizens; talks, lectures, discussions; playreadings to complement the plays being performed; jazz sessions....but let the words of the citation on the occasion of the Prudential's Arts Theatre Award for 1994 speak for it:

> The West Yorkshire Playhouse has put itself at the centre of its community's agenda through the breadth of its vision. It is a 'civic' theatre in the best sense of the word, for not only does it represent the cultural diversity of the region, but the Playhouse also provides its varied audiences with new influences and ideas - a combination which has given a whole community its own particular aesthetic.

The second wave of campaigners finally got there.

But the principal campaigner for the West Yorkshire Playhouse was, of course, Leeds Playhouse. With all its deficiencies and limitations, many of them attributable to the location and to the minimality of facilities beyond the auditorium, it established in Leeds the habit of theatre-going, a sense of the importance of good drama, and the public will to perpetuate it - and to pay £13m to do so. Even allowing for inflation there is a big difference between the capital costs of 1970 and 1990. But the difference was the value that, by 1990, was attached to an enterprise established by a group of reluctant citizens, who never really intended to do it themselves. The decision in 1967 to get re-started, no matter how, was justified, and Leeds at last could throw off the reputation it had acquired in the eighteenth century, of being 'the Botany Bay of actors' and of 'displaying an extraordinary, nay frightful, prejudice against the theatre'.

Perhaps the greatest single triumph of the first theatre was its auditorium. That 'miracle of teamwork' was tested and approved by twenty years of actors and audiences; and when the specification for the new theatre was drawn up, the central feature was an exact replication of the first auditorium. The new, splendid building has two auditoria, great foyers, vast work rooms, rehearsal rooms, committee rooms, assembly rooms, an art gallery and a great, upturned profile in a prominent place in the city. But at its heart is the miracle of teamwork, built on a razor's edge.

*Chatting with Jude Kelly in the new playhouse on the morning of the 'First Night'.*

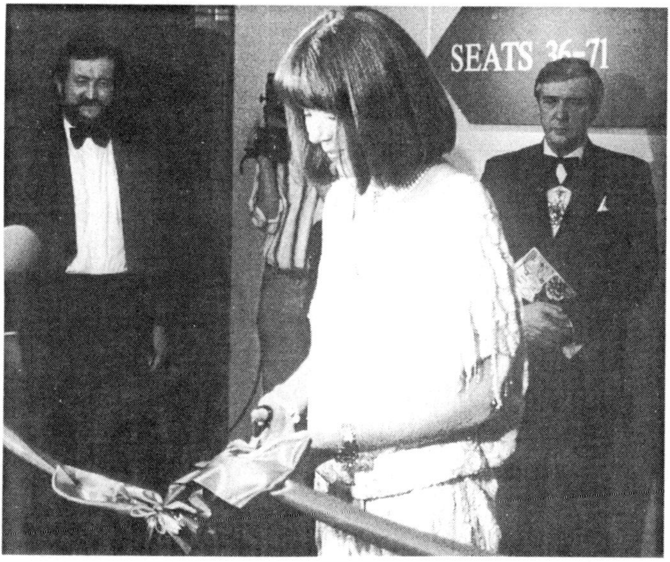


*Dianna Rigg opening the new Playhouse*

# The Epilogue

The stories I have told all happened a long time ago. Many of the actors in them are no longer alive. But the threads of their lives where they crossed mine are woven into the fabric of my memory, and into the things we achieved together. When I remember one I remember all, for all are connected. Those of us who were actors in the central drama in this book have a special meeting place, which resulted from the task that bound us together, and where we may encounter the rich network of memories that links us with those who no longer share moments in time with us. Each one of us followed our own path to the common destination. Each brought to the point of intersection a personal network that thickened the common web.

Even the paths we took after we reached the common destination are often oddly connected. Mine took me, with Walter, to Malaysia, where we became involved with another theatre in the early stages of its life. This was a dazzling venture that was re-creating an ancient form of dance-drama based on Malay folk tales; a friendship with the two who were its inspiration and main protagonists sprang from our shared love of theatre, for each of us rooted in our own culture. For long after we came home from the east we would hear of their growing reputation and of the international engagements that resulted. One such brought them to England, and then we learnt, with near incredulity on both sides, of the linking of our threads with theirs in another network: it was on a tour of Australia where, in Perth, they were hosted by - and, indeed rescued from a crisis by - one of the core campaigners for the Playhouse, who had gone to direct an Arts Centre in Western Australia; neither he nor they had known of the common thread that wove us all into the same web.

Another chance meeting, with one who had shared the Uganda Mystery Cycle in the Kampala school[1], enabled me to follow paths that led back through the dark years of Uganda to many of the theatre-makers there with whom I had worked, and who had enriched so much my experience of theatre. Many had died (including, as I already knew, my dear Zirimu friends); some by nature's hand, some in Amin's rule of terror, some mysteriously. But death is not the end of the story if the life has born fruit. The lives of that special group in the Makerere Travelling Theatre had born astonishing fruit, and in a country that, ten years before their time, gave few signs of a tradition of verbal drama, there now exist some five hundred theatre groups throughout the country, with three hundred in the city of Kampala itself. Drama has become a nation-wide taste, and local writing for it has gone on in spite of years of troubles, wars and censorship. There are still no professional companies, it is true, but the proliferation of amateur groups is perhaps more indicative of theatre concern than a passive enjoyment of officially funded work (though passivity was not one of the audience characteristics that I remember there!). There are now ten theatre buildings in Kampala alone - often small, homely, improvised or dated buildings, but again, more accessible and part of daily life than the National Theatre, for they are alongside markets and busy streets. They house the most active and creative of the drama groups, many of which have taken their work out on tour to other parts of the country - travelling theatres. Even when the wars had destroyed the venues like community halls and school halls, there was always the opportunity of performing in outdoor clearings, in the way that both the Uganda Pilgrim Players and the Makerere Travelling Theatre had done. There must have been many dangers and set-backs - the curfew, the censor, the army -

and their survival into the new Uganda is a great tribute to courage and conviction.

The new Uganda, under a liberising President, attaches great value to drama, although it is not yet in a position to divert resources to it from the compelling primary needs of the country (from the bread to the flowers) except in one specific area. With external aid and resources from UNICEF, the Ministry of Education has sustained a continuous drama programme as part of the battle against AIDS, taking specially written plays to schools and other community centres.

The National Theatre - with a new title, the National Cultural Centre - has a continuing programme of entertainment that includes performances by local groups. It also acts as the focal point for the present leaders and innovators in the local drama. Its Theatre Guild holds conferences, and runs seminars and study groups and practical courses. There is a strong and determined movement to stimulate and encourage writers, directors, actors and technicians. There is considerable pride in the work of several writers who worked through the troubles, and of some who had flowered in the period just after the Makerere Travelling Theatre started. And there is a great concern to seek out the origins of Ugandan drama and to link it with the possible existence of an indigenous tradition shrouded in the mists of history, with the role of the missionaries from the west seen as both destructive of the old and introducing the new. Somewhere, perhaps, there is a folk memory of a tradition introduced not by missionaries but by an odd little racially- mixed group who showed, if nothing else, that drama can operate on a shoe-string in a clearing in the bush.

The status of drama is evidenced by the existence in the University of a Department of Music, Dance and Drama; the linking of the subjects shows perhaps the way in which the unbroken traditions from an earlier past of music and dance are integral to a truly Ugandan form. Certainly, one great advantage of a form that incorporates indigenous non-verbal elements is that it could be a way of overcoming the language differences in the country. For the language problem is not just that of English

*Kampala Theatres*

*Uganda's National Theatre*

versus local language, but of many different local languages. A resolution of that obstacle to the growth of a truly national theatre is a great challenge. Two of the academics to whom the challenge is thrown have a place in my network of threads; for they are two with whom I shared the adaptation and production of Chekhov's *The Proposal* - and both of them were, themselves, in Leeds during the period of the Playhouse campaign: one, Rose, is the Professor of Music, Dance and Drama, and Tim was, until recently, the Professor of English.

At the end of Farndale in Yorkshire there still lives a man who remembers the theatre coming to the village in November 1940. He was sixteen, and a year later he went away to the war. But he remembers the excitement of that unprecedented occasion, which, in the blurred way of memory, he associates with 'the evacuees' - a memory that at long last accounts, to me, for the inexplicably large number of children who were joining in that much repeated version of 'There's a Hole in my Bucket', on the anxious Saturday afternoon when the YRCC Travelling Theatre gave its first performance, and Jane was late. There are no longer any lonely airmen at the end of the wrong fork, where she was so ardently welcomed: only the great, sweet open fell, that stretches away into the lonely heights of the North Yorkshire moors.

The people in the stories will always be there, in the rich network of my memories, all linked together by the threads they share with me: Arnold and Olive and Rose; Geoffrey and the mediaeval barn theatre that inspired a fit-up war-time travelling troupe; a group of people on a simple rostrum in a bush clearing in the middle of Africa; 'the thirteen' in a loved house in Leeds; a gentle scientist in a factory laboratory in Trafford Park and an opera director when he was 'nobbut a lad' in Oxford; most dear of all, the small band of core campaigners who stayed the pace to the end.

No man is an island. We affect and are affected by all whose paths cross ours. Our endeavours are fuelled in part by the endeavours of others, and each of us brings to the point of intersection in the network the fruit of many lives. From some encounters grow deep and abiding friendships that owe their strength to the sharing of endeavour. From others we do no more than make bridges to other men's lives. But sometimes an encounter opens the most important door, shows us where the path can lead, and sends us along it. The door through which I first glimpsed the power, the beauty and the magic of theatre was opened by John Gielgud, on a cold December day nearly sixty years ago. It pleases me to believe that one of the paths in the network of which I am a part thus links the greatest actor of our time to the great civic theatre that stands at the heart of the City of Leeds.

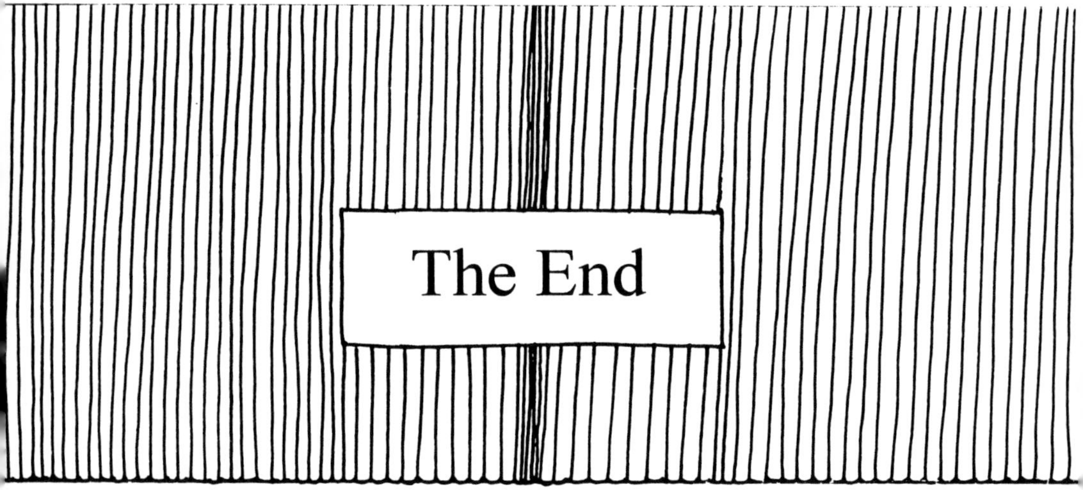


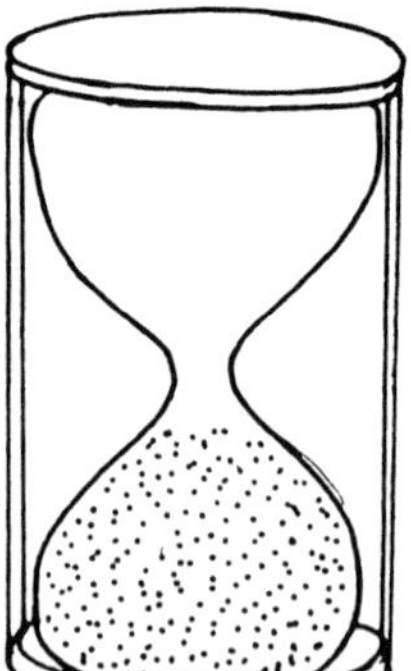

# References

## Prologue

1. G B Shaw, *The Saturday Review*, 14 March 1896

## 1. The First Act: a travelling theatre

1. Giles Brandreth, *John Gielgud*, Pavilion Books, 1984, p.67
2. op. cit., p.65
3. Quoted by Giles Brandreth, op. cit., p.68
4. Giles Brandreth, op. cit., p.71
5. Herbert Farjeon, *The Shakespearian Scene*, quoted by Giles Brandreth, op. cit., p.71
6. Kenneth Tynan, quoted by Brandreth, op. cit., p.85
7. Rowell and Jackson, *The Repertory Movement*, Cambridge, 1984, p.97
8. Jane Ridley, *The Story of a Travelling Theatre in Wartime*: an unpublished report, to which I am indebted for much of the content of this chapter; as I am to Jane, for the original experience, and for a long friendship.
9. Jane Ridley, op. cit.
10. *Yorkshire Post*, 5 May, 1941
11. Jane Ridley, op. cit.
12. *Yorkshire Post*, 12 May, 1941
13. R C S., *Yorkshire Post*, 2 May, 1942
14. A series of devastating air raids made for morale-breaking rather than strategic purposes, on several culturally important cities, such as Exeter, Coventry and York. The name derives from that of the nineteenth century German publisher who produced a set of guide books which bore his name.
15. Jane Ridley, op. cit.
16. J S Purvis, *The York Series of Mystery Plays*, SPCK, 1957, p.7

## 2. Between the Acts: some amateur scenes

1. Kenneth Tynan, *Observer*, 6 January, 1957. With thanks to Michael Billington of the *Guardian* for tracing it for me.
2. Quoted in the *Guardian*,1 September, 1992
3. Peter Ackroyd, *Dickens*, Minerva, 1990, p.568
4. John Osborne, *A Better Class of Person*, London, 1992, p.246
5. Rowell and Jackson, *The Repertory Movement*, Cambridge, 1984, p.60
6. Peter Ackroyd, *Dickens*, Minerva, 1990, p.642
7. op. cit., p.669

## 3. The Second Act: on the road in Uganda

1. Held 5 February, 1993, in the National Theatre, Kampala, under the auspices of the Uganda Theatre Guild.
2. Purvis, op. cit., p.7

## 4. The Third Act: action opens in Leeds

1. Local Government Act 1948, Section 132, HMSO
2. John Russell Taylor, *Anger and After*, Methuen, 1962, p.144
3. Arts Council of Great Britain, *Annual Report*, 1963/64
4. Extract from an issue of *Pegasus Flight*, newsletter of the Pegasus Club; quoted in Leeds Theatre Campaign, *A New Theatre*, p.28
5. G B Shaw, *Our Theatre in the Nineties*, vol.2, pp. 70 and 81; quoted by Rowell and Jackson, op. cit., p.30
6. Sheila Goodie, *Annie Horniman*, Methuen, 1990, p.119
7. Cmnd. 2601, February 1965, *A policy for the Arts*, HMSO

## 5. Between the Scenes

1. A full account of the work of the Makerere Travelling Theatre may be found in a chapter by David Cook in a forthcoming book on Uganda Arts, edited by Rose Mbowa and Eckhard Breitinger, published by Bayreuth University Press. David Cook, one-time Professor of English in Makerere University, was founder of the Travelling Theatre, and I am greatly indebted to him for the photographs of the theatre's work.

## 6. The Action Develops in Leeds

1. Item on a *Report to the Arts Council*, Minutes of Leeds Theatre Trust Ltd., November 13, 1967
2. Leeds Theatre Trust, op. cit.

## 7. The Long Entr'acte

1. Statement by John Beaumont to the *Yorkshire Evening Post*, following a meeting of the Finance Commitee of the Council, April 25, 1968.
2. Councillor Bradley, Chairman of the Finance Commitee of the Council, speaking to the Yorkshire Evening Post, April 25, 1968.

3. *The Queen's Highland Servant by William Douglas Home; The Boston Story by Ronald Gow, based on a story by Henry James; Candida by George Bernard Shaw; The Game by Janet Allen; The Ghenki Boys by Terence Kelly; Whose Baby? adapted by Basil Dawson and Felicity Douglas from the French by Andre Haguet and Jean Valmy.*
4. Letter from Keith Waterhouse in the *Yorkshire Post*, August 8, 1968
5. op. cit., p.106

## 8. Climax: the last chance

1. *Yorkshire Evening Post*, August 15, 1968
2. *Yorkshire Evening Post*, January 9, 1969
3. *Yorkshire Evening Post*, January 14, 1969

## 9. Finale: the razor's edge

1. W T Oliver, *Leeds Playhouse Souvenir Brochure*, published on the occasion of the opening of the theatre, September 1970.

2 - 5. W Houghton-Evans, *Leeds Playhouse Souvenir Brochure*

6. Rowell and Jackson, op. cit., p.106
7. Rowell and Jackson, op. cit., pp.115 et seq.
8. Ben Iden Payne, the first manager of the Gaiety Theatre, Manchester, explained the repertory system thus: 'The dictionary meaning of the word was "storehouse", and this was just what the company aimed at. As a library had books on its shelves waiting to be taken down and used , so would they have plays that had already been produced and justified themselves ready to be used again. By changing the play two or three times a week, the actors would not grow stale, and their supporters would be able to come to the theatre more than once a week. In this way a community spirit would grow between them and their audience. The repertory movement was to be a democratic art, reaching the widest possible public.' Sheila Goodie, *Annie Horniman*, op. cit., p.110
9. Arthur Wise, *The Day the Queen went to Scotland for the Grouse-shooting: a document*, Hodder Paperbacks, London 1969

## 10. The Epilogue

1. Gill Dyer, to whom I am indebted for the photographs of the Mystery Cycle as well as for her careful research on my behalf into the current state of theatre in Uganda.